Green Finance and Investment

Clean Energy Finance and Investment Policy Review of Viet Nam

OECD

BETTER POLICIES FOR BETTER LIVES

Please cite this publication as:
OECD (2021), *Clean Energy Finance and Investment Policy Review of Viet Nam*, Green Finance and Investment, OECD Publishing, Paris, *https://doi.org/10.1787/61c33f7f-en*.

ISBN 978-92-64-58368-9 (print)
ISBN 978-92-64-97613-9 (pdf)

Green Finance and Investment
ISSN 2409-0336 (print)
ISSN 2409-0344 (online)

Photo credits: Cover © Nguyen Quang Ngoc Tonkin.

Corrigenda to publications may be found on line at: *www.oecd.org/about/publishing/corrigenda.htm*.

Preface

As international action against climate change intensifies and global value chains are reshaped as a result, effective clean energy policies will increasingly be a source of competitive advantage. Viet Nam, Asia's major regional manufacturing hub and one of South-East-Asia's fastest growing economies, must act consistently with these trends to maintain its position as a leading destination for foreign direct investment. This will require ever-greater levels of investment in clean energy infrastructure with sector strategies indicating a more than trebling of generation capacity by 2040 and an increasing role for solar and wind generation. Viet Nam's economy also remains highly energy intensive with abundant economic potential for demand-side efficiency. The scale of investment required goes beyond the capacity of public finances. A strong enabling framework to attract private capital is critical to reap the economic benefits of a clean energy transition.

In recent years, Viet Nam has made impressive progress in this regard, with market liberalisation creating opportunities for independent power producers and favourable renewable support mechanisms facilitating high levels of investment, particularly into the solar market. Maintaining sustainable market growth while integrating higher shares of variable generation and securing cost reductions will be a key challenge for Viet Nam's policy makers over the next decade. This OECD Clean Energy Finance and Investment Policy Review of Viet Nam aims to support the effort to achieve the country's clean energy targets.

The *Review* provides a comprehensive overview of the current policy framework in Viet Nam, highlighting successes and identifying areas that can be strengthened. It also contains a number of tailored recommendations for the Government of Viet Nam and development partners to mobilise private finance and investment for clean energy development.

The *Review* is the result of a constructive dialogue between Viet Nam and OECD member countries alongside other clean energy stakeholders. The OECD will continue to support Viet Nam in implementing the report's recommendations as the country builds a stronger, cleaner and more resilient economy. I am confident that this collaborative effort will help in mobilising private finance and investment to support climate action and sustainable development.

Mathias Cormann
Secretary-General, OECD

Foreword

The *Clean Energy Finance and Investment Policy Review of Viet Nam* is one of the key outputs of the OECD Clean Energy Finance and Investment Mobilisation (CEFIM) Programme. The CEFIM Programme aims to support governments in emerging economies in South and Southeast Asia as well as Latin America to unlock finance and investment in renewable electricity and energy efficiency ("clean energy").

The OECD is grateful to the Government of Viet Nam for its co-operation in providing information and for facilitating the virtual review mission conducted in March 2021. Particular thanks is due to CEFIM's focal points Nguyen Ninh Hai, Director of the Department of New and Renewable Energy of the Electricity and Renewable Energy Authority, and Dang Hai Dung, Chief of the Cleaner Production and Sustainable Production and Consumption Office of the Ministry of Industry and Trade. CEFIM is also grateful to all the government institutions involved in the *Review* process, including Ministry of Planning and Investment, Ministry of Construction, Ministry of Finance, State Bank of Viet Nam, Ministry of Natural Resources and Environment, and Ministry of Science and Technology.

The *Review* was managed by Cecilia Tam, Team Leader of the Clean Energy Finance and Investment Mobilisation Programme. Brendan Coleman co-ordinated the research and *Review* process. Authors of the report were Brendan Coleman, Lylah Davies and Cecilia Tam from the OECD Environment Directorate. Matthew Wittenstein, UNESCAP, and Aisma Vitina, the Danish Energy Agency, participated in the review mission and contributed their expertise for the formulation of the assessments and recommendations. Akos Losz, IEA, provided analytical inputs related to international gas markets and implementation of liquefied natural gas to power projects. The *Review* benefited from in-country support, particularly with facilitating coordination with the Government of Viet Nam, from Nhien Ngo and Hoang Anh Tran from Viet Nam Initiative for Energy Transition. Dominique Haleva provided administrative support and copy-editing. OECD Environment Director Rodolfo Lacy launched the virtual *Review* mission.

The report benefitted from the review and feedback of Aayush Tandon and Jens Sedemund of the OECD Secretariat. Various experts also provided review comments including Pablo Hevia-Koch, Paolo Frankl, Gergely Molnar, Jean-Baptiste Dubreuil, Hiroyasu Sakaguchi and Mike Waldron of the IEA; Loui Algren and Stephan Enevoldsen of the Danish Energy agency; Marshall Brown of the Global Green Growth Institute; Rahul Kitchlu of the World Bank; Stefan Bjarne of ETH Zurich; Thanh Long Nguyen of the Vietnam Energy Conservation and Energy Efficiency Association; and Gregor Paterson-Jones, consultant for the Asian Development Bank.

The preparation of the *Review* also benefitted from a broad consultation process with a range of stakeholders. We are grateful to the Viet Nam Energy Partnership Group who supported in facilitating this communication. The OECD is thankful to the numerous experts in OECD member country embassies based in Viet Nam who were consulted throughout the Review process. Lastly, we are also grateful to all the participants in the virtual review mission who also provided invaluable input to the *Review*.

This report was made possible thanks to generous funding from Denmark.

Table of contents

Tables

Figures

Boxes

Follow OECD Publications on:

http://twitter.com/OECD_Pubs

http://www.facebook.com/OECDPublications

http://www.linkedin.com/groups/OECD-Publications-4645871

http://www.youtube.com/oecdilibrary

http://www.oecd.org/oecddirect/

This book has...

StatLinks

A service that delivers Excel® files from the printed page!

Look for the *StatLinks* at the bottom of the tables or graphs in this book. To download the matching Excel® spreadsheet, just type the link into your Internet browser, starting with the ***https://doi.org*** prefix, or click on the link from the e-book edition.

Abbreviations and acronyms

ABIF	ASEAN banking integration framework
AC	air conditioner
AEC	ASEAN Economic Community
AFD	Agence Française de Développement (French development agency)
ART	average retail tariff
APG	ASEAN Power Grid
ASEAN	Association of Southeast Asian Nations
B2B	business to business
B2C	business to consumer
BAU	business-as-usual
BOT	build-operate-transfer
BOOT	build-own-operate-transfer
BQDM	Brooklyn-Queens Demand Side Management Programme
CfD	contract for difference
CIT	corporate income tax
CMSC	Commission for the Management of State Capital at Enterprises
CO2	Carbon Dioxide
Con Edison	Consolidated Edison Company
COVID-19	corona virus disease 2019
CPEE	Clean Production and Energy Efficiency Project
CPTPP	Comprehensive and Progressive Agreement for Trans-Pacific Partnership
DANIDA	Danish International Development Agency
DEESD	Department of Energy Efficiency and Sustainable Development
DEU	designated energy user
DOIT	Department of Industry and Trade
DONRE	Department of Natural Resources and Environment
DPPA	direct power purchase agreement
DPI	Department of Planning and Investment
DSM	demand-side management
E&S	environmental and social
ECA	Export Credit Agency
EE	energy efficiency
EEAP	Energy Efficiency Action Plan
EPC	energy performance contract
EPT	Environmental protection tax
ERAV	Electricity Regulatory Authority of Viet Nam
EREA	Electricity and Renewable Energy Authority
ESCO	energy services company
ESG	environment social and governance
EU	European Union
EVN	Viet Nam Electricity
EVN EPTC	Viet Nam Electricity Power Trading Company
EVN NLDC	Viet Nam Electricity National Load Dispatch Centre
EVN NPT	Viet Nam Electricity National Power Transmission Corporation
FDI	foreign direct investment
FIA	Foreign Investment Agency
FIT	feed-in tariff

FTA	free trade agreement
GDP	gross domestic product
GENCO	generation company
GGU	government guarantee undertaking
GHG	greenhouse gas
GIPI	Global Intellectual Property Index
GMS	greater Mekong subregion
GW	gigawatt (one billion Watts)
IDR	issuer default rating
IE	Institute of Energy
IEA	International Energy Agency
IP	intellectual property
IPO	initial public offering
IPP	independent power producer
IPT	independent power transmission
IRENA	International Renewable Energy Agency
ISDS	investor state dispute settlement
ISO	International Organisation for Standardisation
JBIC	Japanese Bank for International Cooperation
KfW	Kreditanstalt für Wiederaufbau (German state-owned investment and development bank)
kV	Kilovolt
KWh	kilowatt-hour
Ktoe	kiloton of oil equivalent
LCOE	levelised cost of electricity
LED	light-emitting diode
LEED	Leadership in Energy and Environmental Design (green building certification standard)
LNG	liquefied natural gas
LTMS-PIP	Laos PDR, Thailand, Malaysia, Singapore Power Integration Project
LURC	land use right certificate
MEPS	minimum energy performance standards
MOC	Ministry of Construction
MOF	Ministry of Finance
MOIT	Ministry of Industry and Trade
MONRE	Ministry of Natural Resources and Environment
MOST	Ministry of Science and Technology
MPI	Ministry of Planning and Investment
Mtoe	million tonnes of oil equivalent
$MtCO_2e$	million tonnes of CO_2 (carbon dioxide) equivalent
MW	Megawatt (one million Watts)
MWp	Megawatt power
NLDC	National Load Dispatch Centre
NATIF	The National Technology Innovation Fund
NDC	Nationally Determined Contribution
O&M	operation and maintenance
ODA	overseas development aid
PAYG	pay as you go
PDP	Power Development Plan
PPA	power purchase agreement
PPC	Provincial People's Committee
PPP	public private partnership
PSC	New York Public Service Commission
PV	Photovoltaic
QAB	qualified ASEAN bank
R&D	research and development
RE	renewable energy
REDS	Renewable Energy Development Strategy
REIPPPP	South Africa's Renewable Energy Independent Power Producers Procurement Programme
RE-IPP	renewable energy independent power producer
RPS	renewable portfolio standard
RIA-FIN	Roadmap for Monetary and Financial Integration of ASEAN

SBV	State Bank of Viet Nam
SCADA	Supervisory Control and Data Acquisition (system of software and hardware which enables remote control of equipment)
SEC	specific energy consumption
SSC	State Securities Commission
SDG	sustainable development goal
SEDS	Socio-Economic Development Strategy
SOE	state-owned enterprise
STAMTEQ	Directorate for Standards, Metrology and Quality
TVET	technical and vocational education and training
TFC	total final consumption
TOE	tonnes of oil equivalent
TPES	total primary energy supply
TRIMS	trade related investment measures
TWh	Terawatt-hour
U4E	United for Efficiency
UNFCCC	United Nations Framework Convention on Climate Change
USD	United States Dollar
VAT	value-added tax
VECEA	Viet Nam Energy Conservation and Energy Efficiency Association
VEEBC	Viet Nam energy efficiency building code
VEPF	Viet Nam Environmental Protection Fund
VEPG	Viet Nam Energy Partnership Group
VGBC	Viet Nam Green Building Council
VIET	Viet Nam Initiative for Energy Transition
Vinacomin	Vietnam National Coal and Mineral Industries Group
VND	Vietnamese Dong
VNEEP	Viet Nam Energy Efficiency Programme
VNSI	Viet Nam Sustainability Index
vRE	variable renewable energy
W	Watt
WEEE	European Union's Waste Electrical and Electronic Equipment Directive
WIPO	World Intellectual Property Organisation
WTO	World Trade Organisation
WTO TRIM	World Trade Organisation trade related investment measures
WTO TRIPS	World Trade Organisation Trade-Related Aspects of Intellectual Property Rights Agreement

Executive summary

The Clean Energy Finance and Investment Policy Review of Viet Nam supports Viet Nam's efforts to realise a clean energy transition. It provides a comprehensive overview of the current policy environment, highlighting progress and identifying opportunities for strengthening policy interventions that can help to scale up clean energy finance and investment. The following is a summary of the assessment and key recommendations from six policy areas that form the framework for the *Review* and that are elaborated in chapters 2 through 7.

Assessment

The Government of Viet Nam is to be commended for its prioritisation of clean energy development and for the recent progress in becoming one of the largest regional renewable energy markets in just a few short years. Strong incentives have created a boom in solar development and drawn attention to the country's abundant renewable resource potential. To maintain market growth sustainably Viet Nam must resolve critical new challenges over the coming years including the successful integration of higher shares of variable generation; the mobilisation of diversified sources of capital; ensuring continued cost reductions; and maintaining a stable investment environment while managing the transition of its support schemes. Although it has been anticipated that the explosive rate of deployment witnessed over the last two years would slow down, the level and length of reduction in deployment rates signalled in the Power Development Plan (PDP) VIII (still at draft at the time of publication), which sees no significant new, large-scale renewable capacity additions until after 2030, is dramatic and could prove detrimental to local supply chains, green jobs, investor confidence and longer-term cost reductions. Risks associated with the availability and costs of finance for new coal power plants as well as the capacity to achieve timelines for the implementation of complex integrated liquefied natural gas (LNG) to power projects are emerging sources of energy insecurity under the PDP VIII draft. The ability of new thermal plants utilising imported fuels to mitigate fuel price risks will also be critically important as import reliance increases. Fifty percent of electricity supply will rely on imported fuels by 2035 compared to 15% in 2021. Enabling project sponsors to lock in longer-term fuel supply contracts will likely depend on contracting terms such as guaranteed offtake and more generous tariffs that have not been readily provided by EVN to date. Despite tremendous economic potential, the energy efficiency market remains largely untapped and stronger incentives, regulation and new business models are needed to drive the market. As an increasing number of countries and corporates pledge stringent commitments to climate action and sustainable development, Viet Nam will need to continue its clean energy transition if it is to maintain its current position as a leading destination for foreign direct investment.

Planning and public governance

Viet Nam is continuing to strengthen its long-term ambitions for renewable energy and energy efficiency as outlined in the draft PDP VIII, Viet Nam Energy Efficiency Programme (VNEEP) III, and the updated Nationally Determined Contributions. However, the lack of a flexible planning process may hinder the ability to react to the quickly changing context for clean energy and emerging implementation risks. Effective oversight and governance are critical to ensuring that Viet Nam's future power system develops in a manner consistent with the country's overarching policy goals.

Regulatory framework

Viet Nam's energy policy landscape has undergone significant transformation pivoting the sector towards greater levels of private participation, market-based principles, and, more recently, prioritisation of non-hydro renewable and energy efficiency development. The regulatory environment will need to evolve quickly to ensure incentive structures and enabling regulation can drive suitable business models for both renewable energy and energy efficiency development, including the procurement of balancing services and flexible demand and supply side resources.

Investment and competition policy

As the renewable energy market matures, Viet Nam will need to continue to support fair competition and equal access to the market between private developers and state owned enterprises. The upcoming framework for competitive procurement of renewable projects, the full launch of the wholesale market, the continued equitisation of Electricity Viet Nam (EVN) generation companies and the independence of the National Load Dispatch Centre (NLDC) will be important milestones for creating a level playing field. Viet Nam benefits from a particularly open environment for foreign direct investment, and the country's clean energy transition can help attract further investor interest and support the government's ambitions to become a leading manufacturing hub.

Investment promotion and facilitation

The strong action taken to reduce direct fossil fuel subsidies coupled with plans to develop a local carbon market will do much to ensure capital is directed towards projects supporting the country's green growth ambitions. A favourable tax structure providing generous corporate income tax holidays to renewable energy projects and energy efficient equipment manufacturers also provides important incentives. However, the complex regulatory environment and administrative procedures can be challenging to navigate, particularly for foreign investors.

Financial market policy

A major scale up in financing is needed to meet Viet Nam's clean energy transition goals requiring both domestic and international public and private sources of finance. The green banking policies led by the State Bank of Viet Nam are commendable and have played an important role in facilitating domestic finance. The rapid solar expansion over the last two years was financed to a large degree through domestic banks. While there is good appetite to finance clean energy projects, a lack of access to long-term debt capital will limit future growth potential and the absence of non-recourse project finance restricts the funding capacity of developers.

Cross-cutting issues

Without careful, long-term planning, mismanagement of end of life solar photovoltaic waste will have negative environmental effects and deteriorate public confidence in the energy transition. Regional initiatives for grid integration can enable cost effective variable renewable energy integration. Initiatives have progressed slowly to date but renewed focus on overcoming the challenges to establish multilateral trading should be prioritised. Targeted support for innovation in the clean energy sector will be an important cost reduction driver where local conditions necessitate localised technical solutions. In order to enable an inclusive clean energy transition, communities must be supported to benefit from local clean energy investment by improving access to green jobs and increasing opportunities for female entrepreneurship.

Table 1. Actions for Viet Nam to improve its clean energy finance and investment framework

KEY ACTIONS
Near-term
• Strengthen and expand minimum energy performance standards and labelling in Viet Nam to remove inefficient products from the market and improve the availability and certainty of demand for more efficient ones. • Fill regulatory gaps in the energy services market holding back development of those opportunities, ensuring there are transparent conditions for energy service contracting. • Streamline project approval and permitting processes to reduce administrative costs and timelines for renewable energy project development. This could be achieved by establishing a nodal agency (or one-stop shop) that provides a single point of contact for clean energy project developers. • Prioritise implementing an effective framework for corporate sourcing in order to keep-up with global trends on decarbonising supply chains and to provide new routes to market for renewable electricity. • Establish regulations that set a clearly defined green bond framework including definitions for eligibility, reporting and verification protocols. Support the development of green bond issuances for sovereign, sub-sovereign and corporate issuers. • Begin planning for and implementing the enabling framework for the development of a domestic solar photovoltaic recycling industry drawing from the experience of mature solar markets.
Medium-to-long term
• Develop a clear roadmap to move to full cost recovery levels in the tariff structure to provide consumers sufficient long-term visibility to adapt to tariff uplifts and to provide a market signal for the promotion of energy efficiency investment. • Establish a centralised agency (a variant of the Super ESCO model) mandated to support provincial authorities to develop, procure, finance, and monitor public energy efficiency programmes and support private sector ESCO development • Increase frequency of the regular PDP revisions and updates to ensure that the most cost-effective and optimal development of the power system of Viet Nam is continuously ensured. Mechanisms for ensuring optimised course-correction (annual or biennial) should be clear and transparent. • Enhance the independence of the NLDC and strengthen ERAV's independence, so that all market participants view the decisions it makes as fair, objective, and free of political interference. • Clarify renewable energy procurement mechanisms over the course of the PDP VIII period to provide medium-long-term confidence on pipelines. This is particularly important for offshore wind capacity procurement where supply chain development is at a formative stage.

Table 2. Opportunities to enhance development assistance

KEY ACTIONS
• Development co-operation should enhance efforts to support policy makers in designing and implementing policies to facilitate variable renewable integration, design renewable energy auctions, strengthen energy efficiency regulation and support the development of local capital markets to deliver green financial products. • Support skills development in the banking sector for the development and integration of environmental and social management skills and non-recourse project financing. Programmes should also include developing solutions that can be easily replicated or standardised to facilitate project preparation and due diligence by investors. • Develop on-lending schemes or other financing mechanisms that can facilitate access to long-term capital by domestic finance institutions and take advantage of low cost capital from multilateral and bilateral development banks. This could require a re-evaluation of development finance mandates to shift from sovereign lending to be able to facilitate more direct lending to financial institutions without a sovereign mandate. • Improve the availability of clean energy finance and investment data. This will help identify funding gaps, track climate finance flows and help build investor confidence and reduce perceived risks that could potentially lower the cost of finance.

1 Introduction and recent trends in clean energy finance and investment

This chapter examines key trends related to clean energy finance and investment in Viet Nam. It provides a brief overview of key macroeconomic, investment and social developments in Viet Nam over recent decades. It analyses key trends in energy demand and energy efficiency, as well as in the power sector, highlighting progress against clean energy and climate targets. The chapter also provides a snapshot of Viet Nam's clean energy market, looking at recent trends in the cost of clean energy technologies, as well as finance and investment flows.

Economic and social developments

The economy has grown consistently over the last decade

Following a wave of economic and political reforms launched under Đổi Mới in 1986, Viet Nam has developed rapidly into a lower middle-income economy, shifting from centralised planning towards a market economy. Over this period, the country underwent a structural transition away from agriculture towards foreign direct investment (FDI) driven manufacturing. Viet Nam has seen a remarkable increase in FDI with steep year on year growth since 2000, rising from less than 2 billion USD to 14 billion USD by 2019. As a proportion of GDP, FDI inflows far outpace those of peer countries in the region, such Thailand, the Philippines and Indonesia. After a brush with deflation (-0.19%) in 2015, inflation has held between 1.1% and 4.1% since 2016 and high inflation of over 20% has not been seen since 2011. While Viet Nam's GDP per capita is still amongst the lowest of its regional peers, it is growing at one of the fastest rates in the region. GDP growth has been consistent since reforms, averaging 6.5% per annum between 2000 and 2019, and weathering through global economic downturns (World Bank, 2020[1]).

The economy has demonstrated noteworthy resilience during the ongoing COVID-19 pandemic, compared to the rest of the world. This is due to in part to proactive measures, which limited the health impact of COVID-19, but also solid economic fundamentals and policy buffers. This includes strong foreign investment and current account surpluses, a structurally sound banking system which has decreased its non-performing loans since the 2012 debt crisis and, finally, strict public debt management in the years leading up to the pandemic. Though the economy has suffered during the crisis, GDP growth in 2020 was one of the highest rates in the world, at 2.9%, and growth is projected to bounce back towards near pre-COVID-19 levels over 2021 (IMF, 2021[2]). In a context of trade disputes between the United States and China, and global disruptions to supply chains over the course of the COVID-19 pandemic, Viet Nam has maintained strong performance in export-oriented manufacturing. This has further positioned it as an attractive and reliable location for FDI, supporting ambitions for manufacturing and processing to account for 30% of GDP by 2030 (Resolution No. 23-NQ/TW), situating Viet Nam as a leading hub amongst ASEAN economies.

Figure 1.1. FDI as a share of GDP, 2006-2019

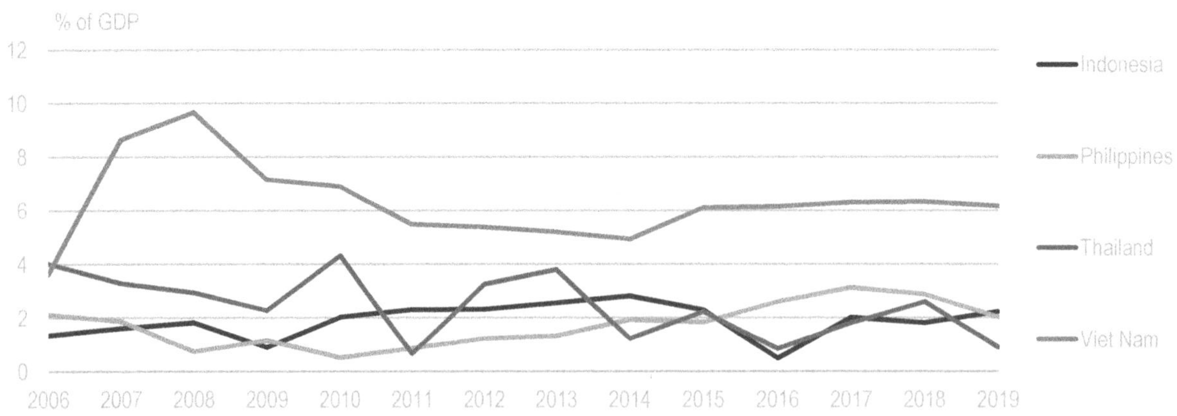

Source: World Bank (2020) World Bank Development Indicators (database)

StatLink https://stat.link/vm93ls

Poverty levels are declining and electricity access has reached 99%

Considered to be amongst the world's poorest countries in the 1990s, after the wave of economic reforms, the World Bank now classes Viet Nam as a lower middle-income country. The country has made strong socio-economic progress and is experiencing rapid demographic growth with the population reaching 97.3 million in 2020 with a life expectancy of 75 years. Moving from a strategy of import substitution to one of export orientation, Viet Nam has seen a decline in agriculture and an increase in industrialisation. This has influenced poverty levels, with a rise in higher wage non-agricultural jobs in rural areas, such as manufacturing, construction and service sectors, accompanied by an overall rise in real wages. In 2018, 6.6% of the population lived under the national poverty line (3.2 USD a day, 2011 purchasing power parity) falling from 70% in 2002 (World Bank, 2020[3]).

Over the last decade, basic services have significantly improved. As of 2011, electricity access reached 100% in urban areas, and as of 2016, it has reached over 99% of the whole population, relying on 8 368 kilometres of 500 kV lines and 18 542 kilometres of 220 kV run by the national power transmission corporation, EVN NPT (EVNNPT, 2020[4]) (World Bank, 2019[5]) . Economic growth and urbanisation are putting increasing pressure on Viet Nam's infrastructure. Despite increased investment from the economic stimulus of the last financial crisis in 2008, there is still a need for large infrastructure investments to expand the current grid and power generation capacity to meet growing per capita electricity consumption. The two extremes of the country, the north around the Red River Delta, home to the country's capital Hanoi, and the southeast, are densely populated and developed regions, which also have the highest concentration of industrial production and therefore the greatest energy demand. However, Viet Nam has a challenging geography for infrastructure. The territory extends from north-to-south across 1 650 kilometres, in an S shape, spanning 500 kilometres across at its widest, and only 50 kilometres at its narrowest. Moreover, about 75% of the country is made up of low mountains and hilly regions which places constraints on land availability for industry and agriculture and utility scale energy projects (Vietnam Embassy, 2020[6]) (OECD, 2019[7]).

Key energy demand and efficiency trends

Energy demand and energy related emissions are increasing rapidly

Viet Nam has a rapidly developing economy with long-term socio-economic forecasts averaging 6.6% GDP growth a year for 2021-2030, and 5.7% for 2031-2045. Since admission into the World Trade Organisation (WTO) in 2007, the country has been regarded as an attractive destination for low-cost, high-volume manufacturers, a trend that has been strengthened by various free trade agreements (FTAs), most recently the European Union-Viet Nam FTA. Whereas the share of agriculture in the economy is steadily shrinking, higher energy-intensive activities are on the rise. In 2020, the value added of industry (including mining, manufacturing, construction, electricity, water and gas) represented 33.7% of GDP, within which, manufacturing represented 16.7% of GDP (World Bank, 2021[8]) (World Bank, 2020[3]).

Keeping pace with economic growth, energy demand (in terms of total final consumption, TFC) has increased rapidly over the last two decades, driven notably by industrialisation and population growth. Demand for electricity is also growing, nearly doubling its share in energy demand between 2010 and 2018, from 15 to 27%. Fossil fuels have played a large role in meeting Viet Nam's growing demand for electricity and consequently have caused energy-related CO2 emissions to grow dramatically (Figure 1.2). In 2018, 24% and 34% of energy consumed was from coal and oil. While 27% of energy demand was electricity consumption, power generation relies heavily on coal and natural gas with a decreasing share of hydropower. In this context, the power sector is increasingly contributing to energy related emissions. Given constraints to domestic coal supplies, Viet Nam relies on imports for coal and for a lesser extent oil, contributing towards a situation of energy insecurity. In 2020 coal imports amounted to 31.57 million tons from countries such as Australia, China, Indonesia and Russia, up by 53.8% from the previous year (IEA, 2020[9]).

Figure 1.2. Energy related emissions, 2000 -2017

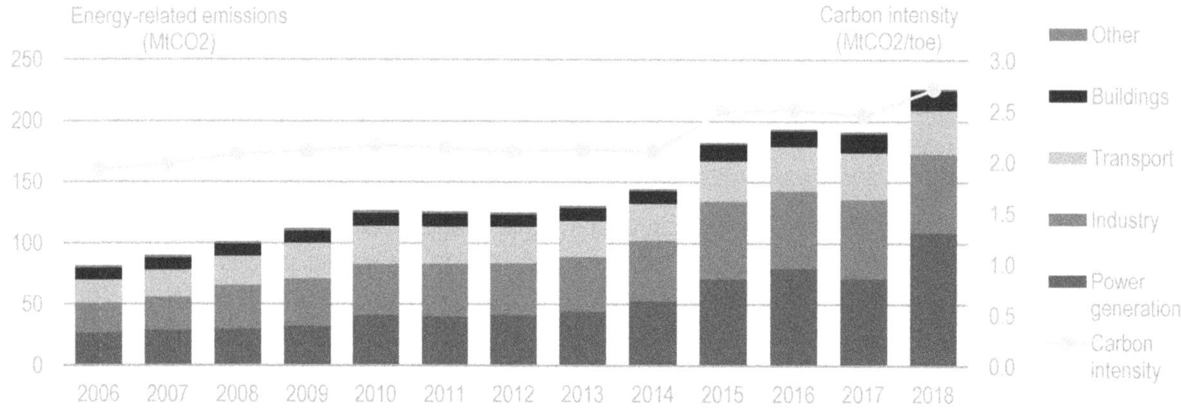

Note: MtCO2 = million tonnes of carbon dioxide. toe = tonnes of oil equivalent
Source: IEA (2020), World Energy Balances (database)

StatLink https://stat.link/6g71pb

Promoting greater investment in energy efficiency will be critical to rationalise fast-increasing energy demand, and therefore expansion plans for power generation, increasing energy related emissions and dependence on energy imports. From about 69 GW in 2020[1], by 2030, the Power Development Plan (PDP) VIII draft aims to increase total installed capacity to 130 GW. However, total energy supply by unit of GDP has remained mostly constant since 2000 and industrial energy demand by unit of GDP has increased in recent years suggesting there remains a large potential for energy efficiency improvements. Moreover, without these improvements, total final consumption could grow over three and half times by 2050, driven not only by industry but also by rapid growth in transport and rising residential demand (Figure 1.3) (EREA & DEA, 2019[10]).

Figure 1.3. Total final energy consumption across sectors

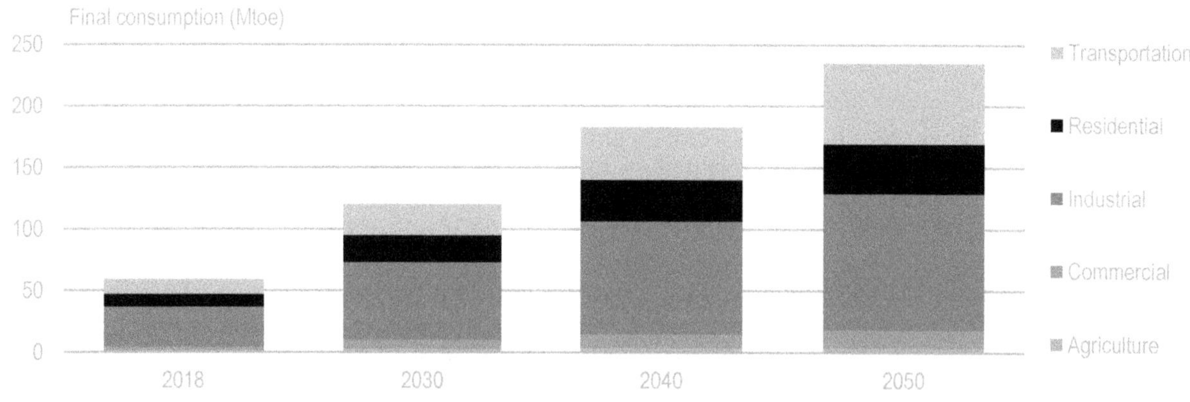

Note: Final energy projections are shown under business-as-usual scenarios. Mtoe = million tonnes of oil equivalent
Source: IEA (2020), World Energy Balances (database), (EREA & DEA, 2019) Vietnam Energy Outlook Report

StatLink https://stat.link/r8bjgd

Industry and buildings are the priority areas for energy efficiency

Viet Nam has a highly energy-intensive economy, ranking amongst the highest in the world. Industry is the largest consumer of energy, accounting for 54% of demand in 2018, a share which has more than quadrupled since 2000 (IEA, 2020[11]). Some of the most important areas for energy efficiency improvements in industry are process heat for cement, iron and steel, pulp and paper, and textiles. Moreover, from low-skilled and labour-intensive industries, such as footwear and textiles, the economy is seeing an increasing share of high-skilled manufacturing such as electrical machinery and equipment, which made up 39% of exports in 2019 (ITC, 2021[12]). Low electricity tariffs by regional standards have provided an added incentive for industry to set up in Viet Nam, but, by the same token, have provided little incentive for energy efficiency practices in the sector. A fast growing economy and population are also driving energy demand in the residential sectors, with cooking, air conditioning and lighting representing important priorities (EREA & DEA, 2019[10]). Additionally, rising household incomes are contributing towards an emerging middle class, which is expected to increase from 13% of the population today to 26% by 2026. This in turn is leading to a rising number of dwellings, growing floor area and increasing ownership of household appliances (World Bank, 2021[13]).

In this context, electricity demand is growing at an astounding rate, rising by 59% between 2015 and 2018 to 227.21 TWh. Industry accounts for nearly 60% of electricity consumption, having more than doubled since 2010. The residential sector accounts for another 33%, with electricity consumption fast replacing the use of biofuels in buildings. For residential users, growing demand for appliances and other electrical equipment, such as air conditioners, will further increase electricity demand, particularly at peak hours (Figure 1.4). Yet, there remain many cost-effective opportunities for energy efficiency measures. A 50% penetration rate of least cost-efficient technologies could cut as much as 12% of energy demand growth to 2030 (EREA & DEA, 2019[10]).

Figure 1.4. Total final consumption by sector and fuel type, growth since 2000

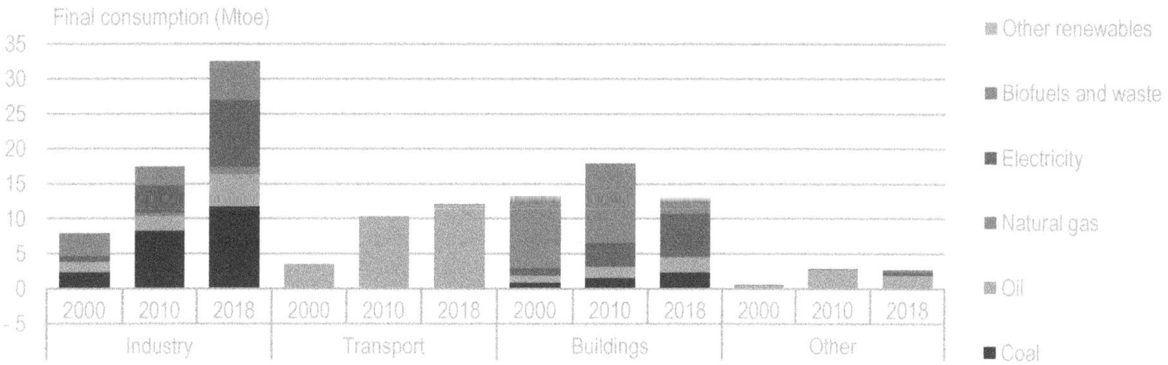

Note: Mtoe = million tonnes of oil equivalent
Source: IEA (2020) World Energy Balances

StatLink https://stat.link/ko7m6n

Progress has been made in energy efficiency through the VNEEP programmes

Energy efficiency has been prioritised in Viet Nam through the National Energy Efficiency Program (VNEEP I and II) for the period 2006-2015, which provided a number of targets and guided the development of a legal and regulatory framework for energy efficiency. VNEEP II set the overall objective for 2011 to 2016 of 5-8% savings of total energy consumption compared to energy demand forecast, equivalent to 11-17 million TOE. This target was met, and at the end of the programme the overall energy savings amounted to 5.81%, equivalent to 12.61 million TOE, with sector specific targets in industry surpassed (RCEE, 2016[14]). Energy intensity in 2015 reduced as compared to 2010 by 10.9% in the cement industry, 24.5% in iron and steel, and 19% improvement in textiles and leather (Ha Dang Son, 2020[15]) (discussed in chapter 3). A delay in between VNEEP II, which ended in 2016, and VNEEP III which started in 2019, led to break in momentum in pushing forward the energy efficiency agenda. The third phase of VNEEP promises to reinvigorate the programme, by strengthening regulation to keep pace with market conditions, and by prioritising the monitoring and enforcement capacity of provincial governments, who are responsible for implementing energy efficiency policy.

Power sector trends

Fossil fuel generation continues to play a key role in Viet Nam's power sector

Hydropower was the dominant generation technology up until the early 2000's. In 1995 it accounted for 72% of generation, dropping to 55% in 2000, and 32% by 2005 (IEA, 2020[11]). Whereas electricity demand has rapidly increased driven by industrialisation and economic growth, the availability of cost-effective hydro resources has decreased as Viet Nam has developed much of its exploitable potential. The development of coal and gas generation therefore became a priority for meeting growing electricity demand, albeit at the cost of increased emissions and public health concerns over air pollution. Coal and gas respectively represented 47% and 17% of power generation in 2018 (Figure 1.5).

In the last years, capacity has struggled to keep up with rapidly growing demand, and concerns have been raised over increased risks of power shortages. Whereas, generous concessions helped attract foreign developers, under build-operate-transfer (BOT) models, tighter controls on state budget have led to less readily available guarantees (Law on State Budget 83/2015/QH13 of 2015). This in turn has led to longer negotiations with developers and significantly delayed projects. In some cases, negotiations have lasted up to 8 to 10 years. The Ministry of Industry and Trade (MOIT) noted that during the 2016-2020 period, only 58% of planned coal-fired capacity came into operation (IEEFA, 2020[16]).

The Power Development Plan (PDP) VIII draft cancels or postpones one-third of its coal power capacity currently in the pipeline, until after 2030, due to lengthy delays, growing reluctance amongst lenders, and negative public opinion. In recent years, there has been increasing socio-environmental concern over pollutants from coal plants, with provincial authorities and communities pushing back against potential plant locations, for instance in Long An, Tien Giang, Bac Lieu, Thua Thien Hue and Quang Ninh (IEEFA, 2020[16]). Nevertheless, with coal-fired thermal power, gas-to-power and oil-fired power coal will jointly represent 52% of installed capacity planned by 2030. This increases the risk of locking into a high emission pathway and investment in stranded assets, as well as reliance on fuel imports given limitations to domestic coal supply.

Beyond meeting greenhouse gas emissions reduction targets set out in Nationally Determined Contributions (NDC), diversifying power generation through renewable energy can help improve the sustainability of Viet Nam's power system. In the face of growing risks of power shortages, renewable energy provides an additional option to keep pace with rapidly increasing electricity demand, and can increase energy security through domestic renewable resources.

Figure 1.5. Power generation mix, 2008-2020

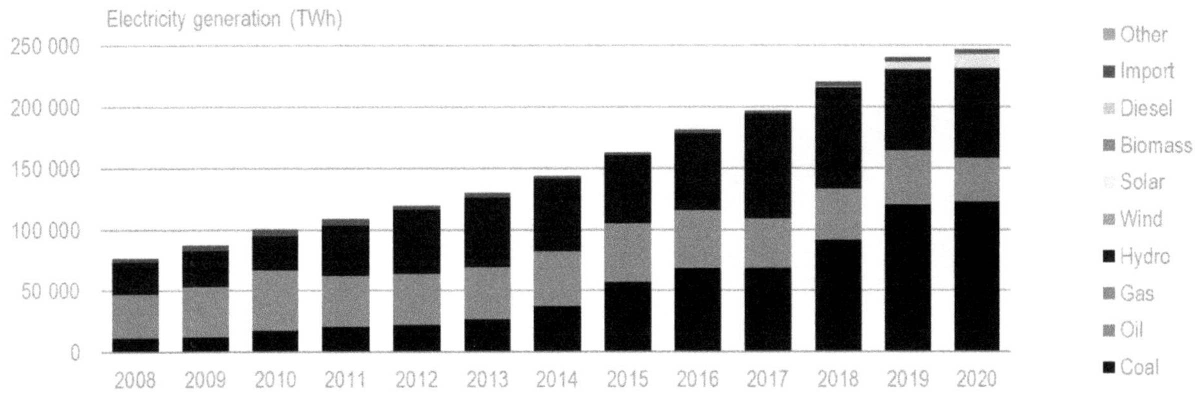

Note: TWh = terrawatt hour
Source: EVN (2020) Electricity Annual Report

StatLink https://stat.link/gv2xch

Renewables deployment has increased substantially over the last years

Viet Nam has become a leading regional solar market, with 17 126 MW of installed capacity at the end of 2020 accounting for 22.9% of total installed capacity (EVN, 2021[17]). Wind capacity represented 537 MW in 2020 with a further 4 480 MW to start operation for 2021. This is an incredible increase since 2017, when Viet Nam had only 8 MW of solar and 205 MW of wind (IRENA, 2018[18]) (Figure 1.6). A first rush of investments was particularly driven by the feed-in tariffs (FIT) regulation on solar which expired in June 2019, benefiting from attractive tariffs by regional standards and a standardised power purchase agreement (PPA) (discussed in chapter 3). Generation targets for solar set through the Renewable Energy Development Strategy and the revised PDP VII were, in fact, surpassed, with MOIT noting that that during the 2016-2020 period, 205% of planned non-hydro renewable capacity came into operation (IEEFA, 2020[16]) (discussed in chapter 2).

A priority moving forward will be to ensure sustainable market growth in the face of challenges around the safe integration of such a rapid increase in variable renewable energy (vRE) capacity over the last two years. Utility scale solar increased from 86 MW in 2018 to 8 852 MW by the end of 2020. In an even shorter time span, from only 378 MW of rooftop solar in 2019, 8 274 MW were installed by the end of 2020, 101 996 rooftop solar power projects were installed and put operation by 31 December, with a total installed capacity of up to 9 296 MWp, just before the solar rooftop feed-in-tariff expired (Tuoi Tre, 2021[19]).

Figure 1.6. Increase in installed solar capacity between 2018 and 2020

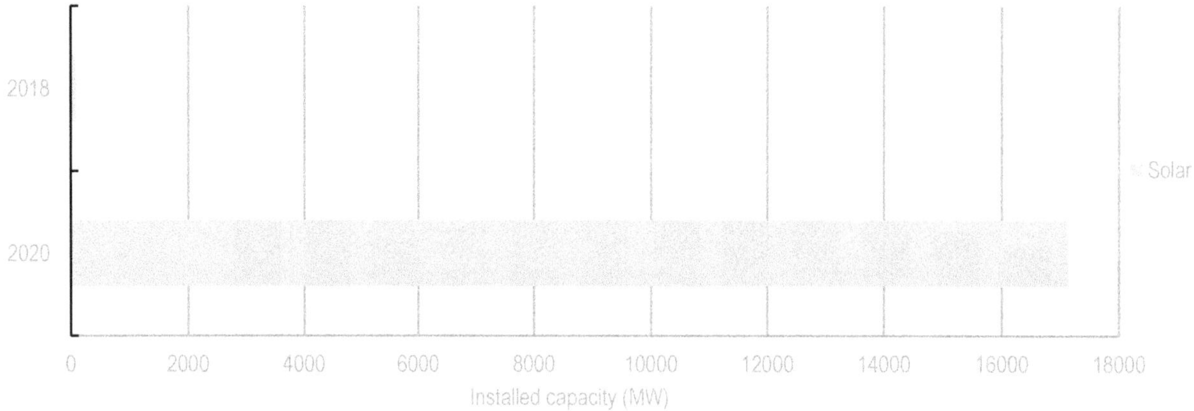

Note: MW = megawatt
Source: Institute of Energy (2021) draft PDP VIII; EVN (2021) CEFIM Review

StatLink https://stat.link/1hn3e4

Comparing 2018 to 2020, the share of solar and wind generation has increased from next to nothing to 5% of total power generation. Yet, over the same period, the share of hydropower generation has decreased (by 5%) and while the share of gas generation has also decreased (by 3%), more emissions-intensive fossil fuel generation from coal and oil has increased (by 3% and 1%). Overall, this means that the share of fossil fuel generation has marginally increased from 64% to 65% (Figure 1.7). This is largely due to difficulty integrating large shares of vRE, a mismatch between periods of electricity demand and solar generation, and lower than expected demand due to COVID-19. At midday, which is a time of low electricity demand, vRE would be equivalent to about 40% of generation, however sufficient solar generation is not available in the evening when electricity demand is at a peak, requiring conventional power plants to remain at hand throughout the day (EVN, 2021[20]).

This is leading to the need for strategic curtailment of generation assets, particularly renewable independent power producers, in low demand periods. The impact of the COVID-19 pandemic on economic activity and suppressed electricity demand has exacerbated this challenge. Even as demand picks up as the economy recovers, significant investments in new grid infrastructure are needed in the near-term, in order to address congestion of the transmission system. In the long term, a range of technical and market-based solutions will be required to enable power system flexibility and the affordable, safe and timely integration of further vRE capacity additions (discussed in chapters 2 and 3) (EVN, 2021[20]).

Figure 1.7. Electricity generation 2018 and 2020

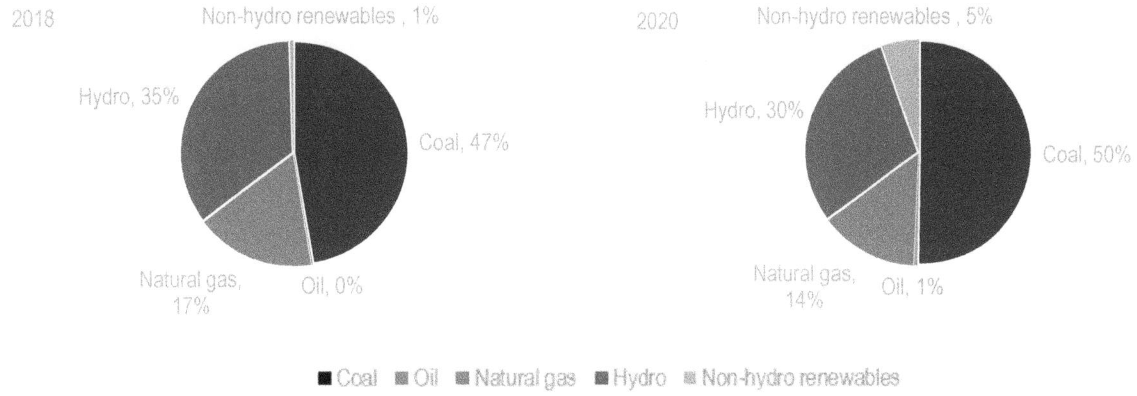

Note: Non-hydro renewables includes solar, wind and biofuels
Source: IEA (2020) World Energy Balances, EVN (2020) Electricity Annual Report

StatLink https://stat.link/o9ry0m

There remains significant untapped wind and solar potential in the country

Viet Nam has high quality solar resources, which until recently had not been exploited for electricity generation. The recent increase in solar deployment has barely scratched the surface of Viet Nam's potential. An economic potential of 380 GW of solar capacity has been identified, mostly concentrated in the South, South Central, and Highland regions (EREA & DEA, 2019[10]). However, the concentration of potential in the southern and central regions has been a significant source of congestion in the transmission network, given low demand in central regions, and high demand in the north, where solar resources are of lower quality.

Viet Nam has some of the best wind resources in Southeast Asia; 217 GW of onshore wind potential has been identified, also located in the South, South Central, and Highland regions (EREA & DEA, 2019[10]) (Netherlands Enterprise Agency, 2018[21]). Viet Nam also benefits from 3 260 kilometres of coastline, excluding islands, with several attractive locations for offshore wind in the north and south. While estimates of the technical potential[2] of fixed and floating offshore wind projects vary, they remain extremely favourable, ranging from 160 GW to as high as 309 GW (Danish Energy Agency, 2020[22]) (Global Wind Energy Council, 2019[23]).

Hydropower has been a cornerstone of economic development for Viet Nam since 1964, with the construction of the first large hydro plant, Thac Ba hydropower plant, with a capacity of 108 MW, supported by the Soviet Union. In particular, the Hoa Binh hydropower plant, with a capacity of 1 920 MW built in 1989, close to the capital Hanoi, was instrumental in accelerating Viet Nam's economic growth (IHA, 2014[24]). Of the roughly 20 GW of economically exploitable resource potential for large hydro, nearly 17 GW was already in operation in 2019 (EVN, 2019[25]). Although technical potential is thought to be around 35 GW, in terms of current economic feasibility, there is already a high utilization rate, leaving limited scope for additional capacity additions. Further potential remains for small hydropower which has a total potential of about 6.7 GW, of which 3 GW is already in operation (EREA & DEA, 2019[10]). Another potential for Viet Nam's hydro resources is pumped hydro storage, which could help integrate renewable generation by providing an important source of flexible, dispatchable power and storage capacity to help balance supply and demand (OECD, 2020[26]). While Viet Nam has notable off-river pumped storage potential, there are also a number of constraints such as costs and proximity to renewable generation and transmission. The

Bac Ai pumped-storage hydropower project, the first of its kind in Viet Nam, is currently under development by EVN with a capacity of 1 200MW and expected to be completed by 2029.

Biomass in the form of wood, bagasse, rice husk, or straw is commonly used in households and industry. With respect to bioenergy, a technical potential for power production of 7 GW is identified for biomass resources and 1.5 GW for solid waste power of which currently only 0.3 GW is utilised (EREA & DEA, 2019[10])

Table 1.1. Renewable potential

Renewable energy	Renewable potential (GW)
Solar	380
On Shore Wind	217
Offshore Wind*	309
Large hydro	20
Small hydro	6.7
Biomass	7
Solid waste power	1.5

Note: Values are expressed as economic potential, which is economically viable renewable generation according to studies. Offshore wind* is expressed as technical potential which establishes an upper-boundary estimate of development potential, given system performance, topographic, environmental, and land-use constraints.
Source: EREA & DEA (2019): Vietnam Energy Outlook Report 2019; Global Wind Energy Council (2018): Global Wind Report 2018; International Hydro Association (2017): Hydropower Status Report 2017

Figure 1.8. Renewable resource potential and utilisation rate

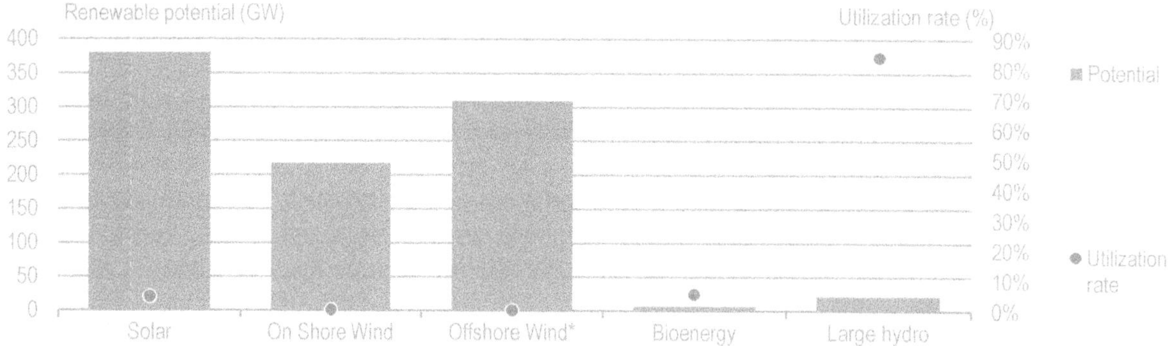

Note: GW = Gigawatt. Based on installed capacity (2020) and economic potentials, except for offshore wind which is expressed in technical potential.
Source: EREA & DEA (2019): Vietnam Energy Outlook Report 2019; Global Wind Energy Council (2018): Global Wind Report 2018; International Hydro Association (2017): Hydropower Status Report 2017, EVN (2021) CEFIM Review, IRENA (2019), Renewable capacity statistics 2019

StatLink https://stat.link/h6aukw

Viet Nam's market for clean energy

Public investment has supported the bulk of power through large hydropower and coal

The majority of generation in Viet Nam is publicly owned through EVN, PetroVietNam and Vinacomin, who together made up 59% of installed capacity in 2020, down from 70% of large-scale installed capacity in 2018 (VIET, 2021[27]). The decreasing share of installed capacity owned by SOEs is due to the development of new solar and wind capacity, the vast majority of which is privately owned (Figure 1.9). Prior to this, local private investment had principally targeted hydropower, while thermal power plants had attracted foreign investment through BOT models under the country's public private partnership laws (Samantha Campbell and Long Huynh, 2018[28]).

To attract international finance and low cost financing from export credit agencies, over the last decades, BOTs have benefited from Government Guarantees and Undertaking (GGU) which could mitigate against certain risks such as non-performance of offtake and supply, Vietnamese Dong convertibility and inflation adjustment, and termination payment obligations. More recently, Viet Nam has had to balance the need to attract overseas financing with tightening fiscal space. Through the Law on Public Debt Management and Resolution 55, which orients the National Energy Development Strategy, much more stringent requirements have been placed on the issuance of state guarantees for power generation projects.

Conversely, investment in gas-fired power plants is increasing. With a declining supply of natural gas from domestic sources, Viet Nam is expected to become an LNG importer, which will require significant international private sector investment and expertise across the LNG to power chain. From 9 GW in 2020, the PDP VIII draft sets a target of 27 GW for 2030, which will increase Viet Nam's dependence on energy imports.

Figure 1.9. Share of installed capacity owned by state owned enterprises in 2020

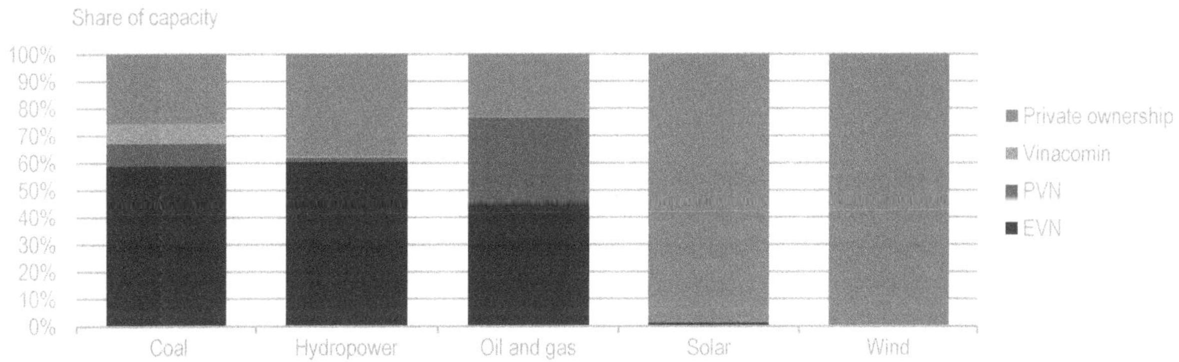

Note: Private investment includes capacity procured under independent power producer or public-private partnership models
Source: VIET (2021) State management role in power sector; EVN (2020) Electricity Annual Report

StatLink https://stat.link/0p4wit

Viet Nam is now the 7th largest renewable energy market

Viet Nam has taken the limelight with two large waves of renewable investments under its FIT programmes, in 2019 and 2020 for utility scale solar PV and again in 2020 for rooftop solar, driving almost all of the 17 126 MW of installed solar capacity. The 8 274 MW of solar rooftop developed in 2020 pushed Viet Nam into the place of third largest solar market in 2020 and 7th largest renewable market, just after France (Bloomberg, 2021[29]). Before this, Viet Nam had remained a small player, with low levels of investment vastly outpaced by neighbours such as Malaysia, the Philippines and Thailand (ADBI, 2018[30]). A review of climate expenditures estimates that over 2011 to 2015, the private sector invested around 9.75 billion USD into renewable energy projects, a majority of which went into 150 small-scale hydropower projects (GIZ, 2019[31]). In 2019 alone, 3.9 billion USD was invested, increasing drastically to 7.4 billion USD in 2020 (Bloomberg, 2021[29]).

The strong interest in the solar market has given MOIT confidence that Viet Nam can attract investment to develop its clean power generation at a faster rate than previously experienced with conventional power plants. Still, this first wave of investment has taken place primarily through domestic and regional investors, and with a lesser proportion of international developers and financiers. For these, concerns have been raised over permits, land availability, the bankability of PPA terms, as well as high risks of curtailment of renewable projects without take or pay agreements, and most recently, market uncertainty over the planned transition to an auction system (discussed in chapter 5). As Viet Nam moves towards larger or riskier projects such as offshore wind, a number of these elements, and in particular the risk allocation between the state utility, EVN, and the renewable developer, may need to be revisited in order to mobilise sufficient investment.

Renewables are increasingly becoming cost competitive

From a new market for utility-scale solar PV, with around 86 MW installed in 2018, Viet Nam has rapidly gained maturity with 5 351 MW installed by the end of 2019, and a further 3 530 MW in 2020. The global weighted-average of the total installed cost of utility-scale solar PVs commissioned in 2019 fell below the USD 1 000/kW mark for the first time, to just USD 995/kW. Thanks to market growth in Viet Nam, average installed costs were already very close to global averages in 2019, amounting to USD 1 054/kW, more than halving since 2016. In line with falling installed costs, over the same period, the levelised cost of electricity (LCOE) of utility-scale solar PV in Viet Nam fell by 55% to 82 USD/MWh (IRENA, 2020[32]).

Although the offshore wind sector is still in its early stages, the Danish Energy Agency has already estimated the LCOE for 24 projects of 500 MW potential offshore capacity distributed throughout a number of shortlisted sites. This exercise determined LCOEs of between 81 EUR/MWh and 120 EUR/MWh, with the best sites located along the South-Central coast. These costs are comparable to early estimates of the LCOE for offshore wind projects in countries such as the UK (Danish Energy Agency, 2020[22]) (BVG, 2015[33]).

Despite the suppressed electricity demand caused by economic impacts of the COVID-19 pandemic, the need for more generation remains a priority to keep up with the demand growth forecast in the socio-economic development strategy. The availability of a diversified pool of investors and new and more affordable renewable technologies has boosted the government's confidence that Viet Nam will be able to develop clean energy generation in a timely manner. Ongoing innovation in renewable technology has made renewables increasingly cost competitive. Attracted by high quality solar and wind resources and stable economic growth, international developers, equipment suppliers and financiers have shown their interest in the Vietnamese market. While it is expected that by 2030, the LCOE for renewable power will fall below that of coal power in most Asia-Pacific markets, this is now forecast for 2021 in Viet Nam, along with China, South Korea, and Thailand, given the falling cost of renewable technology (Wood Mackenzie, 2020[34]).

The domestic market for energy efficiency has ample room for expansion

The energy savings targets established under VNEEP I & II were both achieved despite limited public budget mobilized for the programme, which amounted to approximately 24 million USD (VND 518 billion). However when considering the potential for economic benefits, private investment in energy efficiency has not scaled up sufficiently, particularly in industrial and residential sectors where it is most needed. This is due to several reasons, including low industrial electricity tariffs by regional standards, the need for strengthened institutional capacity for monitoring and enforcement of energy efficiency regulations, and greater technical expertise and understanding by industries, potential service providers, and local financial institutions. For households, the energy performance of appliances, and enforcement of building codes will be increasingly important as Viet Nam's emerging middle class continues to grow. During the VNEEP III phase, there is a need for further strengthening of policy frameworks and regulations, to create an enabling environment for energy efficiency investment. In order to promote energy efficiency across industries, an MOIT assessment on energy efficiency potential in Viet Nam identifies investment needs of 3.6 billion USD (World Bank, 2020[35]). According to a UNDP study, private sector investments in energy efficiency projects in areas such as equipment replacement, energy circulation and technological renovation only amounted to USD 630 million between 2011 and 2015, which is very low for the size of economy (GIZ, 2019[31]).

The Government of Viet Nam is taking a number of steps within VNEEP III to support investment in energy efficiency, including action at the provincial level through the implementation of provincial energy efficiency action plans and increased focus on regulatory enforcement. Existing ESCOs in the market face challenges in accessing finance, given high collateral requirements from commercial banks. Although local banks still have limited experience with energy efficiency projects, the action plan for green banking aims to address these challenges, by making credit available for environmentally sustainable projects including energy efficiency (discussed in chapter 6).

Building certification has increased since 2012. A key milestone has been the revision of the Building Energy Efficiency Building Code (QCVN09:2017/BXD), under the Ministry of Construction, which provides mandatory technical standards for the design, construction and retrofit of buildings with floor areas equal or greater than 2 500m^2. Currently, several green building certification systems exist in Viet Nam, the most popular being, LOTUS which was developed in 2009 by Vietnam Green Building Council, LEED (Leadership in Energy and Environmental Design) developed by the US Green Building Council which has been in the Vietnamese market since 2008, and EDGE (Excellence in Design for Greater Efficiencies) developed by the International Finance Corporation (IFC) for emerging markets and present in Viet Nam since 2015. The number of certified projects is increasing and by 2021, 179 buildings were certified under these systems, accounting for 4 141 266 square metres (Figure 1.10). Since the building code came into force in 2013, government reports of compliant buildings indicate that 130 000 tons of CO2 a year have been saved, equivalent to approximately 28 million USD in annual savings for building owners. The government of Viet Nam has yet to produce a plan for increasing the efficiency of its own building stock, despite being a large owner and investor in real estate. Policies and incentives at both central and provincial level to encourage new green building development remain limited ((IFC, 2021[36]).

Figure 1.10. Growth in green building certification, 2010-2020

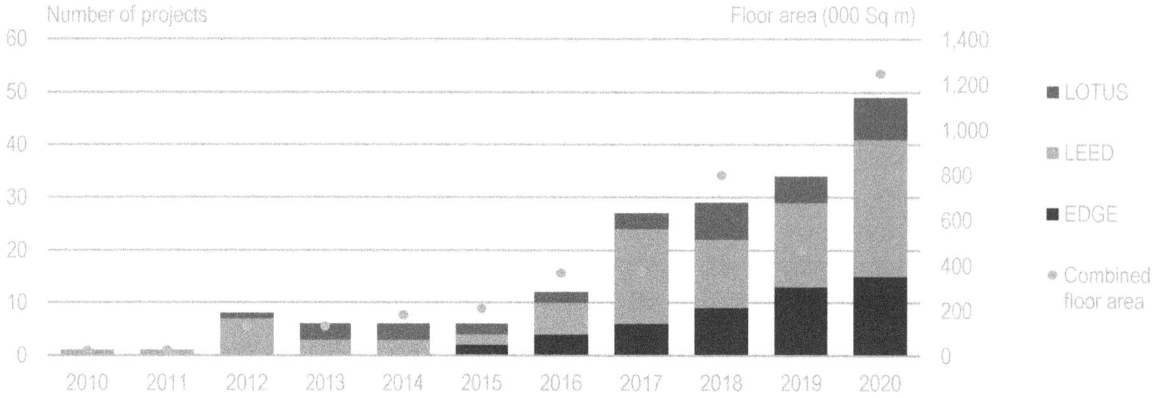

Note: 000 Sq m = thousand square meters
Source: IFC (2021) CEC Workshop Paper: Developing Land and Real Estate Market Meeting Green Criteria

StatLink https://stat.link/byi67k

References

ADBI (2018), *GREEN FINANCE IN VIET NAM: BARRIERS AND SOLUTIONS*, https://www.adb.org/sites/default/files/publication/466171/adbi-wp886.pdf. [30]

Bloomberg (2021), *What Does $500 Billion for Clean Energy Mean for Climate Change?*, https://www.bloomberg.com/news/articles/2021-01-21/what-does-500-billion-for-clean-energy-mean-for-climate-change (accessed on 1 April 2021). [29]

BVG (2015), *Approaches to cost-reduction in offshore wind A report for the Committee on Climate Change*, https://www.theccc.org.uk/wp-content/uploads/2015/06/BVG-Associates-2015-Approaches-to-cost-reduction-in-offshore-wind.pdf. [33]

Cuong, T. et al. (2021), *Renewable energy from biomass surplus resource: potential of power generation from rice straw in Vietnam*, Nature Research, https://www.nature.com/articles/s41598-020-80678-3. [48]

Danish Energy Agency (2020), *Input to roadmap for offshore wind*, https://ens.dk/sites/ens.dk/files/Globalcooperation/d5_-_input_to_roadmap_for_offshore_wind_development_in_vietnam_full_report_english_final_2020-09-21.pdf. [22]

Effigis Geo-Solutions (2018), *Assessment of rooftop photovoltaic solar energy potential in Vietnam.* [47]

EREA & DEA (2019), *The Vietnam Energy Outlook Report 2019*, https://ens.dk/sites/ens.dk/files/Globalcooperation/vietnam_energy_outlook_report_2019.pdf. [10]

EVN (2021), *Presentation during OECD Clean Energy Finance and Investment Review of Viet Nam.* [17]

EVN (2021), *Rooftop solar power boom is underway with a total installed capacity reaching nearly 9,300 MWp*, https://en.evn.com.vn/d6/news/Rooftop-solar-power-boom-is-underway-with-a-total-installed-capacity-reaching-nearly-9300-MWp-66-142-2169.aspx. [20]

EVN (2020), *Performance in the first 9 months of 2020 and objectives and tasks for the last 3 months of 2020.* [49]

EVN (2019), *EVN Overview of hydropower in Vietnam.* [25]

EVNNPT (2020), *National Power Transmission Corporation*, https://www.npt.com.vn/c3/en-US/he-thong-truyen-tai-dien/Operations-5-315. [4]

GIZ (2019), *Measuring private investments into green growth: Vietnam´s Private Climate Expenditure and Investments Review.* [31]

GIZ (2016), *Vietnam Power Development Plan for the period of 2011 - 2020 - Highlights of the PDP 7 revised*, http://gizenergy.org.vn/en/item-detail/highlights-pdp-7-revised. [41]

Global Wind Energy Council (2019), *Market to Watch: Vietnam Offshore Wind*, https://gwec.net/market-to-watch-vietnam-offshore-wind/. [23]

Ha Dang Son, B. (2020), *Industrial Energy Efficiency in Vietnam: From Policy to Implementation*, https://data.worldbank.org. [15]

IEA (2020), *VIETNAM: COAL IMPORTS RISE TO RECORD LEVELS*, International Centre for Sustainable Carbon- News, http://iea-coal.org/vietnam-coal-imports-rise-to-record-levels/ (accessed on 2 July 2021). [9]

IEA (2020), *World Energy Balances*, https://www.iea.org/data-and-statistics. [11]

IEEFA (2020), *New Regulations Threaten Vietnam's Remaining Coal Pipeline*. [16]

IFC (2021), *CEC Workshop Paper: developing Land and Real Estate Market Meeting Green Criteria*, World Bank Group, Washington, https://www.asiapropertyhq.com/vietnam-. [36]

IHA (2014), *International Hydropower Association - country profile Viet Nam*, https://www.hydropower.org/country-profiles/vietnam. [24]

IMF (2021), *Vietnam: Successfully Navigating the Pandemic*, https://www.imf.org/en/News/Articles/2021/03/09/na031021-vietnam-successfully-navigating-the-pandemic. [2]

IMF (2020), *Vietnam's Development Success Story and the Unfinished SDG Agenda1*, https://www.imf.org/~/media/Files/Publications/WP/2020/English/wpiea2020031-print-pdf.ashx. [43]

IMF (2018), *IMF Country Report No. 19/235*, https://www.imf.org/~/media/Files/Publications/CR/2019/1VNMEA2019002.ashx. [38]

Institute of Energy (2021), *Draft Power Development Plan 2021-2030 with a vision to 2045.* [51]

International Renewable Energy Agency (ed.) (2018), *RENEWABLE CAPACITY STATISTICS 2018*, http://www.irena.org. [18]

IRENA (2020), *IRENA Power Generation Costs 2019*, https://www.irena.org/-/media/Files/IRENA/Agency/Publication/2020/Jun/IRENA_Power_Generation_Costs_2019.pdf. [32]

ITC (2021), *Trade Map - List of products at 2 digits level exported by Viet Nam in 2019*, https://www.trademap.org/Product_SelProductCountry.aspx?nvpm=1%7c704%7c%7c%7c%7cTOTAL%7c%7c%7c2%7c1%7c1%7c2%7c1%7c1%7c1%7c1%7c1%7c1. [12]

Netherlands Enterprise Agency (2018), *WIND ENERGY POTENTIAL VIETNAM*, https://www.rvo.nl/sites/default/files/2019/02/Wind-Energy-Potential-Vietnam.pdf. [21]

OECD (2021), *Clean Energy Finance and Investment Mobilisation*, http://www.oecd.org/cefim/ (accessed on 5 March 2021). [44]

OECD (2020), *Multi-dimensional Review of Viet Nam: Towards an Integrated, Transparent and Sustainable Economy*, OECD Development Pathways, OECD Publishing, Paris, https://dx.doi.org/10.1787/367b585c-en. [26]

OECD (2020), *OECD Investment Policy Reviews: Indonesia 2020*, OECD Investment Policy Reviews, OECD Publishing, Paris, https://dx.doi.org/10.1787/b56512da-en. [46]

OECD (2019), *OECD Green Growth Policy Review of Indonesia 2019*, OECD Environmental Performance Reviews, OECD Publishing, Paris, https://dx.doi.org/10.1787/1eee39bc-en. [45]

OECD (2019), *Southeast Asia Going Digital: Connecting SMEs*, http://dx.doi.org/www.oecd.org/going-digital/southeast-asia-connecting-SMEs.pdf. [7]

OECD (2018), *OECD Investment Policy Reviews: Viet Nam 2018*, https://www.oecd-ilibrary.org/finance-and-investment/oecd-investment-policy-reviews-viet-nam-2017_9789264282957-en;jsessionid=l0xqvdqLj4BULwjQE_czV26V.ip-10-240-5-54. [40]

RCEE (2016), *Evaluation of Vietnam Energy Efficiency Program-Phase II.* [14]

Samantha Campbell and Long Huynh (2018), *Client briefing: Renewable energy in Vietnam*, https://www.hoganlovells.com/en/publications/client-briefing-renewable-energy-in-vietnam. [28]

Tuoi Tre (2021), *In the 89th minute of the policy, the solar power project increased "huge"*, Business news, https://tuoitre.vn/phut-thu-89-cua-chinh-sach-du-an-dien-mat-troi-tang-khung-20210101103108829.htm (accessed on 17 June 2021). [19]

UNCTAD (2020), *UNCTAD STAT*, https://unctadstat.unctad.org/wds/ReportFolders/reportFolders.aspx. [37]

UNDP (2018), *Private funding opportunities for renewable energy and energy efficiency investments in Viet Nam*, https://www.vn.undp.org/content/vietnam/en/home/library/environment_climate/private-funding-opportunities-for-renewable-energy-and-energy-ef.html. [42]

VIET (2021), *State management role in power sector*, Vietnam Initiative for Energy Transition, Hanoi, Vietnam. [27]

Vietnam Embassy (2020), *Embassy of the Socialist Republic of Viet Nam in the United States of America*, http://vietnamembassy-usa.org/vietnam/geography. [6]

Wood Mackenzie (2020), *Renewables in most of Asia Pacific to be cheaper than coal power by 2030*, https://www.woodmac.com/press-releases/renewables-in-most-of-asia-pacific-to-be-cheaper-than-coal-power-by-2030/. [34]

World Bank (2021), *Green Climate Fund provide Vietnam with US$86.3 million to spur energy efficiency investments*, https://www.worldbank.org/en/news/press-release/2021/03/08/wb-gcf-provide-vietnam-with-us863-million-to-spur-energy-efficiency-investments. [50]

World Bank (2021), *Vietnam Overview*, https://www.worldbank.org/en/country/vietnam/overview. [13]

World Bank (2021), *World Bank Development Indicators (database).* [8]

World Bank (2020), *International Development Association program document for proposed development policy credit in the amount of SDR 61.5*, http://documents1.worldbank.org/curated/en/580071591668121859/pdf/Vietnam-Climate-Change-and-Green-Growth-Development-Policy-Financing.pdf. [35]

World Bank (2020), *Poverty & Equity Brief: Viet Nam*, https://databank.worldbank.org/data/download/poverty/987B9C90-CB9F-4D93-AE8C-750588BF00QA/AM2020/Global_POVEQ_VNM.pdf (accessed on 15 October 2020). [3]

World Bank (2020), *World Bank Open Data: Vietnam*, https://data.worldbank.org/country/vietnam (accessed on 15 October 2020). [1]

World Bank (2019), *Accelerating Vietnam's path to prosperity*, https://blogs.worldbank.org/voices/accelerating-vietnams-path-prosperity. [39]

World Bank (2019), *Connecting Vietnam for Growth and Shared Prosperity*, http://documents1.worldbank.org/curated/en/590451578409008253/pdf/Vietnam-Development-Report-2019-Connecting-Vietnam-for-Growth-and-Shared-Prosperity.pdf. [5]

Notes

[1] Excluding rooftop solar PV.

[2] Technical potential establishes an upper-boundary estimate of development potential, given system performance, topographic, environmental, and land-use constraints.

2 Planning and governance

This chapter examines governance for clean energy finance and investment and power planning in Viet Nam. It provides an overview of Viet Nam's institutional framework for clean energy and electricity market structure, and identifies areas to improve coordination across institutions, at all levels of government, to ensure effective and consistent goals and policies. The chapter also highlights progress and opportunities to improve the country's clean energy finance and investment-related targets, strategies and power planning mechanisms with a view to sending credible, ambitious and long-term signals to investors.

Viet Nam has already met many of its clean energy ambitions set under the last 10-year socio economic development cycle. Energy savings under the Viet Nam Energy Efficiency Programmes (VNEEP) I and II were achieved, and ambitions for 2030 solar photovoltaic (PV) power have been surpassed. The draft Power Development Plan (PDP) VIII increases long-term renewable deployment targets but signals no significant capacity deployments until after 2030. Although the level of market growth was not expected to be maintained following the recent boom, the length and hiatus outlined may prove disruptive to supply chains, green jobs, and investor confidence.

As the country turns to integrated liquefied natural gas to power projects and additional coal power capacity, unmitigated fuel price risks and implementation delays could be a source of increasing energy insecurity. In this fast evolving energy context, co-ordination between local and central government actors remains a priority, and the flexibility of planning processes will need to increase.

Viet Nam has signalled its intention to steadily develop a competitive power market and, in line with ongoing electricity market reforms, the role and independence of the Electricity Regulatory Authority of Viet Nam (ERAV) should continue to evolve to ensure effective oversight. In order to integrate the rapidly growing share of variable renewable electricity into the power system, Viet Nam Electricity National Power Transmission Corporation (EVN NPT) has already planned substantial upgrades to the transmission system and this can be further supported by adopting a range of technical and market-based solutions.

Assessment and recommendations:

Viet Nam has set ambitious clean energy targets but co-ordination on planning remains a challenge

Viet Nam should be commended for its clean energy ambitions set out its Nationally Determined Contributions (NDCs) and national strategies, such as the National Green Growth Strategy, the Renewable Energy Development Strategy, the National Environmental Protection Strategy, the National Climate Change Strategy and Resolution 55NQ/TW on the orientation of the National Energy Development Strategy. Under Viet Nam's system of top down planning, national master plans are currently being drafted in line with the 10-year Socio-Economic Development Strategy. The new master Planning Law No. 21/2017/QH14, takes a positive step in consolidating the existing framework on planning and provides a new structure for policy coherence and co-ordination. However, the multi-layered process requires a significant level of co-ordination to simultaneously formulate interlinking masterplans, which must be appraised by relevant ministries and authorities, and be put to public consultation.

A number of important planning elements are still in development at the time of this assessment, such as the National Land Use Planning and the National Marine Spatial Planning, which both inform the current Power Development Plan draft, and are important tools for ensuring provincial co-ordination. The master plan cycle runs over 10 years and while the planning law does provide for a review after five years, in light of the extensive formulation, consultation and appraisal process, modifying master plans will represent a significant endeavour. At a time where the context for clean energy is changing extremely quickly, the lack of a flexible planning process may hinder policymaker's ability to react in a timely manner.

Clarity is needed on the process for supplementing the Power Development Plan VIII

The Government of Viet Nam should be commended for their level of ambition in prioritising the sustainable development of the national energy system, as noted in Resolution 55, and the recently published Draft PDP VIII documents. As mandated by the recently updated planning law, the PDP VIII covers a period of 10 years, with a review every five years. Responsive power development planning will be important in light of rapidly changing circumstances, both in terms of high GDP and energy demand growth, as well as renewable energy technology cost reductions. A 10-year power development plan cannot therefore ensure a cost-efficient and optimal power system development trajectory throughout the period. The draft PDP VIII document does include provisions indicating a possibility for more flexible and frequent updates and revisions throughout the planning period, however, the process, criteria, the extent of possible revisions and timeline thereof still appear to be unclear.

The annual growth rate of power consumption is expected to be 9.1% from 2021-2025 and 7.9 % from 2026-2030. As the dependence on electricity increases due to fuel switching and economic growth, it is vital that the number and scale of energy savings programs also increases. The inclusion of energy efficiency in the PDP VIII is a positive development. It outlines current energy efficiency policies under the National Energy Efficiency programme for 2019-2025 with a vision to 2030 (VNEEP III), and the National Program on Electricity Demand Management programme for 2018-2020 with a vision to 2030, as well as analysing the impacts of rooftop solar on electricity demand. Energy efficiency has also been included as a parameter in the electricity demand modelling.

Oversight and governance will be central to creating a competitive power market

Effective oversight and governance are critical to ensuring that the future power system develops in a manner consistent with the country's overarching policy goals. Ongoing and planned restructuring efforts under the 2004 Electricity Law, including the greater operational independence of generation and transmission activities, plans to make the National Load Dispatch Center (NLDC) operationally independent, and the introduction of the wholesale market, will profoundly affect the way in which new generation is developed and integrated into the system.

ERAV's effective oversight of these various interlinking pieces is critical to ensuring success. ERAV already has many tools in place including access to data, analytical capacity, and limited regulatory authority over critical elements such as retail pricing. As the power sector and power markets develop, ERAV's oversight role will need to be strengthened and potentially expanded. For example, ERAV has limited capacity to model the power system. As a result, it must rely on the technical capabilities of the utility, EVN, and other entities such as the Institute of Energy to assess the need for and benefits of new investments.

ERAV will also need to ensure that the costs associated with the energy transition are passed on to consumers in a fair and equitable manner, carefully balancing the need to keep prices cost reflective while working to minimize the economic burden on the country's low income households. ERAV's ability to do so is complicated somewhat by the fact that some significant cost drivers, in particular transmission line development, are outside of its regulatory authority. Other elements, such as the ability to increase tariffs, are constrained by the need to seek the approval of the Ministry of Finance for changes above a certain level.

EVN has strengthened planning and system operation practices

EVN's planning and operation practices, until very recently, were based on running a power system with very high shares of conventional, dispatchable generation. Given the rapidly increasing share of renewable generation, the NLDC is having to quickly adapt its capabilities. Dispatch plans, for example, have been based around hour-long blocks, but under the wholesale market pilot, this has been switched to 30-minute trading and dispatching cycles since September 2020. Load forecasting is also improving; as well as depending on generator schedules, the NLDC has developed in house forecasting[1], and from 2021, uses forecasts from two independent third-party providers[2].

EVN should also be commended for its willingness to experiment with new technologies and practices, for example through its energy services company (ESCO) pilot, demand side management program, and demand reduction program, which have trialled demand side measures for load shaping and demand flexibility. A continued focus on integrating demand side measures into EVN's planning and operational practices can ensure these initiatives can be scaled up to achieve economic benefits. Further modernisation of system operation can also support greater variable renewable energy integration, for example, by further reducing the size of the dispatch windows to 15-minute increments. EVN has improved its capabilities to forecast wind and solar generation but incentives should also be implemented to ensure generators provide regular and accurate forecast updates, especially leading up to dispatch.

Technical and market-based solutions will be required to integrate variable renewable capacity

While investments in new grid infrastructure will be necessary, a range of technical and market-based solutions focused on unlocking and enabling power system flexibility can help ensure that planned solar PV and wind generation is integrated affordably, securely, and in a timely manner. As Viet Nam advances transmission infrastructure planning, the costs and benefits of "non-wires alternatives" such as distributed energy resources, demand-side response, or a range of storage technologies should be evaluated on equal terms with investment in transmission upgrades. These solutions can often provide the same benefits at much lower costs. For example, a New York City utility was able to avoid a USD 1 billion transmission upgrade by investing USD 652 million in a combination of energy efficiency, demand response and distributed generation (Girouard, 2019[11]). While some of these solutions may not yet be implementable under the current policy framework, embedding the assessment of non-wires alternatives into the planning process can help identify opportunities for greater efficiency or cost saving.

Box 2.1. Main policy recommendations on clean energy governance and planning

- Increase NLDC's ability to balance the system efficiently by adopting incentives for renewable generators to deliver accurate and regular forecasts leading up to dispatch.
- Improve ERAV's independence and ensure it is fully resourced to perform its required functions and respond to future regulatory needs. In addition, consider expanding its regulatory authority to cover transmission planning and approval, as well as other areas that impact system costs and which therefore have implications for end-user tariffs.
- Increase frequency of the regular PDP revisions and updates to ensure that the most cost-effective and optimal development of the energy system of Viet Nam is continuously ensured. Mechanism for ensuring optimised course-correction (annual or biennial) should have clear and specific procedure, criteria, timelines and other critical elements to ensure alignment and confidence among all stakeholders, both governmental, provincial and commercial. Streamlining and accelerating the development and approval process of the PDP should also be considered through e.g. earlier involvement of critical stakeholders, mandating more operational matters to be decided at administrative level etc.
- Clearly define and embed the co-ordination processes between governmental and provincial institutions to support effective and timely PDP VIII implementation (e.g. support favourable for renewable energy development from a resource and transmission system perspective), as well as the development of the annual / biennial plans and updates.
- Undertake a strategic review of non-wires-based alternatives within the planning process for transmission infrastructure, such as batteries, demand-side response programs, or other modern technologies. These solutions can help avoid costly investments in transmission line reinforcement throughout the power system, and can be particularly more cost-effective in densely populated areas.

Policy coherence, co-ordination, and monitoring

In the 1980's Viet Nam embarked on the transformation from a centrally planned economy towards a social market economy under state guidance. Key elements of this central planning remain, particularly in Viet Nam's approach to agenda setting, which is led across sectors and government levels by the Socio-Economic Development Strategy (SEDS), decided by the Congress of Viet Nam Communist Party.

Top down planning is the main instrument for policy coherence and co-ordination

Formulated for a 10-year period, the SEDS sets the overarching strategy for economic and social development, which informs a system of master plans that formulate the agenda across all areas of activity. Governance is split between four levels, comprising of a central level, and three sub-national levels, provincial, district, and town. Central and provincial government set and implement policies, and the latter two sub-national levels participate in implementation. National master plans and subsequent budget programmes flow downward to set the agenda for the next sub-national level of master plan and its budget, from regional, to provincial then rural and urban levels (Robiou du Pont and Balanowski, 2018[2]). Information flows upwards from sub-national levels in the form of draft plans, supporting the formulation of national master plans at central government level, and therefore final sub-national plans and budgets. In practice, this will depend on the subnational authority's planning capabilities and resources, and the alignment with current policy priorities.

In combination with a hierarchical system of decision making authority, Viet Nam's clean energy sector has a complex institutional structure, directly involving several government agencies. The Prime Minister holds final authority as head of government, and the Ministry of Industry and Trade (MOIT) occupies a central position in energy policy. Fiscal policy and financial markets fall under the Ministry of Finance (MOF) and its subsidiaries: the State Bank of Viet Nam (SBV) and State Securities Commission (SSC). Investment policy falls under the Ministry of Planning and Investment (MPI). Responsibility is shared with other line ministries, in particular the Ministry of Natural Resources and Environment (MONRE), which is responsible for the environment and leads the Climate Change Strategy and the NDC update, and the Ministry of Construction (MOC), which is responsible for building standards, as well as other areas of clean energy policy related to the construction sector. However, the authority for the formulation and implementation of clean energy finance and investment policy and legislation is centralised in MOIT, MOF, and MPI.

Figure 2.1. National system of master planning

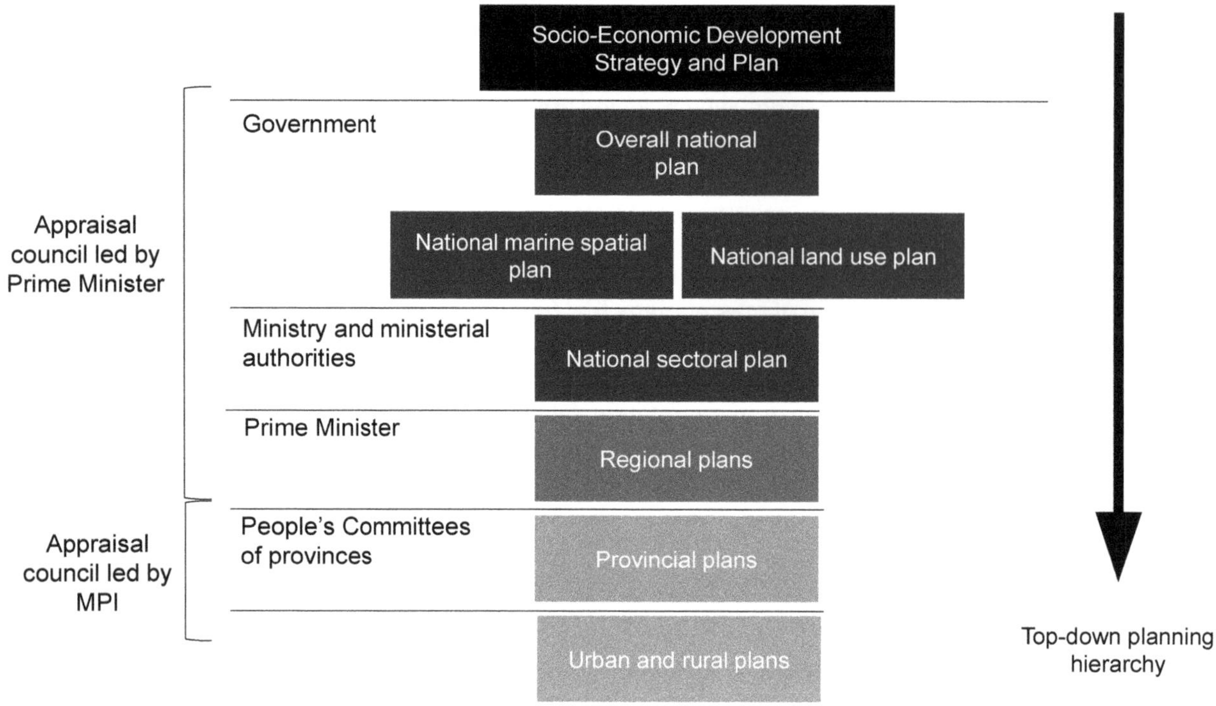

Note: MPI = Ministry of Planning and Investment
Source: The National Assembly - Government of Viet Nam (2017) Law No. 21/2017/QH14

MOIT, MPI and MOF are key actors in formulating and implementing clean energy policy

Responsible for the energy sector as a whole, MOIT formulates policy and national plans, subject to the Prime Minister's approval, and issues circulars and guidelines implementing the Prime Minister and National Assembly's laws, resolutions and decrees. Moreover, by leading on planning and implementation of energy sector mitigation activities, MOIT plays an important role in achieving Viet Nam's NDC targets.

Under the former national Power Development Plan (PDP), renewable energy projects under 50 MW are approved by MOIT and anything over that by the Prime Minister. This process is yet to be determined under the draft PDP VIII, which moves from a system of pre-approved pipelines of projects to competitive bidding. Under MOIT, the Electricity and Renewable Energy Authority (EREA), advises on electricity and renewable energy and designs renewable energy support mechanisms including feed-in tariffs. Also under MOIT, the Energy Efficiency and Sustainable Development Department (EESD) advises on energy efficiency and conservation and the Electricity Regulatory Authority of Viet Nam (ERAV) regulates the power sector. As fully funded departments and subsidiaries, all three bodies remain closely bound to MOIT's decision-making authority.

MOF and MPI hold important positions in not only clean energy finance and investment but in Viet Nam's governance structure generally. Together the two line ministries coordinate the state budget allocated to the implementation of master plans. Private Public Partnership and investment laws are formulated by MPI, who is also responsible for administrating investment and enterprise registration, leading the implementation of the green growth strategy, and investment promotion activities. MOF has authority over taxation and exemptions, approves changes to electricity tariffs over given thresholds, and through SBV regulates financial market policy and leads the promotion of green banking.

At sub-nation level, the Peoples Provincial Committee play a pivotal role

The governance of clean energy finance and investment is a multi-layered co-ordination process with decentralised planning at sub-national level. The Provincial People's Committee (PPC) acts as the executive arm, implementing national strategies, regulations and laws at provincial level. They are supported by regional offices of key ministries who provide technical expertise in their respective fields. Although decentralisation reforms have given provinces more planning authority, they remain strongly dependent on central planning where much of the final authority is concentrated. Planning, co-ordination and financing capacity varies across provinces, which has consequences for local implementation capabilities. An example of this is the investment registration certificate, which should serve as a tool to ensure new projects align with sectoral strategy, however, without sufficient resources or competences to fully evaluate projects the registration process becomes less effective and transparent (OECD, 2018[3]).

For renewable energy, the appraisal process has up till now been dependent on the size of the project. For projects over 30 MW MOIT undertakes the appraisal, whereas for projects under 30 MW, its regional office, the Department of Industry and Trade (DOIT) can appraise and grant generation licenses. Equally, depending on the size of the project, appraisal of investments or environmental impacts will either respectively be in the hands of MPI and MONRE, or their regional offices, the Department of Planning and Investment (DPI) and Department of Natural Resources and Environment (DONRE). Provincial authorities will also formulate and execute plans for ground clearance and resettlement compensation for land lease agreements. For energy efficiency, provincial authorities are responsible for developing and implementing provincial action plans, which requires significant data and technical capabilities. Outside of allocated state budget, the respective province will be responsible for raising capital for the plan's implementation.

Figure 2.2. Governance of renewable energy

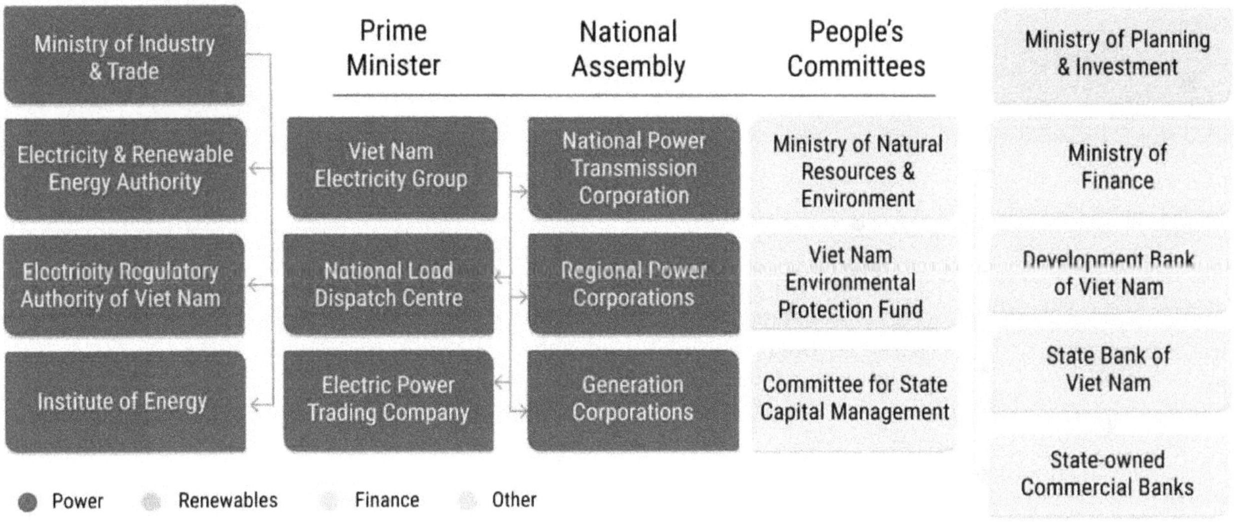

Source: OECD (2021) Viet Nam Country Page CEFIM webiste

Figure 2.3. Governance of energy efficiency

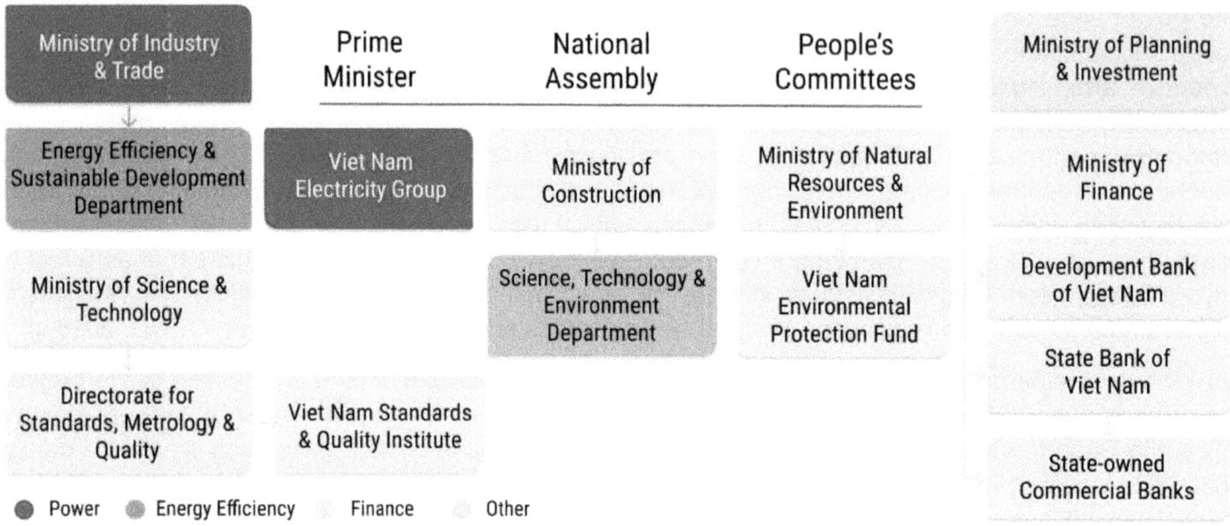

Source: OECD (2021) Viet Nam Country Page CEFIM webiste

Table 2.1. Co-ordination bodies

The National Assembly	Highest body of state power of the Socialist Republic of Viet Nam, the sole body that has the constitutional and legislative rights.
The Prime Minister	Head of Government, which is the supreme state administrative agency of the Socialist Republic of Viet Nam. Appointed by the National Assembly.
National Committee for Climate Change	Highest-level institutional body and inter-ministerial committee in charge of climate change policy, formulating, co-ordinating and implementing climate policies, and providing advice to government on climate change issues.
Cross-sectoral initiatives	• Viet Nam Energy Efficiency Programme (VNEEP) steering committee • Green Growth Strategy steering committee • Power development steering committee

Table 2.2. Line ministries and subsidiaries

The Ministry of Industry and Trade (MOIT)	MOIT has overall responsibility for energy sector policy and regulation. • Electricity Regulatory Authority of Viet Nam (ERAV) is the department managing and regulating electricity market-related activities, including the development of all power projects. • Electricity and Renewable Energy Authority (EREA), agency acting as main regulator for renewable energy, with authority and responsibility for regulating feed-in tariffs. • Energy Efficiency & Sustainable Development Department (EESD), department advising on energy efficiency and conservation. • Institute of Energy, institute conducting research for power development planning and renewable energy.
The Ministry of Planning & Investment (MPI)	MPI coordinates the country's overall development strategies, planning and national investments, and mobilises and manages ODA and climate finance. • Foreign Investment Agency (FIA), investment promotion agency providing information and guidance on investment in Viet Nam. It is the agency responsible for issuing investment registration certification. • The Central Institute for Economic Management (CIEM), national institute researching and providing proposals and recommendations on economic laws, regulations and reforms, planning and management mechanisms and business environment.
The Ministry of Finance (MOF)	MOF formulates state budgets, fiscal policy, and financial market monitoring and regulation and co-ordination with MPI to formulate relevant financial legislation and state budget. • State Bank of Viet Nam (SBV), ministerial agency, undertaking state management of monetary and banking activities and foreign exchange, money issuance, bank of credit institutions. • State Securities Commission of Viet Nam (SSC), commission responsible for regulation and supervision of securities and the securities market, and for management of public services around these markets.

The Ministry of Construction (MOC)	MOC is responsible for construction, building materials, housing and office buildings, architecture, urban and rural construction planning, and urban infrastructure.
The Ministry of Science and Technology (MOST)	MOST is responsible for scientific research, technology development and innovation activities, including intellectual property, standards, metrology and quality control. • Directorate for Standards, Metrology and Quality (STAMTEQ), responsible for advising in the fields of standardisation, metrology and quality.
The Ministry of Natural Resources and Environment (MONRE)	MONRE is responsible for natural resources such as land, water, and minerals. It works on the formulation of climate policy, planning of land use on the national level, and acts as the focal point to the UNFCCC and leads NDC Review and Update. • Department of Climate Change coordinates climate action within the ministry. • Viet Nam Environment Protection Fund (VEPF), national fund that operates as a state financial institution to support climate adaptation and mitigation and environmental protection through concessional loans, interest-rate support or loans.

Table 2.3. Regional authorities

Provincial People's Committee	Executive arm of government at provincial level with budgetary and administrative authority. Develops provincial renewable-energy development and energy efficiency action plans subject to central government approval.
Provincial People's Council	Represents the authority of the state at local level. Elects and oversees Provincial People's Committee.
Provincial offices of central line ministries	Supports the Provincial People's Committee and acts as line ministry representative at provincial level (e.g.: the Department of Industry and Trade is the regional office of the Ministry of Industry and Trade)

Long-term goal setting to promote clean energy investment

Viet Nam is particularly vulnerable to the effects of climate change, ranked 14th most climate vulnerable country by HSBC in 2018 (HSBC, 2018[4]), particularly due to its exposure to flooding, tropical cyclones and drought. A number of comprehensive climate change strategies, many of which predate the Paris Agreement, demonstrate a commitment to mainstreaming mitigation and adaptation across socio-economic plans. High oil prices and declining hydroelectric power, linked to adverse weather, contributed to the energy shortages in the early 2000's. Priority has since been given to opening the energy sector to private investment and increasing the role of clean energy technologies over long and medium term horizons. Initial targets for solar power have been surpassed and progress has been made on energy efficiency, but a clear long term and ambitious strategy for clean energy should remain a priority.

Clean energy plays a key a role in Viet Nam's long term energy security strategy

Climate and clean energy strategies are integrated into the country's system of planning by informing the 10-year socio-economic development strategy, which in turn informs socio-economic development plans. Key milestones in the clean energy agenda have been the 2004 Electricity Law, which formalised the move away from a centrally planned monopoly to market liberalisation and private sector investment. This was followed by the 2007 National Energy Development Strategy up to 2020 with a vision to 2050 (Decision No. 1855/QD-TTg), which prioritised diversification of energy sources, energy saving technologies, restructuring the electricity market and supporting renewable technologies. Initial targets for clean energy were set through the 2015 Renewable Energy Development Strategy 2016-2030 with an outlook to 2050 (REDS), and the two phases of the Viet Nam Energy Efficiency Programmes (VNEEP) from 2006 to 2015. Clean energy has also been a key feature of the Green Growth Strategy 2011-2020 with a vision to 2050 (Decision No. 1393/QĐ-TTg) and the more recent Resolution No. 55NQ/TW (Resolution 55) which orients the design of the upcoming National Energy Development Strategy of Viet Nam to 2030 with a vision to 2045. Resolution 55 lays out the priorities for an energy system focusing on sustainable energy development, decarbonisation, diversification and competitive energy markets. It reinforces Viet Nam's intention to increase private participation in electricity generation, with articles around eliminating distorting policies, increasing competition and restructuring state owned enterprises (SOE), as well as improved use of market based instruments

Although these strategies have supported private sector investment and increased supply, Viet Nam is still facing energy security challenges and has remained heavily dependent on thermal power and large hydroelectric resources. Growing energy demands are fast outpacing domestic supply, leading to increasing dependence on energy import. With an average 6.6% GDP growth for 2021-2030, and 5.7% for 2031-2045, forecast by MPI, energy demand is expected to continue to grow significantly. In this context, Viet Nam's medium and long-term energy efficiency and renewable energy strategy are an opportunity to ensure a secure and affordable domestic supply of energy, whilst also addressing environmental and climate change concerns.

Ambitions set out in renewable energy strategies have met with early success

The Renewable Energy Development Strategy (REDS) to 2030 with a vision to 2050 was established to guide renewable energy development in the country, particularly focusing on biomass, on-shore wind and solar development through 2030, and offshore wind potential thereafter. REDS aimed for generation from solar and wind power to increase from next to nothing to represent 0.5% and 1% of total generation by 2020, and 6% and 2.7% by 2030. In the revision of the Power Development Plan for the period of 2016-2020 (PDP VII-revised), targets were reflected by a pipeline of new renewable projects with capacity targets for solar and wind of 800 MW and 850 MW by 2020, and 12 000 MW and 6 000 MW by 2030.

By the end of 2020, solar power had overtaken its 2030 targets under the PDP VII revised, after over 17 GW of installed capacity were recorded. Conversely, wind power had fallen short of its 2020 targets with only 538 MW installed (Institute of Energy, 2021[5]). Yet, the overall target set for installed renewable capacity (excluding large hydro) under the PDP VII-revised (of 9.9%) was surpassed. Solar alone represented 25% of total capacity, which is by 2.5 times this target. In terms of generation, according to EVN generation reports, solar power accounted for 5% of total generation, which is eight times greater than the REDS solar target for the same year.

Renewable energy continues to feature prominently in new strategies. Resolution 55, which orients the development of the upcoming National Energy Development Strategy to 2030, confirms an increasing commitment to investment in clean energy. Published in 2020, in the midst of the solar boom, Resolution 55 takes a broader approach by targeting 15-20% renewable energy sources in the total primary energy supply mix by 2030 and 25-30% by 2045. While electricity from renewable sources is prioritised, the strategy notes that wind and solar power development should be undertaken while ensuring the safety of the national power system and reasonable costs. Resolution 55 aims for overall greenhouse gas emissions reductions from energy activities compared to the business-as-usual (BAU) scenario of 15% by 2030 and 20% by 2045. Renewable energy development also features in the new strategy for the sustainable development of Viet Nam's marine economy by 2030, with a vision to 2045, highlighting Viet Nam's interest in supporting new developments in marine renewable energy and new marine economic sectors.

Energy efficiency features across different strategies but progress has been slower

Viet Nam has a highly energy-intensive economy, ranking amongst the highest in the world. The importance of energy efficiency as a policy goal has been highlighted in numerous economic and sectoral development strategies such as the Green Growth Strategy to 2020 and the Industrial Development Strategy to 2025. Much of this focuses on manufacturing and industry, which has been a core component of economic development strategy and a large factor in increasing energy demand. Energy price policies have not been reflective of costs and rapidly increasing industrialisation has benefited from particularly low energy tariffs by regional standards, and has tended towards inefficient use of power. Viet Nam is aware of this, as highlighted by objectives within both strategies, which aim to increasing the use of energy efficient and energy saving technologies in industry. However, early ambitions set under the 2012 Green Growth Strategy of reducing energy consumption per unit of GDP by 1-1.5% per year have not been met. A review of this strategy is upcoming.

Specific energy efficiency targets have been set through the Viet Nam Energy Efficiency Programme (VNEEP), which have been broadly successful. The VNEEP I and II covering the 2006-2010 and 2011-2016 periods, respectively targeted a 3-5% and 5-8% reduction in total commercial energy consumption over their periods. Cumulative commercial energy savings in the first phase of VNEEP reached 3 733 KTOE, equivalent to 3.4% of the total final energy consumption, and in the second phase reached 10 610 KTOE, equivalent to 5.65% of the total final energy consumption (RCEE, 2016[6]).

After a short implementation gap, the third phase of the VNEEP programme (VNEEP III) was launched in 2019 and will run through to 2025. Over the period, the VNEEP III aims to achieve 5-7% savings on national energy consumption, power losses of less than 6.5%, and set targets to reduce average energy consumption across certain industrial sectors (Table 2.4) (Decision No: 280/QD-TTg of 2019) (PwC, 2017[7]). Resolution 55 sets longer term targets of 7% ratio of energy efficiency on total final energy consumption by 2030, compared to the business-as-usual scenario, and approximately 14% by 2045.

Table 2.4. VNEEP III energy consumption savings across industrial sectors compared to the period of 2015-2018

Industrial sectors	Energy consumption savings
Steel industries (depending on production process)	3-10%
Chemical industry	7 %
Plastic manufacturing industry	18-22.46 %
Cement industry	7.5%
Textile and garment industry	5%
Alcoholic beverage industry	3-6.88%
Paper industry (depending on production scale)	8 to 15.8%

Source: RCEE (2016) Evaluation-of-Viet Nam-energy-efficiency-program-phase-ii

A comprehensive climate agenda is reinforced through international commitments

The governance structure is strengthened by a comprehensive set of national climate change policies. The three core climate change strategies are the 2011 National Climate Change Strategy (Decision No. 2139/QĐ-TTg), the Green Growth Strategy 2011-2020 with a vision to 2050 (Decision No. 1393/QĐ-TTg), and the National Environment Protection Strategy to 2020 with visions to 2030 (Decision No. 1216/QĐ-TTg) established in 2012 with the view of limiting pollution and environmental deterioration. The Climate Change Strategy sets a number of targets up to 2050, with the objective of developing a low-carbon economy, and a focus on sustainability, adaptation and resilience. Established to support implementation of the Climate Change Strategy through fast, efficient and sustainable growth, the Green Growth Strategy aims to achieve a low carbon economy whilst enriching natural capital.

In 2020, Viet Nam became the ninth country to submit a revised Nationally Determined Contribution (NDC) under the 2015 Paris Agreement. The NDC places a heavy focus on the energy sector for mitigation potential, and in alignment with the latest socio-economic development forecasts for up to 2030, emission reductions targets were marginally revised up from 8 to 9% unconditionally and from 25 to 27% conditionally compared to a business as usual (BAU) scenario from a 2014 base (Figure 2.4). The conditional targets are dependent on international support received through bilateral and multilateral cooperation and through mechanisms under the Paris Agreement. Due to the incredible surge of renewable projects since 2019 following the feed-in tariff regulations, Viet Nam is already well on track to meet its mitigation targets. The government has indicated an update of the NDC will be developed, after the PDP VIII for the period of 2021-2030 has been finalised (E3G, 2021[8]).

Figure 2.4. Viet Nam's updated NDC targets, by 2030

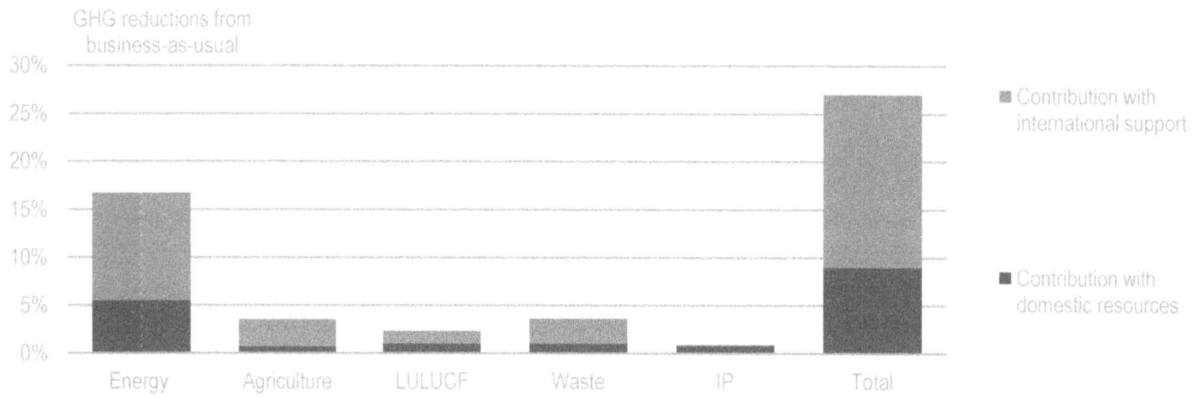

Note: LULUCF reductions represent increase in GHGs sequestration

Source: The Socialist Republic of Viet Nam (2020) Update Nationally Determined Contributions

StatLink https://stat.link/kvazwj

Energy efficiency planning

In the face of energy shortages in the early 2000s, Viet Nam shifted its focus to improving the efficiency of its exploitation and use of primary energy, prioritised in law through the Decree on Energy Efficiency and Conservation promulgated in 2003, and the Electricity Law in 2004. In 2006, the first national energy efficiency action plan, known as the Viet Nam Energy Efficiency Programme (VNEEP), was approved (Figure 2.5).

Figure 2.5. Viet Nam Energy Efficiency Programme (VNEEP)

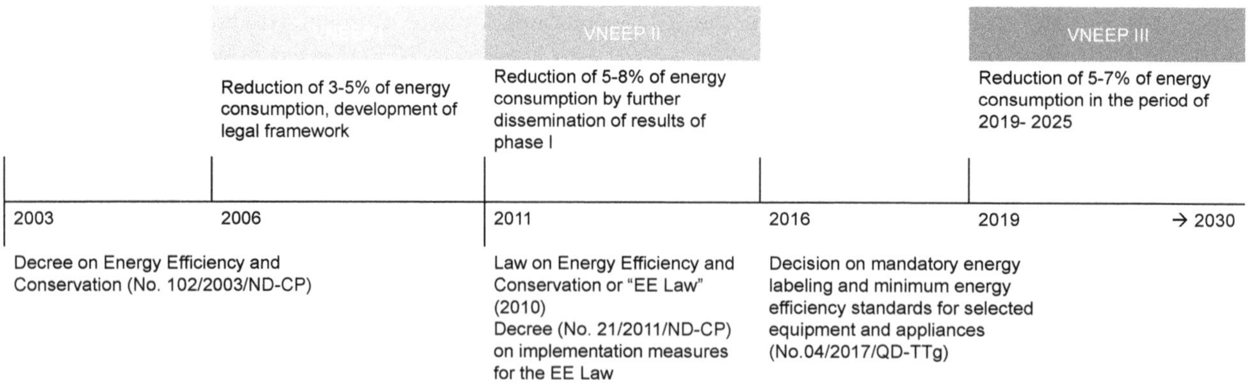

Source: Government of Viet Nam (2019) Decision 280/QD-TTg

VNEEP is the main instrument for energy efficiency planning

VNEEP has been the main instrument for planning the promotion of energy efficiency. All energy efficiency and conservation activities across sectors were integrated into the VNEEP programme, which acts as a co-ordination tool for sub-projects and programmes funded by international development partners. Many important legislative milestones were achieved during VNEEP I and II, including Law No. 50/2010/QH-12 on Economical and Efficient Use of Energy (the Energy Efficiency Law) and its implementing decrees (Decision 1427/QĐ-TTg of 2012). Over the period, voluntary and mandatory energy labelling requirements and building energy performance standards were also introduced.

Arguably, the momentum built-up by these early successes suffered due to a delay in approving an updated programme at the end of the VNEEP II implementation period. This led notably to a loss of human resource capacity in government, particularly at the provincial level. VNEEP III was approved in 2019 setting out planned activities over the period 2019-2025 with a view to 2030. VNEEP III seeks to build on the achievements of VNEEP I and II with medium-term energy efficiency targets for both the overall economy and industry sectors, and by further development of the regulatory environment, strengthening monitoring and compliance enforcement, and building the skills in the market through training and certification (Box 2.2).

Box 2.2. Viet Nam National Energy Efficiency Programme 2019-2025 with a view to 2030 (VNEEP III)

Prioritised Activities

- Reviewing, developing and finalising mechanisms and policies on efficient use of energy
- Providing technical and financial assistance
- Building a Viet Nam energy data centre
- Enhancing capacity for economical and efficient use of energy
- Strengthening inspection and supervision
- Communication to raise community awareness
- Strengthening international cooperation
- Scientific research and technological development
- Establishing funds to promote economical and efficient use of energy

Source: MOIT (2018) VIETNAM - NATIONAL ENERGY EFFICIENCY PROGRAM 2019 – 2030

VNEEP III places a stronger emphasis on co-ordination

A review of VNEEP I and II pointed to a need for better central and local co-ordination, as well as co-ordination across ministries and national strategies. In particular, energy efficiency policies did not feature sufficiently in sector master plans. The inclusion of energy efficiency in the PDP VIII is an important tool for ensuring greater co-ordination and prioritisation.

VNEEP has received support from international organisations such as the World Bank, JICA, DANIDA, UNIDO and the IFC, in the form of financial assistance, technical assistance and development human resources training. Low co-ordination of this support over VNEEP I and II led to some overlaps and potential inefficient use of resources. One of VNEEP III's primary objectives is the co-ordination tool for mobilising national and international resources for policy implementation, technical assistance, research, product development, market transition and capacity building.

VNEEP III involves a number of different actors, including the prime minister, line ministries, associations working on energy efficiency and energy conservation, local authorities and energy groups. Under VNEEP III, a programme steering committee has been set up to co-ordinate this, comprising of participating line ministries and associations, led by the Prime Minster, with MOIT as Standing Deputy. Additionally, an assisting office is located within MOIT, who assume primary responsibility for co-ordinating with ministries and sectoral authorities on the VNEEP programme to determine annual plans and tasks. MOIT coordinates with MOF and MPI to finalise the list of tasks and projects to be implemented.

Within the steering committee, the elaboration of tasks and allocation of responsibilities is split between a number of different ministries and their departments, including MOIT's EESD, or MOST's Directorate for Standards, Metrology and Quality, to name a couple. Non-governmental associations also have prominent roles, such as the Viet Nam Energy Conservation and Energy Efficiency Association (VECEA), the Viet Nam Green Building Council (VGBC) or consulting firms, such as the Energy Conservation Research and Development Center (Enerteam) and the Viet Nam Initiative for Energy Transition (VIET), which provide inputs for the design of clean energy policies and regulations.

The steering committee works directly with other energy sector stakeholders such as EVN who consult on the content of plans and implement their own energy efficiency activities under their demand side management programme.

Figure 2.6. VNEEP III Steering Committee

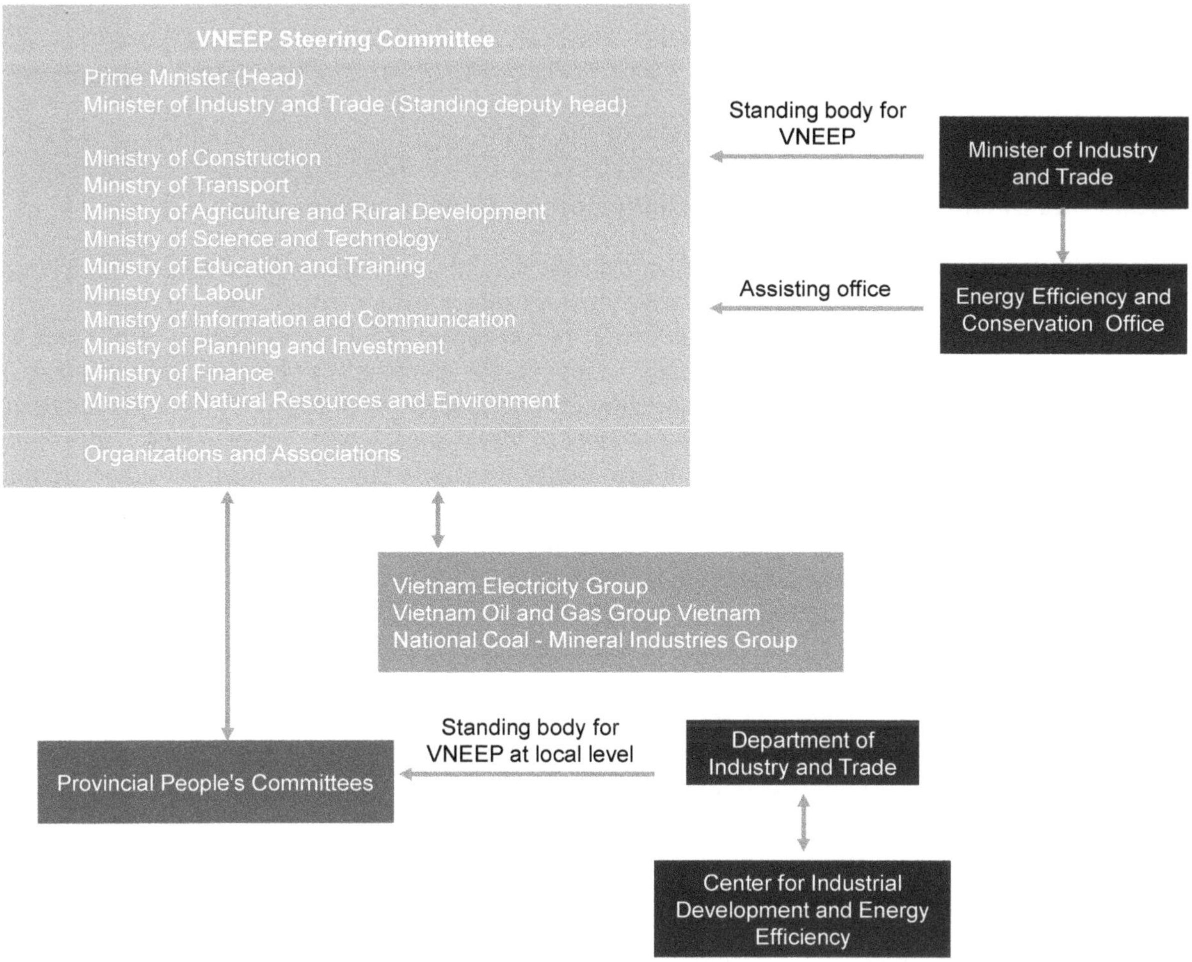

Source: Government of Viet Nam (2019) Decision 280/QD-TTg

Provincial and municipal authorities play a larger role in VNEEP III

Whereas VNEEP I and II consisted predominantly of centrally-led initiatives, VNEEP III places greater emphasis on actions at the provincial and municipal level. MOIT proposes the overall VNEEP III target across provinces based on current implementation of energy consumption, forecast of energy demand according to the local socio-economic development scenario, the potential implementation of energy efficiency through technology solutions, and energy saving potentials in various fields. Provinces are accordingly grouped under seven target brackets ranging from 4.75% to 7.25% energy savings targets from 2020-2025. This approach aims to provide provinces with greater autonomy in determining actions based on their specific and often very different contexts; whereas some provinces may be large industrial hubs, others may be agricultural or rural locations. The PPC develops plans for the implementation of the VNEEP in local authorities, known as provincial energy efficiency action plans (EEAP), sets roadmaps and targets in accordance with their authorities, and allocates funds to implement, inspect, and supervise local programmes. After plans have been approved, MOIT will allocate budget towards the determined activities. In March 2021, 40 out of 63 localities had submitted an EEAP to MOIT for approval for the period of 2020-2025, with the remaining still under development. At provincial level, MOIT's regional office DOIT, presides over the supervision and reporting of results. This planning process requires both data and experts, which can be challenging for provinces. The success or failure of VNEEP III therefore is highly dependent on local level capacity both in terms of human and financial resources. MOIT is supporting this by recruiting more experts to these provinces to help develop plans and developing improved data collection procedures where there are gaps. A new unit of MOIT is planned that would act as an additional support facility for this purpose.

Institutional framework for the electricity market

Progress has been made towards a partially competitive power market

The Electricity Law of 2004 formalised Viet Nam's intention to move away from a centrally planned monopoly, towards a competitive power market with private sector investment in power generation. Since the 1990's Viet Nam has worked towards reforming the power sector in order to ensure efficient and affordable power and long-term security of supply. To enable the liberalisation of the electricity market, the reform process has required restructuring of the state utility, Electricity Viet Nam (EVN), and importantly, the establishment of the Electricity Regulatory Authority of Viet Nam (ERAV). The electricity law sets out three distinct phases of liberalisation of the electricity market, starting with a competitive generation market, then a competitive wholesale market, and finally the introduction of a competitive retail market. The wholesale market is currently in pilot phase, with 53% of the total installed capacity already participating in 2019 (EVN, 2020[9]). Full operation is planned for 2021. In 2020, 97 power plants participated directly to the wholesale market and 26 plants participate indirectly (ERAV, 2020[10]). When fully introduced, the wholesale market will play a key role in unlocking and incentivising system flexibility, as well as efficient generation based on least cost, allowing emissions and pollution to be minimised due to the lower cost of renewable generation. Prices that reflect actual system conditions can incentivise generation to ramp-up or ramp-down as necessary. This is true not only for traditional dispatchable generation, but also for renewable generation, which can also respond flexibly (for example, by choosing to self-curtail) when incentivised to do so.

EVN's role in generation is evolving as the market liberalisation process continues

While the structure and role of EVN and its subsidiaries is evolving, there remains a significant concentration of power within EVN's central management and close ties to the state (MOIT) through both legal structure and corporate governance. Under the current structure, the government directs EVN's investments, and appoints the members of its board of directors and its senior management. EVN management in turn appoints the management board of EVN's subsidiary. Moreover, EVN owns and sets service and output targets for Power Corporations (regional distribution and retail subsidiaries) and their Management Boards report directly to EVN. Management and control of EVN and subsidiaries, by virtue of the governance structure, is therefore centralised in EVN headquarters (World Bank, 2020[11]).

Today EVN exists as a holding company for a number of its subsidiaries, comprising generation companies (GENCOS), the National Load Dispatch Centre (EVN NLDC), the National Power Transmission Corporation (EVN NPTC), EVN Power Corporations and the EVN Electric Power Trading Company (EPTC). Moreover, at the end of 2018, EVN owned 59 % of total installed generation capacity held either within the three GENCOs, or in the case of strategic hydropower resources under EVN corporate. Consequently, EVN still holds a monopoly over operation, transmission, distribution, and retail albeit in a partially unbundled structure.

Although EVN's separation into different entities may enhance operational independence, such a structure will not entirely reassure private sector investors, given that EVN's capacity as owner of generation assets and parent company to crucial electricity market actors. This includes the EPTC and the NLDC who respectively purchases all renewable electricity from independent power producers (IPP), and determines dispatch and curtailment (discussed in chapter 4). As there is no framework for an ancillary service market for frequency regulation, it is primarily EVN's multi-purpose hydro plants that provide ancillary services.

EVN has played a lead role historically in developing, owning, and operating all electricity system assets, however, the scale of investments required over the PDP VIII to meet energy demand growth surpasses its investment and financing capacity. Attracting private investment to the generation sector will continue to be a priority as seen in sectoral master plans as well as the National Energy Development Strategy. Specifically, it is planned that in the future, EVN's presence in the generation sector would be restricted to ownership of only strategic assets such as multi-purpose hydro plants, which play a role in irrigation or flood management. In order to help realise this ambition, new investments are supervised by the Commission for the Management of State Capital at Enterprises (CMSC) to ensure compliance with regulations related to the use of capital and assets. Thus far, EVN's role in investment in non-hydro renewable generation has been limited, leaving this market open to the private sector.

Authorities within the electricity market need to be strengthened

To deliver on these ambitious goals, Viet Nam will need to develop new generation rapidly, securely, and at least cost to consumers. Effective oversight and governance are critical to ensuring that Viet Nam's future power system develops in a manner consistent with the country's overarching policy goals and that it effectively and efficiently serves the needs of consumers and society more generally. Crucially, the transformation of Viet Nam's power sector extends beyond just the generation mix. Ongoing and planned restructuring efforts, including the unbundling of generation, plans to increase the independence of the National Load Dispatch Centre, and the introduction of the wholesale market, will profoundly impact the way in which new generation is developed and integrated into the system.

ERAV's effective oversight of these various interlinking pieces is critical to ensuring success. Its role includes setting grid codes and standards, issuing licenses, and establishing tariff-setting principles, as well as overall monitoring of the power system. Given the rapid increase in renewable electricity, ERAV's system planning and system operations capabilities are not yet prepared for a power system with high shares of variable energy. Moreover, ERAV's authority is at times limited in scope, with clear boundaries on where its mandate ends, and where that of EVN or EREA starts. For instance, although ERAV reviews master plans around the development of electricity sources, transmission and distribution grids, and their financing needs, the focus of its advice is particularly around security of supply (ADB, 2015[12]). Transmission line development falls outside of its regulatory authority. Part of ERAV's role is to carefully balance the need to keep prices cost reflective while also working to minimise the economic burden on the country's low-income households. Such limitations to its authority complicate its ability to do so. Its authority to increase tariffs is equally constrained by a structured system. Fixed tariff can only be in accordance with Decision 24/2017/QĐ-TTg, with increases of between 5-10% to be approved by MOIT, and anything above 10% submitted to the Prime Minister for approval.

Given the hierarchical structure of governance, ERAV is very closely bound to MOIT in its decision making, and its activities (World Bank, 2020[11]). ERAV's mandate includes monitoring and enforcement of compliance with power market regulation and it serves as the main arbitrator for dispute resolution for power purchase agreements. As Viet Nam's power system continues to evolve, including particularly the move away from the feed-in tariff program to the new, but still undefined, auction system, ERAV's dispute resolution role is likely to grow in importance. By virtue of ERAV's budget, which is fully funded by government, there is a structural dependence on MOIT. Given that EVN is also almost entirely government owned and closely tied to MOIT, this will create uncertainty for investors around whether ERAV's decisions are fair, objective, and free of political interference.

Figure 2.7. Electricity market structure

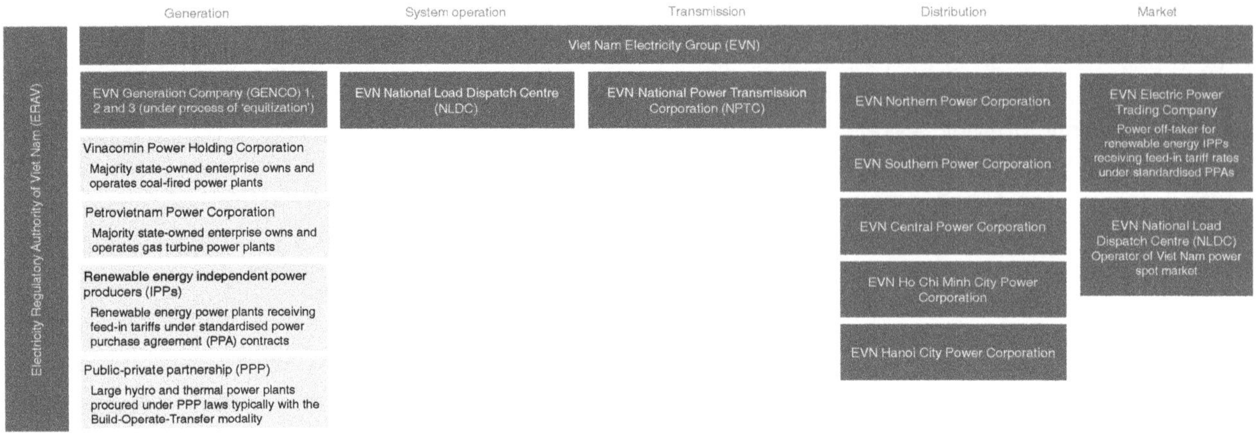

Source: MOIT

Electricity planning

While the electricity market progresses towards liberalisation, electricity planning remains an immense government undertaking, requiring significant co-ordination between line ministries and government agencies. Within the top down master planning system, electricity planning falls within a national sectoral master plan, known as the Power Development Plan (PDP). This is the most significant planning document for clean energy investors and developers, which defines a prescriptive, medium-term plan for capacity additions across all generation technologies.

PV capacity additions boomed in 2019 far beyond the PDP VII Revised 2020 target

For the period of 2011 to 2020 with a vision to 2030, electricity planning was governed by the PDP VII, which in 2016 was reviewed and re-formulated as PDP VII-revised through Decision No. 428/QD-TTg. The review was in response to global renewable technology cost reduction trends, delays in conventional power plant development, and worsening energy security. The most prominent change in PDP VII was a stronger emphasis on renewable energy development, the removal of planned nuclear power plant capacity for 2020 and a reduction in planned imports over the long term. There is also an increased emphasis on market liberalisation, on providing balanced capacity of power sources among the regions and on ensuring the reliability of the power supply system.

Under the PDP VII-revised, a generation project's inclusion in the PDP was a key step in the project approval process and as such, is designed not only as a strategic plan but also a tool for top-down control over system planning and capacity additions. Notwithstanding, solar PV capacity additions overtook the 2025 target, highlighting important considerations around co-ordination and flexibility under the PDP process (Figure 2.7, Figure 2.8). Whereas PDP planning is top-down, taking a medium to long term approach, investments decisions arise from the bottom-up under short time spans in reaction to favourable policy conditions. Driven by generous feed-in tariff support that was set to expire, nearly 4 GW of solar capacity were connected to the national grid taking total capacity from 0.86 MW in 2018, to 4.4 GW by June 2019. IPP selected project location and submitted gird integration studies to EVN, who evaluated these on a case-by-case basis, without a full picture of which would reach commercial operation. At the provincial level, a lack of clarity and consensus around evaluation parameters or provincial caps led to a vastly higher than planned number of projects obtaining investment licences (World Bank Group, 2019[13]). Such rapid deployment of variable renewable energy (vRE), within an incumbent model of large centralised base load power, has led to high levels of grid congestion and curtailment. This is particularly the case in the central regions where there is low demand, and in areas with strong potential in the south, such as Ninh Thuan, Binh Thuan, Dak Lak, Gia Lai, and Quang Tri (Vietnam Energy, 2020[14]). This highlights the need for greater planning flexibility in order to adapt to a fast changing environment.

Figure 2.8. Power Development Plan VII revised deployment targets and capacity installed in 2020

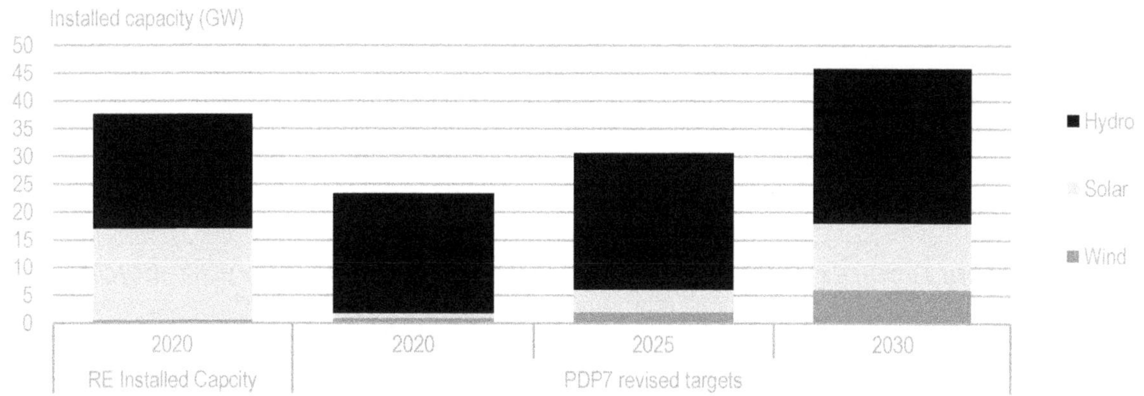

Note: GW = gigawatt
Source: Government of Viet Nam (2016), Prime Minister's Decision No. 428/QD-TTg approving the revised PDP VII EVN (2020)

StatLink https://stat.link/ps1wd9

Figure 2.9. Development of wind and solar sectors (installed capacity) by 2030

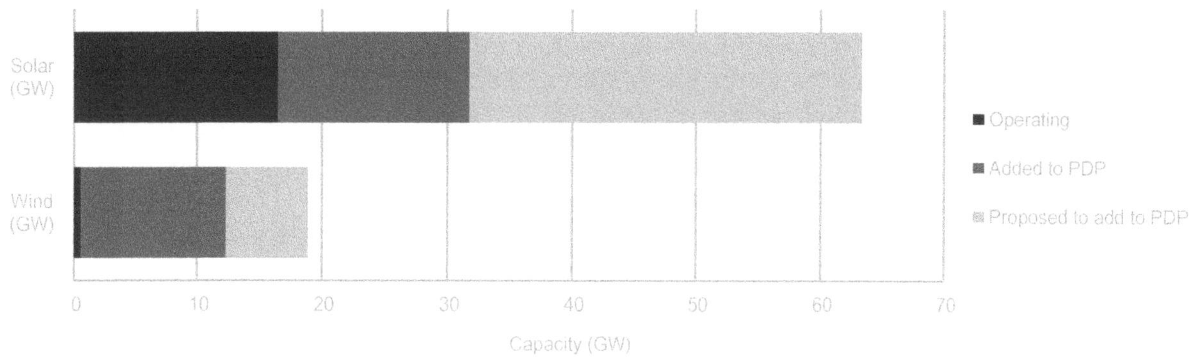

Note: GW = gigawatt. Solar includes rooftop solar
Source: Government of Viet Nam (2020) Letter 10052/BCT-ĐL dated 28/12/2020 and Document 196/TTg-CN dated 18/02/2021 on wind development, Government of Viet Nam (2020) Letter 84/BCT-ĐL dated 07/01/2021 on solar development

StatLink https://stat.link/78jzki

Co-ordination between master plans remains an issue under the new planning law

In its review of the PDP VII, MOIT highlighted issues around co-ordination and inconsistency between master plans leading to overlaps and poor linkages between infrastructure, energy and electricity plans, which were developed at different times and coordinated by different stakeholders, ultimately leading to an inefficient prioritisation of investments (Institute of Energy, 2021[5]). The current series of master plans are being formulated under the new Law on Planning (No. 21/2017/QH14) and Decree No. 37/2019/ND-CP (Decree 37) on guiding its implementation. In the review of the former PDP, MOIT acknowledges that adjusting and supplementing planning has not been timely, with implications for the development of power system and private sector investment. Although the new planning law provides structure with respect to co-ordination, the implementation is still unclear at the central level, delaying the development of socio-economic development plans for the period.

Under the updated top-down hierarchy of plans, national sectoral plans, such as the PDP, must be informed by the overall national plan, the national land-use plan, and the national marine spatial plan. National sectoral plans, in turn, inform regional, provincial, and urban and local level plans. The PDP should also align with other sectoral plans, such as the National Energy Master Plan, which oversees energy infrastructure, and the Master plan for seaport system development, which is relevant for LNG and coal imports, and urban and rural system planning which provides direction for power source and grid development to meet power consumption demand. At the time of the draft PDP VIII submission in February 2021, the overall national plan, the national land-use plan, and the national marine spatial plan had not yet been finalised, implying the need for a subsequent update of the PDP in order for plans to align.

PDP development requires extensive coordination between various stakeholders

The development of the PDP still requires a vast a number of stakeholders in different ministries, who are often responsible for overlapping activities. At the national level, this process is led by MOIT who is responsible for coordinating with MPI, MONRE, MOF and EVN, to formulate and implement the plan and then submit it to the Prime Minister for approval. The Institute of Energy (IE), a research institute under MOIT, undertakes system modelling for cost-optimised technology selections to support the overall PDP design. MPI is responsible for regulations and related guidance on investment and planning policies around power supply and grid expansion and its research institute, the Institute of Development Strategy supports the IE on forecasting. MONRE is responsible for matters concerning land use and marine spatial planning for PDP projects, as well as impacts on the environment, including water resources and forests. The MOF leads on matters related to national PDP budget, and regulations on taxes and fees for renewable power projects. At the provincial level, the PPC is a focal point for elaborating provincial power development plans and submitting them to MOIT, where EREA is responsible for appraisal of regional power development plans. The provincial DOIT coordinates the preparation of the plan and budget, consulting DPI, DONRE, DOF and EVN's subsidiaries before submitting to the PPC for approval (Figure 2.10).

In light of rapidly changing circumstances, both in terms of high GDP and energy demand growth, as well as renewable energy technology cost reductions, an update and revision of the power development plan every ten years cannot ensure the most cost-efficient and optimal power system development trajectory throughout the period. This need for a forward looking, adaptive and responsive planning which can respond to evolving market needs and opportunities was also highlighted in the OECD's recent Multi-dimensional Review of Viet Nam. The review pointed to the use of tools such as the dynamic adaptive policy pathways (DAPP) approach which can help respond to future uncertainties by using scenario analysis to develop appropriate policy responses (OECD, 2020[15]).

Like all masterplans, the new planning law foresees a review of the PDP after five years. The significant resource commitment required to coordinate the simultaneous update interlinking plans, raises concerns about the ability to adjust policy in a timely manner. This has been recognised by the government of Viet Nam in the draft PDP VIII, which proposes a possibility for more flexible and frequent updates and revisions throughout the planning period. However, the process, criteria, extent of possible revisions and timeline thereof still appear to be unclear.

Figure 2.10. Actors involved in PDP process

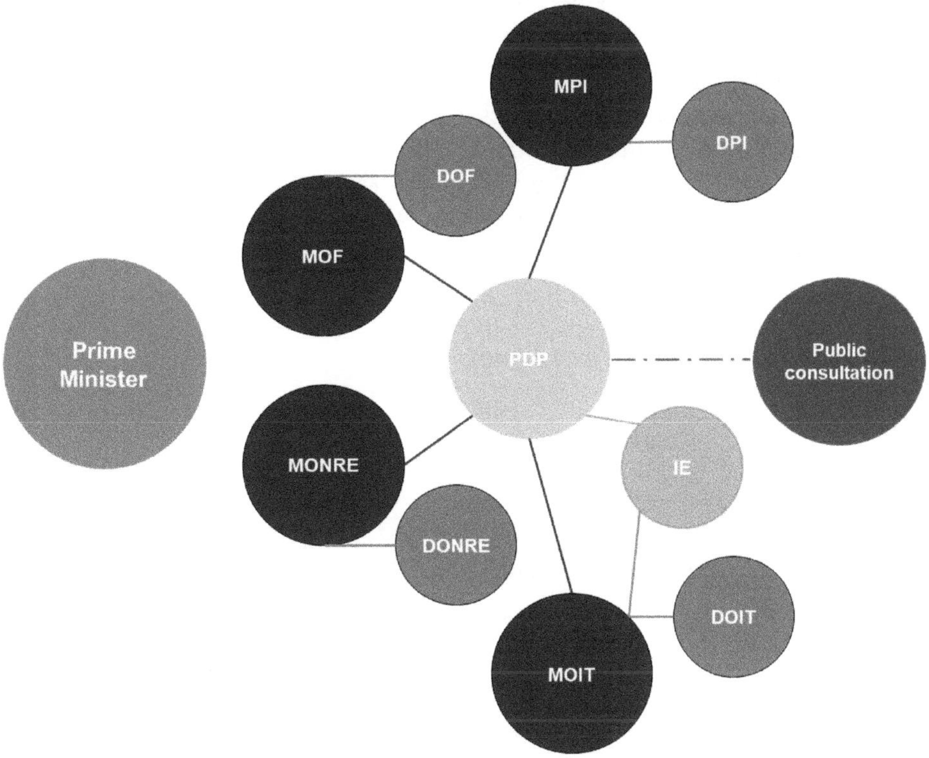

Source: The National Assembly - Government of Viet Nam (2017) Law No. 21/2017/QH14
Note: MOF = Ministry of Finance; DOF = Department of Finance; MPI = Ministry of Planning and Investment; DPI = Department of planning and investment; MONRE = Ministry of Natural Resources and Environment; Department of Natural Resources and Environment; MOIT = Ministry of Industry and Trade; Department of Industry and Trade; IE=Institute of Energy; PDP = Power Development Plan

PDP VIII sets power sector development targets over the coming decades

The draft PDP VIII, which was released for public consultation in February 2021, and a revised version released again in September 2021, presents Viet Nam's strategy for the electricity sector from 2021 to 2030, with a vision to 2045. This plan is notable compared to its predecessors as no prescriptive pipeline of individually approved projects has been included. Such a list had previously been included for all projects with the exception of longer-term, strategic projects such as LNG to power, offshore wind and nuclear. Such a change supports the transition to competitive auctions where projects will be identified and tendered on a rolling basis. Consistent with this approach, the PDP VIII draft sets capacity targets for each province.

The ratio of renewable energy (excluding hydro) in the PDP VIII has increased to 24% in 2030, while in the PDP VII-revised it was lower at 16%. Wind power is set to increase from 0.5 GW in 2020 to around 11.8 GW in 2030 and 48.1 GW in 2045, accounting for 9% and 18% of the total installed capacity in 2030 and 2045 respectively. By 2030, 18.6 GW of solar PV is planned and this will increase to around 51.5 GW by 2045, accounting respectively for 14% and 20% of installed capacity.

The draft PDP VIII features a higher share of renewables compared to the revised PDP VII and a lower deployment of coal power plants. The share of coal power capacity has been reduced to 31% in 2030, down from 43% in the PDP VII-revised and no new coal power capacity is planned after 2035. There is also a large shift to imported LNG to power with gas-fired capacity targets for 2040 more than doubling compared to the previous PDP reaching 62 GW by 2040, and much of this new capacity is set to utilise imported LNG. Comparing the recent draft to the February version, it includes a postponement of some wind capacity (6 GW), biomass, and other renewables (2 GW) until after 2030, and increases coal power capacity (3 GW) over the same period. This is due to a short-term reduction in forecasted demand due to the economic impacts of COVID and concerns in the capacity to integrate higher levels of variable generation over the short term.

The ambitious build out of integrated LNG to power projects and a continuing development of coal power plants brings inherent implementation and fuel price risks (Box 2.3). The level and length of reduction in market growth for renewable energy until 2030 could also prove disruptive to established supply chains and local capabilities developed throughout the FIT period. Moreover, the PDP VIII draft will continue to drive up power sector emissions, in a context where Viet Nam is aiming towards reducing 27% of energy related emissions as outlined under its conditional NDCs under the Paris Agreement.

Table 2.5. Targets set in the draft PDP VIII

Source	Installed capacity	PDP VII revised (2016)	PDP VIII first draft (02/2021)		PDP VIII revised draft (09/2021)	
	2020	2030	2030	2045	2030	2045
Coal-fired	22 077	55 477	37 323	49 918	40 649	50 699
Gas-fired and oil-fired	8 977	19 016	28 871	66 504	27 471	61 933
Hydro (including small-scale) + Pumped storage hydro	20 859	27 871	25 992	33 492	26 684	35 677
Wind	538	5 990	18 010	39 610	11 820	48 110
Solar	17 126	11 765	18 640	55 090	18 640	51 540
Biomass and other renewables	325	3 444	3 150	5 310	1 170	5 250
Power import	1 236	1 508	5 677	5 677	3 936	8 743
Nuclear	0	4 600	0	0	0	0
Total installed capacity	69 258	129 671	137 663	276 601	130 370	261 952

Note: values expressed in Megawatt capacity
Source: MOIT (2021) Draft PDP VIII February 2021; MOIT (2021) Draft PDP VIII September 2021

Box 2.3. Energy security and the Power Development Plan VIII

Viet Nam's upcoming Power Development Plan (PDP) VIII will govern power sector investment over the 2021 to 2030 period and provide a long-term vision to 2045. The approval of this masterplan has met delays since late 2020 pending two rounds of consultations, one in February 2021 and one in September 2021. The current draft maintains a dominant role for thermal generation, more than doubling coal capacity by 2035 (but with no planned capacity additions after this year) and envisioning a significant build out of gas power plants using imported liquefied natural gas (LNG) as fuel. Following Viet Nam's boom in solar deployment in recent years it is also eye catching that no significant increase to solar capacity is planned until after 2030. Similarly, of the 12 GW of wind capacity planned before 2030, 4.5 GW will start commercial operation in 2021. Such a build out of thermal generation capacity, particularly coal, will not only have adverse environmental impacts but could lead to a disruption of Viet Nam's energy security if implementation is delayed, as has been experienced in the recent past. Ensuring fuel price risks can be adequately mitigated will also be critical as reliance on coal and LNG imports increases. By 2035 almost 50% of electricity supply will rely on imported coal or LNG, up from 15% in 2021.

Figure 2.11. PDP VIII draft planned capacity and electricity generation by fuel type

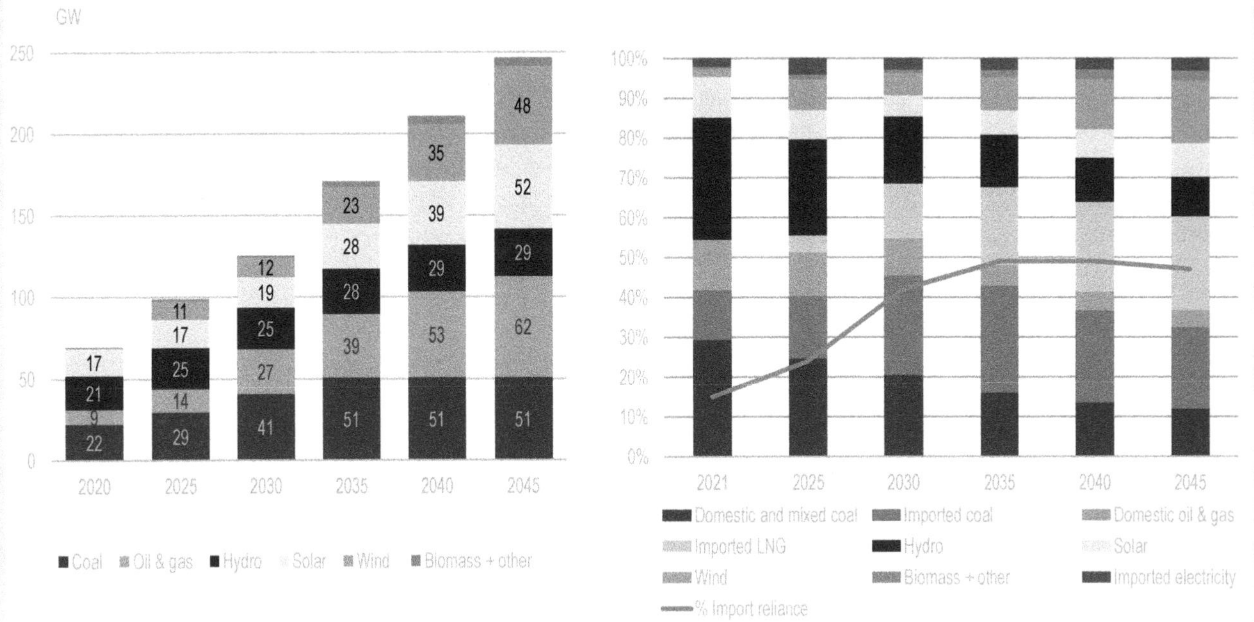

Note:'% import reliance' is calculated as the sum of electricity imported and electricity generated from power plants wholly utilising imported fuels, divided by total electricity supply. The category 'domestic and mixed coal' includes electricity generated from power plants utilising domestic coal or a mix of domestic and imported coal. Plants in this category are excluded from the calculation of '% import reliance'.
Source: VIET based on PDP VIII draft.

StatLink https://stat.link/syxt4d

In principle, natural gas-fired power plants, fuelled with imported LNG, offer a cleaner and more flexible source of firm generation capacity than coal-fired (or oil-fired) plants. However, the ambitious scale of development presents two sets of challenges related to project implementation and price volatility. Viet Nam's plans to develop LNG import infrastructure date as far back as 2008, and the first floating LNG terminal (with an expected start date in 2012 at the time) was proposed in 2010 but never came to fruition (International Oil Daily, 2008[16]) (Reuters, 2010[17]). In the intervening years, and particularly since 2017, investor interest grew substantially in LNG-to-power schemes, and as of September 2021 an estimated 140 GW of LNG-fuelled generation capacity (spread across more than 40 power projects) was in various stages of planning and development (ACSV Legal, 2021[18]). Of this, only nine projects with a combined capacity of about 18 GW were formally endorsed in the amended PDP VII, the plan in effect until the adoption of the final PDP VIII, although more is under review by the government (Thu Vu, 2021[19]). So far, only two projects with a combined capacity of 2.7 GW have reached the construction phase and are expected to come online in the coming year: the Hiep Phuoc and Nhon Trach 3 and 4 power developments, which are expected to be supplied via the Hai Linh and Thi Vai LNG terminals, respectively. This relatively slow progress towards the government's 18 GW target by 2030 outlined in the amended PDP VII speaks to the complexity of structuring and financing LNG-to-power projects in general, and to certain features of Viet Nam's investment framework in particular.

Global experience with integrated LNG-to-power infrastructure is limited to a handful of projects, which are primarily located in South America and the Caribbean. Only two projects have been completed in the Asia Pacific region to date. LNG-to-power projects include two main infrastructure components: an LNG import facility and a gas-fired power plant. Additional elements can include connecting pipelines and transmission lines, for example. This increases complexity, requiring additional permitting and approvals and the management of project-on-project risk. In the case of Viet Nam, the LNG and power components are subject to two different national master plans, two different sets of laws and two different regulatory authorities (Freshfields Bruckhaus Deringer, 2021[20]). Financing such projects with non-recourse project finance debt also involves lengthy negotiations on risk allocation. Guaranteed offtake under a PPA is often a pre-requisite for project financing, but this is not readily offered by EVN (Watson Farley & Willams, 2021[21]). In addition, some elements of Viet Nam's legal framework for LNG-to-power investments, especially provisions on sovereign guarantees, currency convertibility and applicable law fall below bankability requirements of project finance lenders. These challenges mean that the rollout of LNG-fuelled power generation in Viet Nam could continue to progress slowly and fall short of government targets, potentially leaving a gap in the country's electricity supply.

Figure 2.12. Asian spot LNG prices and forward curve

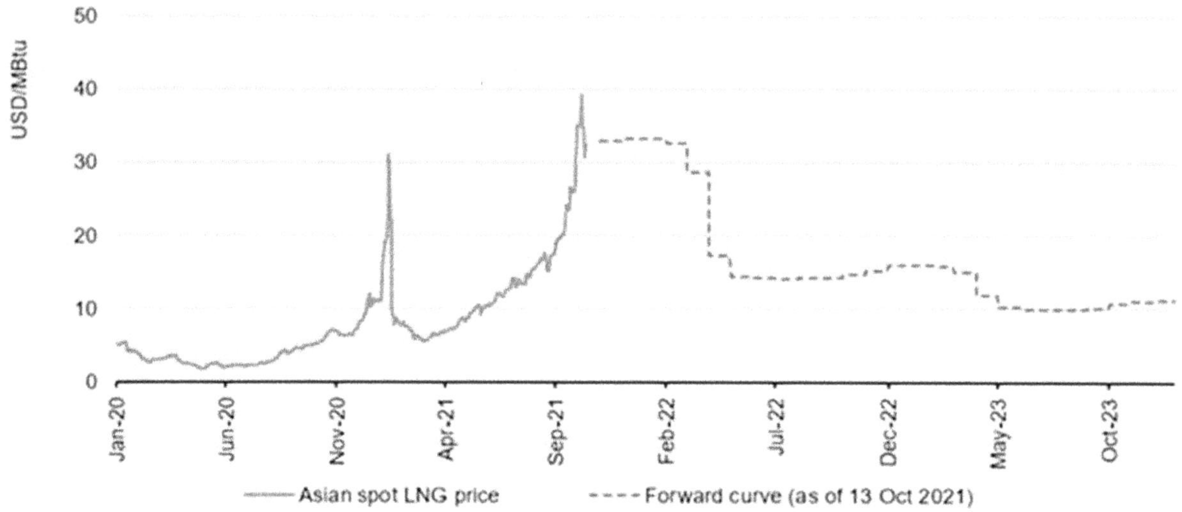

Source: ICIS, CME Group

The second challenge is related to Vietnam's potential exposure to excessive price increases on the spot LNG market. Asian spot LNG prices have spiked twice in 2021 and have recently reached all-time highs as a robust post-COVID recovery, extreme weather patterns and supply shortfalls have led to an unprecedented tightness in the global gas market. Under such circumstances, price sensitive emerging economies (where utilities have limited ability to pass through surging fuel costs to customers or shoulder the financial burden themselves) may be forced to curtail fuel purchases on the spot market. During the earlier price spike in January 2021, for example, India, Pakistan and Bangladesh each registered sharp year-on-year declines in LNG imports (down by 15%, 5% and 32% in January, respectively) as price-sensitive buyers left several spot LNG tenders unawarded due to astronomical bid prices. This, in turn, contributed to gas shortages and a mix of load shedding and fuel switching away from gas in each countries (IEA, 2021[22]). It is possible to hedge against excessive spot LNG price spikes by locking in volumes under term contracts. These can smooth out volatility by indexing prices to oil or gas hub benchmarks (or a hybrid formula combining several price references), by using 3 to 6-month moving averages and s-curves in the formula, and by introducing upward and downward volume flexibility to enable greater optimisation between contracted supplies and spot market purchases. The majority of LNG sold into the Asia Pacific region is, in fact, purchased under long-term oil-indexed contracts and have limited exposure to today's volatile spot prices. However, EVN's wariness to assume market risk (e.g. in the form of PPAs with a high share of guaranteed power offtake) could limit the ability of project sponsors to lock in the majority of their fuel supply with long term contracts. This, in turn, would raise the risk of periodically being priced out of the spot LNG market and unable to generate electricity.

Coal projects also face significant uncertainties particularly related to the availability and cost of finance. Important regional partners for infrastructure lending, namely South Korea, China, and Japan, have all recently pledged net zero climate commitments and have signalled their intention to end coal financing in overseas markets. The cost of financing upstream coal extraction and power generation is also on an upward trend with analysis by Oxford Sustainable Finance Programme showing increased loan spreads for the period 2011-2020 compared to the previous decade. Data from emerging markets in Latin America, China, and Southeast Asia, show spreads for coal mining rising by 56%, 32% and 12% respectively, and a steeper trend is witnessed in OECD markets with spreads in Europe, North America and Australia up by 134%, 80% and 71%. The same applies to the cost of financing coal power plants, which has increased by 63% in Southeast Asia over the same period (Zhou, Wilson and Caldecott, 2021[23]). The tightening financing landscape for coal infrastructure will create inflationary pressure on the levelised cost of electricity from coal sources, which will likely intensify as global action accelerates to meet the Paris climate commitments.

Analysis by the Rocky Mountain Institute shows that the share of coal plants worldwide, which are uncompetitive with renewable alternatives will reach 56% by 2022 and 78% by 2025 (Benn et al., 2018[24]). Such a tipping point could be seen in Viet Nam too, with utility-scale solar experiencing a 55% cost reduction over recent years with LCOEs estimated at 0.082 USD/kWh in 2020 (IRENA, 2020[25]). This is approaching the average LCOE of a coal generator utilising imported coal, which stood at 0.074 – 0.076 USD/kWh in 2016. At the same time, the cost of Viet Nam's domestic coal is increasing, as more costly extraction is required in the face of declining reserves. In deregulated electricity markets, the risk of such price trends is that a wave of fossil generation assets could become stranded, unable to compete on cost terms with cheaper renewables. In the case of Viet Nam with regulated markets and long-term power purchase agreements, there is a significant risk that scarce capital could be similarly locked into long-lived, uneconomic assets.

Due to the issues highlighted above, the implementation risks associated with the PDP VIII draft are judged to be high, putting the country at risk of supply deficits if delays and bottlenecks materialise. Viet Nam's planning system does not currently have the flexibility and nimbleness to quickly adapt to changes in market realities. Implementing processes to enable more timely and reactive changes to the PDP, as has been recommended in this review, will go some way to mitigate these risks. There should also be a recognition that the long delays experienced in the development of privately financed power sector infrastructure to date has stemmed in part from the hesitancy in providing risk allocations aligned with international investor and lender requirements. Providing such assurances would support a more frictionless implementation and will likely lower the cost of capital. These benefits should be fully evaluated against the additional costs and contingent liabilities that EVN and the government would need to shoulder as well as the overall economic risk of deployment delays and supply shortages. Lastly, significant progress has been made in recent years in the development of a thriving renewables market. PDP VIII draft continues to prioritise renewables over the long-term but with a decade-long hiatus between 2021 and 2030 when only limited deployment is planned. Although it has been anticipated that the explosive rate of deployment witnessed over the last two years will slow down, the level and length of reduction signalled in the PDP VIII draft is dramatic and could well prove detrimental to local supply chains, green jobs, and investor confidence.

Source: OECD and IEA analysis

Energy efficiency features in the PDP VIII

Given that annual growth rates of electricity demand are expected to be 9.1% from 2021-2025 and 7.9 % from 2026-2030, the PDP VIII draft takes an important and necessary step in recognising the multiple benefits that energy efficiency offers. The draft PDP VIII outlines current programmes, which includes targets of the Viet Nam Energy Efficiency Program (VNEEP). Also featured is the National Program on Demand Side Management 2018-2020, with a vision to 2030 (Decision No. 279 / QD-TTg 2018), which aims to reduce the national power system's peak load capacity of compared to the power load forecast in the national electricity development plan (300 MW by 2020, 1 000 MW in 2025 and 2 000 MW in 2030). It also includes Viet Nam's strategy for rooftop solar PV, as a solution for reducing grid loss, increasing power supply, and contributing to reducing local electricity consumption.

Forecasting electricity demand in the period of 2021-2030 takes both a top down and bottom up approach, combined with the synthesis and review of electricity demand at national, regional, provincial and EVN power corporation levels. In line with previous PDPs, the top-down approach forecasts electricity demand for the period of 2021 to 2030, for the whole country, for regions and for EVN's power corporations. The bottom-up approach reviews the electricity demand of provinces in the country from 2010 to 2019 based on provincial electricity consumption plans prepared by the EVN's power corporations, and information from large electricity consumers for the period until 2025.

A greater focus on mechanism for integrating a higher share of renewable is needed

The increased share of variable renewable generation already has significant implications for how the power system is planned and operated. Meeting long-term demand growth and targets for new generating capacity – especially variable renewable generation – will require significant amounts of new transmission development. Transmission planning processes were developed with a centralised electricity system architecture and large centralised power plants. The north and the south use up most of the power while the central part acts mainly as a transmission corridor and production site. As renewable capacity is mostly located in the south and central zones of Viet Nam, with only a very small amount of solar in the north, the transmission between the central and southern zones has been put under a lot pressure.

In the short-term, Viet Nam will need to address the oversupply in generating capacity that has resulted from COVID-19's impact on economic activity, in particular suppressed demand for electricity. The relative oversupply of capacity has led to increased congestion of the transmission system during low-demand periods such as weekends and holidays and, therefore, increased curtailment of renewables. This is particularly the case in the central and southern part of the country, where most of the deployment of solar PV is concentrated. Though part of the cause of this current state of oversupply is temporary, the current situation nevertheless provides a valuable preview of Viet Nam's higher renewables future.

Equally, a range of technical and market-based solutions, implemented in particular by EVN, focused on unlocking and enabling power system flexibility can help ensure that existing solar PV and wind are integrated affordably and securely. "Non-wires alternatives" such as expanding demand-side response, energy efficiency and distributed generation programmes, as well as use of batteries or other modern technologies can offer many of the same benefits of transmission development at much lower costs. As a notable example of this, the New York City utility was able to avoid a USD 1-billion transmission upgrade by instead investing USD 652 million in a combination of non-wires alternatives (Box 2.4). Aspects of these technical and market-based solutions can already be incorporated into long-term planning, investment decisions and consideration around increased resource flexibility.

Box 2.4. Consolidated Edison Company Brooklyn Queens DSM program

In 2014, Consolidated Edison Company (Con Edison), a regulated utility providing electric and gas services in New York, highlighted that by 2018, 69 MW of demand growth above existing distribution capacities in Brooklyn and Queens would lead to capacity constraints on a portion of its grid, overloading existing infrastructure and leading to reliability concerns. The proposed solution had an estimated cost of 1 billion USD for upgrading infrastructure, including a new distribution substation, expanding an existing 345 kV switching station, and constructing a sub-transmission feeder to connect the two stations. Instead, the New York Public Service Commission (PSC), ordered Con Edison to look at non-traditional investments as a way to manage demand growth, and offered innovative incentives to encourage their adoption. This led to the Brooklyn Queens Demand Management (BQDM) programme, which aimed to reduce 52 MW of peak demand, from noon to midnight by the summer of 2018.

While traditional capital investments in infrastructure can earn a rate of return, non-traditional solutions are often treated as operating expenses which are passed on to customers. PSC set up a number of performance incentives designed to encourage the utility to contract third-party services that could lower project costs. Con Edison was able to earn an authorized rate of return on BQDM programme costs, and receive up to 100 basis points above their authorized rate of return in performance incentives on BQDM investments. During the programme, an additional shared savings mechanism was designed to let the utility earn 30% of the annual net benefits accrued.

The BQDM programme aimed to defer the need for traditional infrastructure investment for at least seven years and was approved by the PSC with a USD 200 million budget in 2014. It sought to obtain 41 MW of customer-side electricity demand reduction solutions, and 11 MW of utility-side electricity demand reduction solutions such as distributed energy generation and voltage optimization. The utility achieved 52 MW peak load reduction target for summer 2018, but through a different mix, with 34 MW of peak load reduction from customer-side and about 18 MW from utility-side solutions, indicating further opportunities for load reduction. Through 2017, Con Edison spent USD 70 million, leaving USD130 million remaining in its budget. Based on its initial success the utility continued the BQDM programme beyond 2018, without additional funding or changes to the incentive mechanisms. One of the traditional investments, the Glendale substation project, planned for 2018 was postponed to after 2026

This BQDM programme offers an example of how the utility, third-party companies and customers can each benefit from "non-wires alternatives". The traditional utility revenue framework discourages utilities from investing in non-traditional solutions, such as demand management programs and distributed energy resources. Without the proper incentives, these are treated as operating expenses, passed through to customers, whereas traditional "poles and wires" solution, provide an opportunity to earn a rate of return. While investments in new grid infrastructure will be necessary in Viet Nam, expanding "non-wires alternatives", such as Viet Nam's demand-side response programme, battery storage, or other modern technologies can offer many of the same benefits of transmission development at much lower costs, whilst also enabling system flexibility to accommodate for vRE generation.

Source: Girouard (2019) BQDM program demonstrates benefits of non-traditional utility investments. AEE and Rocky Mountain Institutes (2019) Brooklyn Queens Demand Management Program-Employing Innovative Non-Wire Alternatives

Following the IEA's (IEA, 2020[26]), six phases of variable renewable electricity (vRE) integration (Figure 2.13), Viet Nam jumped from phase I to phase II to III between 2019 and 2020. According to this breakdown, phase I, where there is less than 3% of generation from vRE, there is little or no impact on the power system. In phase II, which is between 3% to 15% vRE, there is a noticeable effect on power system operations, which is manageable through upgrading planning and operations practices, particularly in terms of forecasting capabilities in order to balance flexible resources along with electricity demand. From phase III, which is between 15-25%, vRE has a greater influence on system operations requiring additional investments in flexibility. In Phase IV which is between 25-50% of generation, structural surpluses of vRE generation lead to curtailment, and thereafter, sector coupling is required to adjust for structural imbalances in energy supply at seasonal and inter-year periods. Given the rapid increase of vRE, Viet Nam is already experiencing high levels of curtailment. In low demand periods, such as public holidays and weekends, driven yet lower by the economic slowdown caused by COVID-19, the share of solar generation, at peak, could rise to the equivalent of 40% of total generation. However, given the difficulties integrating this sudden increase in variable renewable electricity, much of this solar power has been curtailed, and over the year, renewable generation amounted 5% of total generation. As more of this generation is integrated, Viet Nam will face greater technical challenges for the stability of the power system's operation in very short timescales.

Figure 2.13. Key characteristics and challenges in different phases of system integration

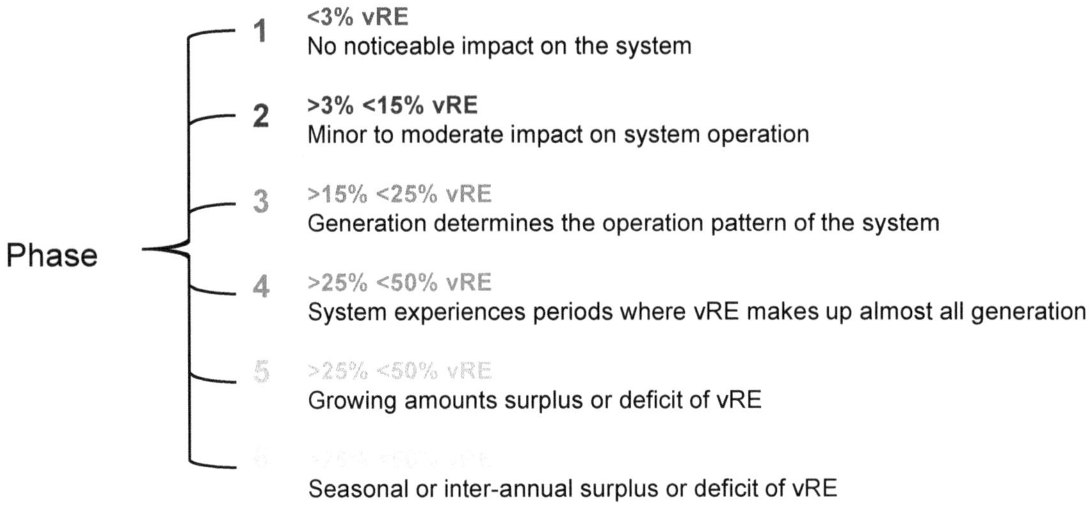

Note: vRE = variable renewable electricity
Source: IEA (2020) Introduction to System Integration of Renewables

USAID highlight seven criteria for assessing readiness for integrating vRE in power systems, in which Viet Nam has quite low to moderate preparedness considering the high share of renewables it already has to integrate (USAID, 2020[27]). Viet Nam has little operational experience integrating wind and solar power and the transmission infrastructure has not kept pace with the development of electricity production. While good progress has already been made on strengthening planning and system operation practices, Viet Nam still needs to develop a number of different areas in order to fully prepare for integrating high shares of vRE (Table 2.6). The rapid strengthening across areas particularly around dispatch rules, storage and ancillary services, will be essential.

Table 2.6. Preparedness for integrating vRE in Viet Nam

Criteria	Situation in Viet Nam	Preparedness for integrating vRE
Market protocols to access system flexibility	Viet Nam established a pilot wholesale electricity market, which aims to be operational by 2021. The next stage will be a competitive retail market.	Moderate, the wholesale electricity market and retail market are key milestones. This could be supported by a framework for the forward capacity market.
Clear dispatch rules for vRE	vRE is dispatched on priority when available. In situations of over-supply there are high rates of curtailment	Low, economic dispatch and commitment tools should be use to effectively integrate vRE.
Grid code requirements for vRE	Best practices capabilities for renewables to be controllable are not specified in grid codes and contracts.	Moderate, an integrated grid code is being developed under DEA's programme with ERAV.
Long-term agreements for regional interconnection	The question of expanding to a regional market or maintaining an only domestic market is under discussion.	Low, regional interconnection is not sufficiently available to support vRE integration.
Sufficient transmission capacity/planned investment	Due to continued load growth, transmission resources are operating near their capacity limits, increasing risk of brownouts or blackouts involving significant loss of load (Deloitte, 2019[28]).	Low, according to PDP VIII, between 2021 and 2045 Viet Nam will need to invest around USD 85 billion in grid infrastructure.
Ancillary services market products to reward flexibility	Multi-purpose hydro plants provide ancillary services. NLDC manages ancillary services and requirements, but there is no framework for an ancillary services market.	Moderate, a clear framework for the ancillary market is needed.
vRE forecasting integrated into system operations	vRE forecasting is provided by generators, 2 third party providers and in-house forecasting within EVN developed with DEA.	High

Source: USAID (2020) Grid Integration Series: Impact of variable renewable energy on system operations

References

ACSV Legal (2021), *Annex 3 (Schedule 9.1 of the draft PDP8) Proposed LNG-to-Power Projects*, https://cdn-se.mynilead.com/2c8bf258f12ee1b2538bb25067eaf6e3/assets/media/acsv-legal-update-draft-pdp8-annex-3_1621998490.pdf (accessed on 20 October 2021). [18]

ADB (2015), *Assessment of Power Sector Reforms in Viet Nam*, https://www.adb.org/sites/default/files/institutional-document/173769/vie-power-sector-reforms.pdf. [12]

AEE Institute and Rocky Mountain Institute (2019), *BROOKLYN QUEENS DEMAND MANAGEMENT PROGRAM-EMPLOYING INNOVATIVE NON-WIRE ALTERNATIVES - Navigating Utility Business Model Reform — Case Studies*, http://www.rmi.org/insight/navigating-utility-business-model-. [29]

Benn, A. et al. (2018), *Managing the Coal Capital Transition: Collaborative Opportunities for Asset Owners, Policymakers, and Environmental Advocates*, Rocky Mountain Institute, https://rmi.org/wp-content/uploads/2018/09/RMI_Managing_the_Coal_Capital_Transition_2018.pdf (accessed on 20 October 2021). [24]

Deloitte (2019), *USAID VIETNAM LOW EMISSION ENERGY PROGRAM (V-LEEP)*, https://pdf.usaid.gov/pdf_docs/PA00WFR7.pdf. [28]

E3G (2021), *COP26 Energy Transition Campaign Country Dialogue Summary Report: Viet Nam*. [8]

Egli, F., B. Steffen and T. Schmidt (2018), "A dynamic analysis of financing conditions for renewable energy technologies", *Nature Energy*, Vol. 3/12, pp. 1084-1092, http://dx.doi.org/10.1038/s41560-018-0277-y. [30]

ERAV (2020), *Decision 120/QD-DTDL 2020 list of power plants participating in the electricity market in 2021 năm*, https://thuvienphapluat.vn/van-ban/Thuong-mai/Quyet-dinh-120-QD-DTDL-2020-danh-sach-nha-may-dien-tham-gia-thi-truong-dien-nam-2021-469150.aspx. [10]

EVN (2021), *Rooftop solar power boom is underway with a total installed capacity reaching nearly 9,300 MWp*, https://en.evn.com.vn/d6/news/Rooftop-solar-power-boom-is-underway-with-a-total-installed-capacity-reaching-nearly-9300-MWp-66-142-2169.aspx. [35]

EVN (2020), *Performance in the first 9 months of 2020 and objectives and tasks for the last 3 months of 2020*, https://en.evn.com.vn/d6/news/90-power-plants-have-participated-in-the-competitive-generation-electricity-market-66-163-1400.aspx. [9]

Freshfields Bruckhaus Deringer (2021), *LNG-to-power – new complexities*, https://www.freshfields.com/4a1b53/globalassets/what-we-do/markets/asia-pacific/vietnam/our-blogs/freshfields-lng-to-power-outlook-paper-june-2020.pdf (accessed on 20 October 2021). [20]

Girouard, C. (2019), *BQDM program demonstrates benefits of non-traditional utility investments | Utility Dive*, https://www.utilitydive.com/news/bqdm-program-demonstrates-benefits-of-non-traditional-utility-investments/550110/. [1]

GIZ/MOIT (2016), *Wind Power Investment Guidelines for Vietnam*, https://www.german-energy-solutions.de/GES/Redaktion/DE/Publikationen/Finanzierungsstudien/2016/investguide_Vietnam_Vol-1_2016.pdf?__blob=publicationFile&v=6. [32]

HSBC (2018), *Fragile Planet - Scoring Climate Risks Around The World - Long Finance*, https://www.longfinance.net/programmes/sustainable-futures/london-accord/reports/fragile-planet-scoring-climate-risks-around-world/. [4]

IEA (2021), *Gas Market Report Q4-2021 including Global Gas Security Review 2021*, https://iea.blob.core.windows.net/assets/261043cc-0cb6-498b-98fa-a1f48715b91f/GasMarketReportQ42021.pdf (accessed on 20 October 2021). [22]

IEA (2020), *Introduction to System Integration of Renewables*, https://www.iea.org/reports/introduction-to-system-integration-of-renewables. [26]

Institute of Energy (2021), *Draft Power Development Plan 2021-2030 with a vision to 2045.* [5]

International Oil Daily (2008), *Vietnam Seeks LNG Terminal By 2013 to Meet Growing Gas Demand*, Energy Intelligence. [16]

IRENA (2020), *IRENA Power Generation Costs 2019*, https://www.irena.org/-/media/Files/IRENA/Agency/Publication/2020/Jun/IRENA_Power_Generation_Costs_2019.pdf (accessed on 20 October 2021). [25]

OECD (2020), *Multi-dimensional Review of Viet Nam: Towards an Integrated, Transparent and Sustainable Economy*, OECD Development Pathways, OECD Publishing, Paris, https://dx.doi.org/10.1787/367b585c-en. [15]

OECD (2019), *OECD Green Growth Policy Review of Indonesia 2019*, OECD Environmental Performance Reviews, OECD Publishing, Paris, https://dx.doi.org/10.1787/1eee39bc-en. [34]

OECD (2018), *OECD Investment Policy Reviews: Viet Nam 2018*, OECD Investment Policy Reviews, OECD Publishing, Paris, https://dx.doi.org/10.1787/9789264282957-en. [3]

OECD (2015), *Policy Guidance for Investment in Clean Energy Infrastructure: Expanding Access to Clean Energy for Green Growth and Development*, OECD Publishing, Paris, https://dx.doi.org/10.1787/9789264212664-en. [33]

PwC (2017), *Power in Indonesia - Investment and Taxation Guide*, http://www.pwc.com/id (accessed on 11 January 2019). [7]

RCEE (2016), *Evaluation of Vietnam Energy Efficiency Program-Phase II.* [6]

Reuters (2010), *SE Asia to start LNG imports in next 3 yrs*, https://www.reuters.com/article/asia-lng-idUSSGE6510AV20100602 (accessed on 20 October 2021). [17]

Robiou du Pont, Y. and J. Balanowski (2018), *MULTI-LEVEL CLIMATE GOVERNANCE IN VIETNAM Bridging national planning and local climate action*, http://www.localclimateaction.orgwww.adelphi.de. [2]

THE SOCIALIST REPUBLIC OF VIET NAM (2020), *UPDATED NATIONALLY DETERMINED CONTRIBUTION (NDC)*, UNFCCC, Ha Noi, https://www4.unfccc.int/sites/ndcstaging/PublishedDocuments/Viet%20Nam%20First/Viet%20Nam_NDC_2020_Eng.pdf (accessed on 16 June 2021). [36]

Thu Vu (2021), *Beyond the Noise: Setting the Right Expectations for Vietnam's LNG Project Pipeline Regulators and Market Realities Will Give Investors No Easy Route To Success*, The Institute for Energy Economics and Financial Analysis (IEEFA), https://ieefa.org/wp-content/uploads/2021/01/Setting-the-Right-Expectations-for-Vietnams-LNG-Project-Pipeline_January-2021.pdf (accessed on 20 October 2021). [19]

USAID (2020), *Grid Integration Series: Impact of variable renewable energy on system operations*, https://www.usaid.gov/sites/default/files/documents/1865/USAID_SURE_VRE-Impact-System-Operations.pdf. [27]

Vietnam Energy (2020), *Principles and processes for adjusting, supplementing power projects into PDP Vietnam Energy Online*, http://nangluongvietnam.vn/news/en/policy-planning/principles-and-processes-for-adjusting-supplementing-power-projects-into-pdp. [14]

Watson Farley & Willams (2021), *Update on Developing LNG to Power Projects in Vietnam*, https://www.wfw.com/articles/update-on-developing-lng-to-power-projects-in-vietnam/ (accessed on 20 October 2021). [21]

World Bank (2020), *Learning from Power Sector Reform Experiences: The Case of Vietnam*, https://documents.worldbank.org/en/publication/documents-reports/documentdetail/757761583166223011/learning-from-power-sector-reform-experiences-the-case-of-vietnam. [11]

World Bank (2015), *Making The Whole Greater Than The Sum Of The Parts: A Review of Fiscal Decentralization in Viet Nam*. [31]

World Bank Group (2019), *Viet Nam Solar Competitive Bidding Strategy and Framework*, http://www.worldbank.org. [13]

Zhou, X., C. Wilson and B. Caldecott (2021), *The energy transition and changing financing costs*, University of Oxford, Sustainable finance Programme, https://www.smithschool.ox.ac.uk/research/sustainable-finance/publications/The-energy-transition-and-changing-financing-costs.pdf (accessed on 20 October 2021). [23]

Notes

[1] https://ens.dk/sites/ens.dk/files/Globalcooperation/deliverable_1.1_-_forecasting_of_renewable_energy_generation_in_the_vietnamese_power_system_-_final_27042021.pdf.

[2] https://www.renewableenergymagazine.com/panorama/solargis-supports-vietnamese-renewables-with-advanced-forecasting-20210315.

3 Regulatory framework

This chapter examines clean energy policies and regulations in Viet Nam. It analyses Viet Nam's evolving clean energy policy environment and how regulatory developments have been shaping the market landscape for clean energy investment. The chapter reviews the role of expanding energy performance standards and labelling schemes, energy management obligations, and regulatory conditions for energy service companies. It also considers the impact of regulations on renewable electricity generation and identifies opportunities to align with international best practice.

Viet Nam's energy policy landscape has undergone significant transformation over the past two decades pivoting the sector towards greater levels of private participation, market-based principles, and, more recently, prioritisation of non-hydro renewable and energy efficiency development. The government of Viet Nam has made laudable progress implementing the regulatory framework to achieve these overriding policy objectives. The Government must continue to strengthen these reforms in a transparent, consultative process to ensure the regulatory framework evolves to address emerging challenges and remaining market barriers. Particular focus should be paid to building the enabling framework to attract diversified sources of capital to deliver the deployment targets set in the Power Development Plan (PDP) VIII and Viet Nam Energy Efficiency Programme (VNEEP) III.

Assessment & Recommendations

Recent success attracting renewable energy investment brings urgent new regulatory priorities

Viet Nam's feed-in tariff (FIT) support mechanism, particularly for grid-scale and rooftop solar photovoltaic (PV), incentivised rapid capacity deployment over the course of 2019-2020. By end of 2020, variable renewable energy (vRE) capacity reached 17.6 GW (for wind and both grid-scale and grid-connected rooftop installations) accounting for 23.6% of total generation capacity. Such rapid deployment was prioritised due to a tightening electricity supply margin caused by strong demand growth coupled with delays in planned thermal power plant procurement. However, the economic impacts of COVID-19 supressed electricity demand causing an oversupply situation, particularly in the southern regions where deployment of solar PV is concentrated. Oversupply led to congestion of the transmission system, magnified during low-demand periods. Under such operational conditions strategic curtailment of generation sources, including renewable independent power producers, was unavoidable. Such large shares of vRE has made operation of the power system more complex and provided a preview for Viet Nam's higher renewables future. Integrating high levels of vRE is not only an operational challenge but also a regulatory one. Viet Nam's regulatory environment will need to evolve quickly to ensure incentive structures and enabling regulation are in place for the procurement of balancing services and flexible demand and supply side resources that will be required to facilitate the continued clean energy transition.

A shift in approach to renewable energy procurement creates market uncertainty

The Prime Minister's Notification No. 402/TB-VPCP issued in November 2019 set the course for a transition from FIT based procurement to competitive auctions for solar. Motivations for this decision include the need for more carefully managed deployment in line with available grid capacity and the desire to harness the cost reduction potential of competitive bidding. The solar FIT programme (Decision No. 13/2020/QD-TTg) expired on 31 December 2020 and there are no plans to introduce a transitional support scheme for grid-scale solar PV projects. This creates a significant regulatory vacuum and uncertainty given the auction system is still at a relatively early design phase and few details are available yet to market participants. Onshore and offshore wind FITs (Decision No. 39/2018/QD-TTg) expire on 1 November 2021 and likewise there are no details available confirming procurement arrangements after this date. Abrupt changes to renewable energy (RE) support mechanisms can have detrimental stop-and-go effects on industry, local supply chain development, investor confidence and risk perception, and local employment effects. All of which could ultimately set back the cost of development of RE projects in Viet Nam as higher levels of deployment are planned after 2030.

Risk allocation in standard power purchase agreements restricted international capital

FIT regulations introduced mandatory standardised power purchase agreements (PPAs) with fixed terms for electricity sale between independent power producers and the national power transmission corporation, Viet Nam Electricity (EVN) as sole off-taker. Aspects of the PPA were highly attractive to investors including the indexing of payments in Vietnamese Dong to the USD exchange rate. However, other aspects fell short of requirements for bankability, particularly for lenders in OECD markets. This includes the provisions for termination compensation, step-in rights, lack of curtailment protection, and lack of international arbitration. Flows of international capital from OECD countries into Viet Nam's clean energy sector have therefore been restricted to date while domestic and regional sources more comfortable with the PPA risks have been predominant. The large investment requirements for PDP VIII implementation, increased sector exposure of domestic banks, and shift to competitive auctions point to the growing need to review the risk allocations in the PPA. Continued barriers to international capital flow may restrict auction price competition and cost reduction while the financing needs for PDP VIII implementation goes beyond the capacity of domestic banks. This is particularly relevant for highly capital-intensive offshore wind projects requiring large economies of scale for price competitiveness and careful risk allocations in the PPA to enable non-recourse project finance led by international loan syndications in partnership with local lenders.

Regulation for energy efficiency promotion has advanced quickly but processes for monitoring, enforcement, and impact evaluation can be improved

Viet Nam has taken important steps to implement the legal and regulatory framework to promote energy efficiency investment during the VNEEP I & II periods. This includes passing the energy efficiency law, introduction of appliance minimum energy performance standards (MEPS) and energy labelling, mandatory sub-sectoral specific energy consumption targets, energy auditing and reporting obligations, and energy performance building codes. The VNEEP III period offers an opportunity to take stock and build from these achievements. There should be a focus on enhancing the monitoring and enforcement capacity at provincial levels, evaluating effectiveness, and strengthening regulation where required to keep pace with market conditions. It is noted, for example, that a 2019 assessment by CLASP found 76% of air conditioning models available in the market met the two highest star ratings indicating the market was ready for a rebalancing of the energy rating scale.

Dedicated regulations that guide energy performance contracting will build market confidence

The uptake of energy performance contracting (EPC) business models has been limited in Viet Nam to date. Development of the EPC market has been a key driver of energy efficiency improvement in mature energy efficiency markets globally. Although there are no regulatory barriers restricting EPC modalities between two private enterprises, the lack of awareness and the novelty of EPC creates significant hurdles leading to long business development cycles. A dedicated framework providing clear guidance on accounting and taxation treatment, third-party monitoring & verification, and specialised arbitration procedures would be an important step to foster confidence. Regulatory barriers related to public budgeting and procurement restrict the possibility for EPC-based procurement across state agencies and state owned enterprises. These regulations should be reviewed to allow multi-year EPC contracting under guaranteed or shared savings modalities. The public sector can take an important 'first adopter' role to demonstrate the EPC model and to allow energy services companies (ESCOs) to build stronger balance sheets and technical competencies.

Box 3.1. Main policy recommendations on clean energy regulatory framework

- A range of technical and market-based solutions will be required to deliver the power system flexibility to integrate higher levels of variable renewable energy generation. A regulatory framework should be developed to enable the procurement of ancillary services through technology neutral, market-based mechanisms. Forward looking and inclusive ancillary services procurement can ensure changing system needs meet at least cost by allowing all possible solutions among generation, grids, and demand, to compete on a level playing field. Vietnam may also consider including incentives for flexibility in long-term PPAs, and even, at some point, the development of dedicated markets for flexibility services.
- Regulatory uncertainty related to RE procurement mechanisms over the course of the PDP VIII period should be resolved to provide medium-long-term confidence on pipelines for investors and new market entrants. This is particularly important for offshore wind capacity procurement where significant regulatory uncertainty exists and supply chain development is at a formative stage.
- A review of PPA terms for renewable energy independent power producers (RE-IPPs) should be carried out once the auctioning mechanism has been developed to ensure appropriate risk mitigation and optimum allocation of remaining risks between bidders and other sector stakeholders. The review process should be consultative and transparent to build investor confidence. Cost-benefit analysis of contractual de-risking options should be undertaken to inform the auction design and maximise cost-effective tariff reduction potential.
- Prioritise implementing an effective framework for corporate sourcing in order to keep-up with global trends on decarbonising supply chains and to provide new routes to market for renewable electricity.
- Minimum energy performance standards and labelling in Viet Nam should be strengthened and expanded to remove inefficient products from the market and improve the availability and certainty of demand for more efficient ones. Viet Nam can build upon its past experience with product MEPS and work with partners such as the United for Efficiency and ASEAN Shine initiatives to increase the stringency and coverage of existing standards.
- The Government should address the regulatory gap in the energy services market holding back development of those opportunities, ensuring there are transparent conditions for energy performance contracting (EPC). Regulations and guidelines should cover accounting procedures, incentives, public procurement and public budgeting barriers, EPC loan terms, and arbitration procedures.

Energy Efficiency Policies and Regulations

Significant progress has been made developing the regulatory framework for industrial energy efficiency promotion but monitoring and enforcement needs to be strengthened

During the course of VNEEP I & II several legal and regulatory milestones were achieved to promote energy efficiency in the industrial sector. Most importantly, this includes the passing of the Energy Efficiency Law which obligated Designated-Energy Users (DEUs) to appoint a qualified energy manager to undertake energy audits every 3 years and to implement energy managements systems that include annual and five yearly energy reduction plans. Implementing Decree No. 21/2011/ND-CP later defined DEUs as industry and agricultural facilities with total energy consumption over 1 000 TOE per year and any non-industrial (including residential, commercial, hospital and education) buildings with over 500 TOE or higher. The first list of obligated DEUs was released in 2018 with MOIT Decision No. 1221 and set the requirement of MOIT to release updated lists yearly. The latest list is based on 2019 consumption (Decision No. 1577/2020/QĐ-TTg) and contains 3 006 DEUs (2 441 industrial facilities, 15 agricultural facilities, 84 transportation units, and 466 buildings). Implementing and enforcing energy audit and energy management obligations can be complicated due to treatment of shared ownership, leased equipment, multi-occupancy, and tenant-landlord split incentives. Defining DEUs at the building or facility level rather than at the enterprise level may exacerbate this issue. Circular No. 9/2012/TT-BCT elaborates on the method for the establishing and reporting of energy management plans but does not provide detailed guidance on these issues.

Enforcement provisions were also introduced with Decree No. 134/2013/ND-CP giving a number of state actors authority to impose warnings and financial sanctions for breach of these obligations. Currently, no enforcement notices or sanctions have been issued and the monitoring and enforcement regime for these obligations have yet to be fully implemented. It was noted in a VNEEP II evaluation carried out by the Danish International Development Agency in partnership with MOIT that DEUs generally do not follow the requirements of developing energy management plans or with yearly reporting to the provincial Department of Industry and Trade (DOIT). VNEEP III has prioritised greater focus on compliance enforcement with a specific target of 100% of DEUs applying energy management systems by 2025. Integrating energy management processes into the core business operation and investment processes of large energy users is a key demand-side driver for energy efficiency market development. The government must be commended in the significant progress made to date establishing the legal framework to drive such uptake, and the platform this provides going into VNEEP III with which to consolidate these achievements through renewed focus on strengthening the compliance environment. The reporting obligations that come with the Energy Efficiency Law also provide valuable information flows from enterprises to government on efficiency opportunities, technology diffusion, progress against sub-sectoral targets, etc. This data should be utilised for impact assessment, evaluation, and to support further refinement of the regulatory environment.

Since the passing of the Energy Efficiency Law, mandatory specific energy consumption (SEC) targets for several energy-intensive industries have also been introduced. Mandatory targets were introduced from 2014 following pilot voluntary agreements developed under the Global Environment Fund (GEF) funded Vietnam Clean Production and Energy Efficiency Project (CPEE) implemented by the World Bank (2011-2016). Mandatory targets have now been set for chemicals, plastics, steel, paper, sugar, and seafood processing industries[1]. These industries must develop and invest in energy reduction plans to meet the SEC targets by 2025 or face potential enforcement action. Industry inputs were gathered during the benchmarking and target setting process, but despite careful industry consultations, the setting of mandatory targets can risk unintended effects if inefficient investment decisions are promoted or where access to investment capital is restricted. These risks can be pronounced if the investment case for deep energy efficiency retrofits is weakened due to low or subsidised energy tariffs; Viet Nam has some of the lowest industrial tariffs in the region (Figure 3.1).

Access to finance was highlighted as a key barrier during the CPEE program with companies keen to implement low-cost measures (small maintenance, improvement of production processes, and innovation), but struggled to prioritize capital intensive actions (e.g. equipment replacement) over other operational and investment needs (e.g. capacity expansion). This was more prevalent for the companies with the lowest profitability margins and/or in the most competitive market segments (World Bank, 2018[1]). This is likely to be exacerbated due to COVID-19 impacts; a survey of firms across a number of sectors, including manufacturing, reported an average 36% revenue reduction in 2020 compared to the previous year due to payment delays, cancellation of existing orders, and falling demand (Tan and Tran, 2020[2]).

Figure 3.1. Comparison of industrial electricity tariffs in selected regional countries 2018

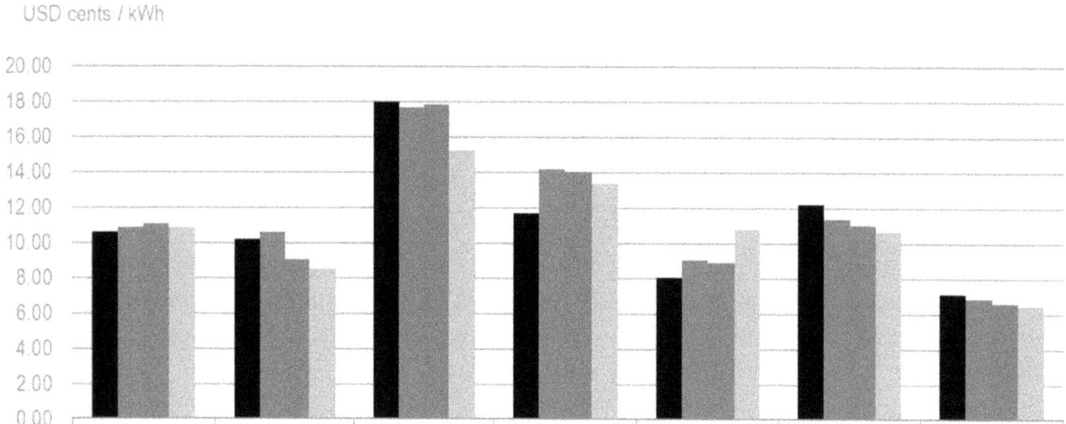

	People's Republic of China	Malaysia	Philippines	Singapore	Republic of Korea	Thailand	Viet Nam
Small	10.59	10.20	17.96	11.68	8.03	12.20	7.13
Medium	10.85	10.59	17.66	14.17	9.08	11.37	6.83
Large	11.06	9.06	17.81	14.05	8.91	11.01	6.61
Very Large	10.83	8.52	15.19	13.36	10.81	10.67	6.45

Note: Industry size defined with monthly consumption and maximum load thresholds: Small 5 000 kWh, Medium 65 000 kWh & 180 kW load, Large 270 000 kWh & 600 kW load, Very Large 1 050 000 kWh & 2,250 kW load
Source: (ADB, 2018[3])

StatLink https://stat.link/ft7o0b

It will be important for MOIT to closely monitor progress against these targets, to continue dialogue channels with industry actors, and to provide supplementary support in the form of technical assistance, tax or other fiscal incentives and facilitating access to finance throughout the target period. Regular tariff uplifts that keep pace with inflation and increasing costs of electricity production will also be crucial. To date these have only happened sporadically and have not kept up with rising costs (Lee and Gerner, 2020[4]). The wider support and facilitation environment available to industries participating in China's top-1000 Programme was a key driver of diffusion of best available technology and energy intensity improvements over the implementation period when energy intensity of GDP fell by nearly 4% per year. The government of China implemented tax exemptions for approved energy saving projects and equipment and direct fiscal incentives to enterprises between USD 26 to USD 33 per ton of coal equivalent saved (Rock et al., 2013[5]). The Scaling Up Energy Efficiency for Industrial Enterprises Programme co-financed by the Green Climate Fund and World Bank is targeted to begin full operation in Viet Nam in Q2 2021 setting up a risk sharing facility to support access to commercial energy efficiency (EE) loans for industry coupled with expanded technical assistance resources.

Energy management system certification to international standards is increasing

Promoting the uptake of internationally recognised standards such as ISO50001 Energy Management, ISO9001 Quality Management and ISO14001 Environmental Management is a key area to ensure energy and environmental management practices are properly integrated into companies' operational processes. This is not just relevant for improving Viet Nam's energy intensity and industrial competitiveness but will have growing importance for attracting foreign direct investment and trade as multinational corporations increasingly scrutinise the environmental impacts of their global supply chains (discussed in chapter 4).

Viet Nam is making progress in this area with holders of ISO50001 certification increasing from five in 2012 to 84 in 2019 (ISO, 2019[6]). This uptake has been supported through VNEEP I & II periods with awareness raising, training, and conducive regulations such as the Designated Energy User obligations described above. Around 150 enterprises received direct support during VNEEP 1 & 2 for the implementation of an energy management system, among which 20 enterprises went on to successfully achieve ISO50001 certification. This was coupled with training and certification to 2 200 energy management staff and the development of standardized training materials on energy management. The government may consider providing further incentives for ISO50001 uptake, for example, through exemptions or relaxation of energy auditing requirements under the energy efficiency law. This is a similar approach taken across EU countries under the Energy Efficiency Directive.

Figure 3.2. ISO50001 energy management system certifications for selected countries

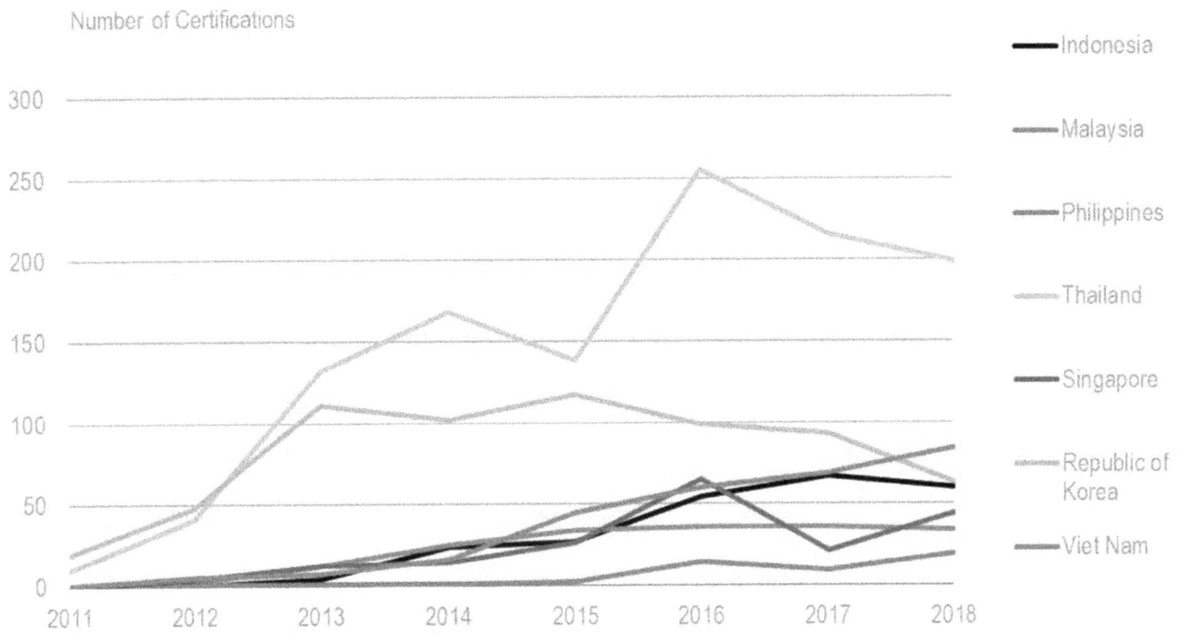

Note: ISO50001 is an internationally recognised certification standard for energy management system quality
Source: (ISO, 2019[6])

StatLink https://stat.link/uf201c

Minimum Energy Performance Standards & Labelling can be tightened in line with market conditions

Energy labelling regulations were introduced by Circular No. 08/2006/TT-BCN mandating a voluntary introductory phase to develop labelling procedures, label design and the technical standards underpinning performance tiers. Technical standards were introduced for five equipment classes, Group 1: lighting, residential appliances and air conditioners; Group 2: commercial and office appliances; Group 3: industrial three phase motors, transformers and chillers; Group 4: cars with less than seven seats; and Group 5: solar water heaters and public lighting. A mix of endorsement labels and comparative labels were introduced depending on technology type. During this time testing facilities were set up (QUATEST 1, 2 & 3), and marketing campaigns undertaken to increase consumer awareness. Decision No. 51/2011/QĐ-TTg later introduced the shift to mandatory labelling for some appliances, as well as the introduction of

MEPS and a roadmap for their implementation. Decision No. 04/2017/QĐ-TTg later supplemented this with five additional products subject to mandatory energy labelling: LED lights, laptops, water heaters with storage, cars with 8-9 seats and motorcycles.

Table 3.1. Timelines for mandatory labelling and minimum energy performance standards

Equipment type	Mandatory labelling Implemented	MEPS introduced
Household appliances and lighting	1 January 2013 various lighting and household appliances 1 January 2020 LED bulbs, kettles	Incandescent bulbs over 60 W banned 1 January 2013 Household appliances 1 January 2014
Industrial equipment	1 January 2013	1 January 2015
Commercial & office equipment	1 January 2014 commercial freezers 1 January 2020, laptops	1 January 2015
Transport	25 April 2017 cars up to 7 seats 1 January 2018 cars 8-9 seat cars 1 January 2020 motorcycles	none

Source: Decision No. 51/2011/QĐ TTg & Decision 04/2017/QĐ TTg

In 2015, shortly after mandatory labelling was introduced, MOIT had approved energy labels for over 8 000 different products and by 2019 this number has grown to 15 000 with labelled products accounting for 90% of all household appliance purchases (Tap Chi Tai Chinh Online, 2019[7]). A market survey in 2014 found impressive uptake and compliance rates for the labelling regulations only six months following the introduction of mandatory labeling requirements; 68% of air conditioners (AC) and washing machines were found to be correctly labelled whereas endorsement labels for compact fluorescent lamps were all found to conform to the regulations. The survey did however highlight that the distribution of washing machines and fans available in the market were highly skewed towards the highest 5 star rating and therefore provided little differentiation in the market and limited incentives for manufacturers and retailers to supply better performing products (Australian Government, 2014[8]). A 2019 survey of the air conditioners market found 76% of all ACs in the market achieved a 4 or 5 star rating, a remarkable improvement compared to the earlier 2014 survey result of 33% (CLASP, 2019[9]). This suggests that Viet Nam has an opportunity to rescale the star rating system and revise the MEPS introduced in 2015 to drive continued market transformation over VNEEP III. It is also recommended that Viet Nam timetable regular market reviews and regrading of MEPS/labelling benchmarks to provide consumers with updated guidance on latest energy efficient technologies.

Figure 3.3. Market share of new appliances for sale by energy performance rating 2014

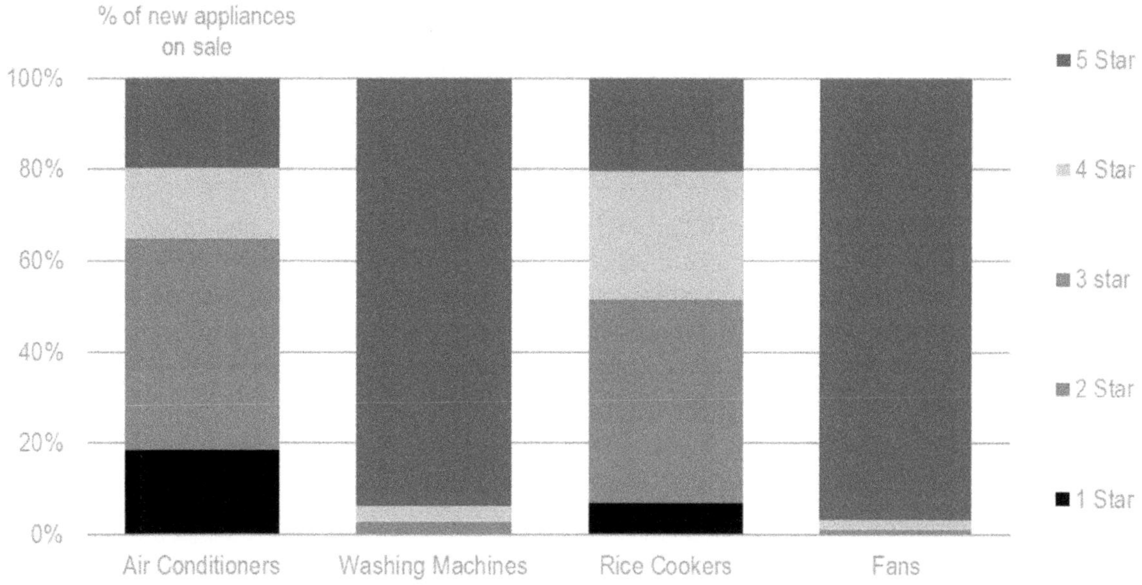

Note: Star ratings corresponding with Viet Nam's appliance energy labelling regulations with 5 star the most energy efficient
Source: (Australian Government, 2014[8])

StatLink https://stat.link/g9ki1u

Energy services companies are active in Viet Nam but a regulatory framework guiding energy performance contracting modalities would build market confidence

Energy services companies (ESCOs) provide technical expertise, project implementation services and, depending on the market conditions, upfront financing or guarantees for energy efficiency projects. ESCO business models have played an important role in facilitating the scale-up of energy efficiency investments in various OECD markets. Their business model mitigates technical and financial barriers faced by project hosts through various forms of energy performance contracts (EPCs) that allow upfront project costs to be paid over time with a share of the savings achieved or by guaranteeing a minimum savings performance. There are thought to be more than 200 ESCOs active in Viet Nam, but the use of EPCs is rare with the vast majority providing consultancy or conventional supply and install services (Viet Nam News, 2020[10]).

Although there are no regulatory barriers restricting EPC modalities between two private enterprises, the lack of awareness and novelty of EPC creates significant hurdles and long business development cycles. A dedicated regulatory framework providing clear guidance on accounting and taxation treatment, third-party monitoring and verification, and specialised arbitration procedures would be an important step to foster confidence. Regulatory barriers related to public budgeting and procurement restrict the possibility for EPC-based procurement across state agencies and state owned enterprises. These regulations should be reviewed to allow multi-year EPC contracting under guaranteed or shared savings modalities. The public sector can take an important "first adopter" role to demonstrate the EPC model and to allow ESCO businesses to build stronger balance sheets and technical competencies. Vietnamese ESCOs are typically small enterprises that lack the balance sheet to provide the collateral required by corporate lenders and therefore have restricted access to financing. It is also relevant for project hosts such as industrial clients who may have weak profitability and high existing debt leverage and who therefore prioritise their remaining investment capacity for what is considered core operational investments. Viet Nam can incorporate learnings from China's successes in ESCO market development as outlined in the case study below (Box 3.2).

Box 3.2. Case Study: People's Republic of China regulatory drivers for ESCO development

The Energy Services Company (ESCO) market in China has seen remarkable growth over the last two decades to become the leading market globally, accounting for 59% of global ESCO revenues in 2017. Over 80 ESCOs were operating in the country in 2005, rising exponentially to over 6 500 in 2019 with ESCOs now providing over 750 000 jobs (Zhu, 2020[11]). China's market development has taken a private sector focused development pathway with 90% of ESCO revenues in the private sector particularly centred in industry. This is a similar market trend to Korea, and to a lesser extent Japan, compared to the United States, the EU, and Canada, where public programmes make up the majority of market activity. It should be noted however that given the level of state support for industry, the line between private and public enterprises in China could be difficult to draw.

Figure 3.4. ESCO market revenue private vs. public sector 2016-2017

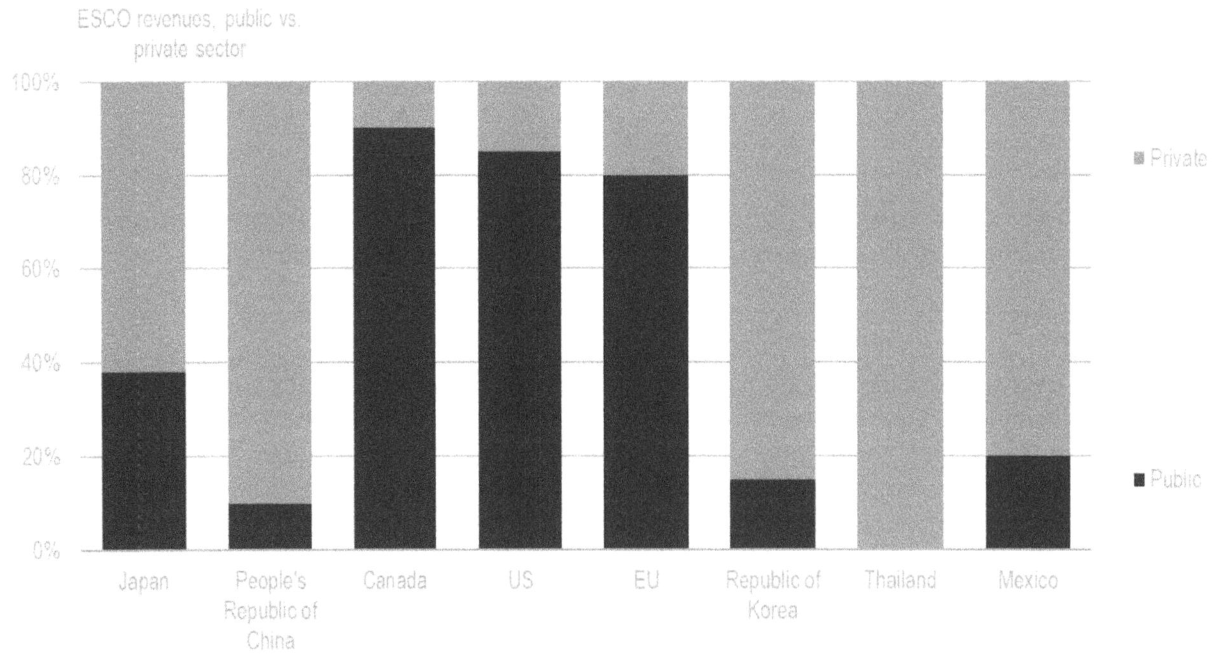

Source: (IEA, 2018[12])

StatLink https://stat.link/rhn4e8

China's ambitious and long-running industry targets set under the Top 1 000 and Top 10 000 programmes implemented since 2005 effectively kick started the market for energy services. This market-making policy was later supported with a range of regulations that fostered the growth of ESCOs and energy performance contracting (EPC). These can be categorised under the following themes in Figure 3.5:

Figure 3.5. Components of a conducive regulatory environment for ESCO development

The range of regulatory actions and guidelines in China targeting EPC development are listed in Table 3.2. Supportive ESCO regulations in China. A critical aspect for ESCO development is access to finance; in China, this was achieved by providing dedicated capital to banks for on-lending but also by focusing on adapting underwriting procedures to overcome barriers specific to ESCOs. The ability for ESCOs to pledge fixed assets and future revenues under EPC projects as security was important and not commonly found in other markets. Supporting ESCOs to develop a credit history in this way has enabled ESCOs to grow their balance sheets and businesses. In 2010, 78% of ESCOs in China were micro or small enterprises, changing to 40% in 2019 (Zhu, 2020[11]).

Table 3.2. Supportive ESCO regulations in China

Financial Incentives	ESCO projects are eligible for incentives of at least RMB 300 (USD 47) per tonne of CO_2e mitigated
Tax Incentives	ESCO revenue from EPCs exempt from paying VAT Income from EPCs exempt from paying corporate income tax for three years and 50% for next three
Accounting Rules	Government agencies permitted to use energy budgets to pay multi-year EPC and accounted as energy-expenditure Fixed assets transferred to users at the end of an EPC treated as a donation and VAT exempt Payments to ESCOs under EPC accounted as a cost
Green Finance	Fixed assets invested by ESCOs under an EPC project can be used as security for loans Banks encouraged to consider future revenues from EPC as security for loans
Certification and Standards	Voluntary ESCO certification based on technical competence, economic capacity and credit record A blacklist system is established for defaulting ESCOs, energy users, and third-party organizations An online EPC registry is established and ESCOs encouraged to register their EPCs in the registry Various technical standards introduced and updated including for rules of EPC, energy auditing, savings monitoring and verification, and energy management systems

Source: adapted from (Zhu, 2020[11])

A private sector led approach to ESCO market development has been achieved successfully in China thanks to the development of a clear regulatory framework that created clarity for contract parties while incentivising market activity. The Government of Viet Nam has made important first steps to create the market through industry targets and energy auditing obligations, however, the supportive regulatory environment to foster market development for ESCOs remains relatively weak. There is no ESCO-specific regulation establishing financial or tax incentives, clarifying EPC accounting treatment, EPC loans, or certification. Viet Nam has prioritised further development of the regulatory environment over the VNEEP III and can incorporate learnings from China to continue to make progress in this area.

Energy Efficiency Regulation in the Building Sector

Vietnam is undergoing rapid urbanisation and a rising middle class. The number of people living in cities is projected to increase from 34.7 million in 2018 to 65.7 million by 2050. This represents more than half of the population relocating to an urban area, spurring demand of 12 million square meters of additional floor space every year (IFC, 2019[13]). In September 2013, the Ministry of Construction adopted the Viet Nam Energy Efficiency Building Code (VEEBC) QCVN 09:2013/ BXD, which set mandatory technical standards for the design, construction or retrofitting of civil buildings (office buildings, hotels, hospitals, schools, commercial buildings, services buildings, apartments buildings, among others), with a gross floor area of 2 500 m2 or larger. VEEBC was updated in 2017 (QCVN 09:2017/BXD) however, the level of compliance is believed to be low. VNEEP III sets a specific goal to verify that 100% of newly built or refurbished buildings comply with the 2017 standard. Decree No. 15/2021/ND-CP has set out important new procedures for the design, appraisal, and inspection of construction projects, which will provide a valuable updated framework to improve the compliance environment.

Figure 3.6. Yearly green building certification 2010-2020

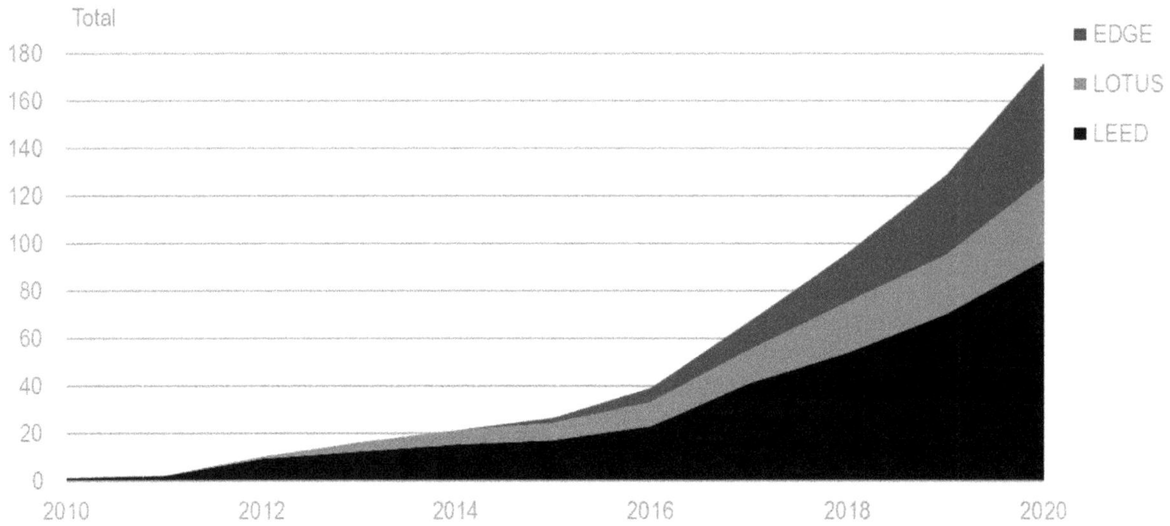

Note: LOTUS is Viet Nam's national green building certification system developed by the Viet Nam Green Building Council. LEED is a green building certification system developed by the U.S. Green Building Council, EDGE is a green building certification system developed by IFC
Source: Viet Nam Green Building Council & IFC

StatLink https://stat.link/gzsi7l

There is positive momentum in Viet Nam with the uptake of green buildings but numbers still remain low. In 2020, there were 23 newly certified LEED buildings (U.S Green Building Council's green building certification standard) and nine LOTUS certified buildings (Viet Nam's domestic green building certification developed by the Viet Nam Green Building Council). To provide further momentum for the green building market the government should consider establishing appropriate incentive programmes, for example, through tax exemptions or support for preferential green mortgage rates. The Ministry of Construction is expected to introduce a new green building legal framework in 2021 that will give authority to provincial level governments to establish localised incentive policies.

Electricity market design and renewable energy policies and regulations

Recent success attracting renewable energy investment brings urgent new priorities to adapt regulatory frameworks for facilitating grid integration

Viet Nam's FIT support mechanism, particularly for grid-scale and rooftop solar photovoltaic (Solar PV), incentivised rapid capacity deployment over the course of 2019-2020. By the end of 2020, variable renewable energy (vRE) capacity reached 17.6 GW (for wind and both grid-scale and grid-connected rooftop installations) accounting for 23.6% of total generation capacity (EVN, 2021[14]). Such rapid deployment was prioritised due to a tightening electricity supply margin driven by strong demand growth coupled with delays in planned thermal power plant procurement. However, the economic impacts of COVID-19 quickly supressed electricity demand causing an oversupply situation, particularly in the southern regions where most of the deployment of solar PV is concentrated. Oversupply led in turn to congestion of the transmission system, magnified during low-demand periods. Under such operational conditions strategic curtailment of generation sources, including RE-IPPs, was unavoidable. During the 2021 Tet holiday (Vietnamese lunar New Year) 5.5 GW of renewable capacity was curtailed whereas ongoing curtailment of RE IPPs to levels up to 30-40% in the most affected localities is also reported. NLDC reports that vRE sources can account for up to 40% of total generation sources during periods of regular grid operation. Over the entire year the average share of vRE on the system accounted for 4.85% of the total which will likely rise to over 10% by the end of 2021 (EVN, 2021[15]). This would put Viet Nam's vRE integration rate above the rate in 2018 of leading renewables markets such as Japan, Australia, the United States and China (Figure 3.7).

Figure 3.7. Variable renewable energy share and phase of integration selected countries 2018

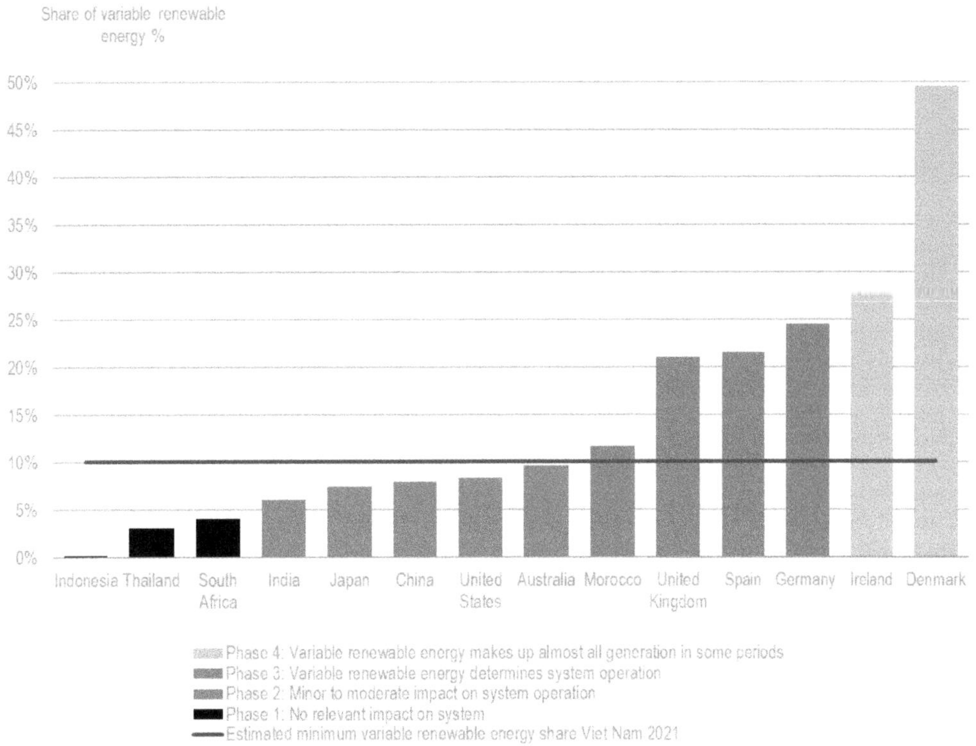

Source: (IEA, 2020[16])

StatLink https://stat.link/okhpqs

Such large shares of vRE has made operation of the power system more complex and provided a preview for Viet Nam's higher renewables future. Integrating high levels of vRE is not only an operational challenge but also a regulatory one. Viet Nam's energy regulatory environment will need to evolve quickly to ensure incentive structures and enabling regulation are in place for the procurement of balancing services and flexible demand and supply side resources that will be required to facilitate the continued clean energy transition. Such measures will also require embedding into the overall market reform process, development of competitive electricity markets and investment plans for grid upgrades.

Viet Nam's competitive power market is developing but a single buyer model remains for renewable energy independent power producers

Viet Nam's Electricity Law, passed in November 2004, set out the legal basis for power sector reforms including the establishment of a competitive power market, the restructuring of Viet Nam Electricity (EVN) and a reformed governance structure (see chapter 2). The Prime Minister's Decision No. 63/2017/QD-TTg (revising earlier decisions passed in 2006 and 2013) approved the reform roadmap (Conditions and Power Sector Organisation Structure for Vietnam Power Market Stages Formation and Development) that plotted the path from a competitive generation market, to a competitive wholesale market, and finally to fully competitive wholesale and retail markets beyond 2023.

Figure 3.8. Planned phases of Viet Nam's electricity market development

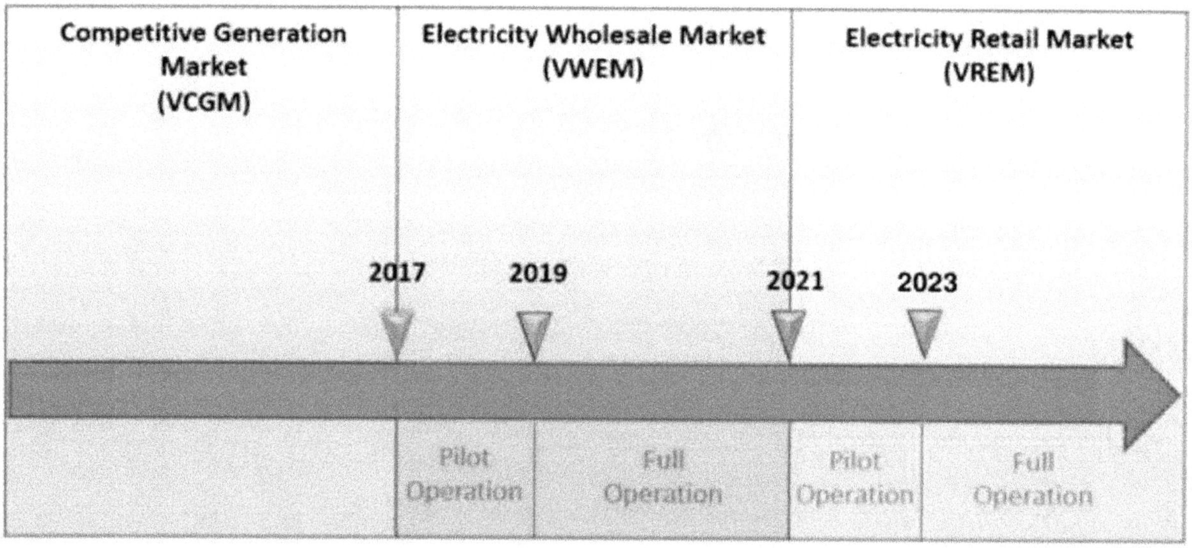

Source: Decision No. 63-2013- QD-TTd

The electricity wholesale market (VWEM) has been in operation since 2019 with the overall design set out by MOIT Decision No. 8266/2015/QD-BCT and rules of participation further developed since. The VWEM implemented the transition from a single buyer model allowing power corporations (and some larger consumers) to participate in the spot market and to also hedge market risks with bilateral contracts directly with generators. This is in contrast to the single buyer model during the competitive generation market period where EVN Electric Power Trading Company (EPTC) purchased all power and supplied it to power corporations at regulated bulk supply tariffs. Hydro and non-renewable generators above 30 MW are now required to participate in the wholesale market whereas renewable energy generators receiving FITs remain under a single buyer arrangement selling power to EPTC without exposure to market prices.

The wholesale market, when fully developed, can play a key role in unlocking and incentivizing system flexibility. Prices that reflect actual system conditions can incentivise generation to ramp-up or ramp-down as necessary, so long as those generators are fully exposed to price signals. This is true not only for traditional dispatchable generation, but also for renewable generation, which can also respond flexibly (for example, by choosing to self-curtail) when incentivised to do so. Price signals should have a high-resolution, both in terms of time (e.g. in 30- or 15-minute increments aligned with dispatch windows) and space (i.e. reflecting local conditions in regions or grid nodes). This means not only carefully considering the design of the wholesale electricity market, but also ensuring that long-term power purchase agreements (PPAs) are market-friendly – that is, exposing generators under long-term contracts to short-term price signals. Contracts for difference (CfDs) or other modern remuneration mechanisms can ensure long-term profitability while also incentivising system friendly operations. As RE-IPPs make up an increasing proportion of installed capacity, their integration into the power market will be of increasing importance to ensure adequate liquidity for efficient market operation. The development of the wholesale market should also be designed to create an environment that enables the technical integration and commercialisation of storage assets by creating price signals that reflect system needs.

Improved ancillary services will be required to maintain power quality and reliability

Power systems with significant vRE penetration require additional ancillary services to maintain power quality and reliability. Ancillary services can be split into different service types: synchronised regulation that corrects short-term electrical imbalances, contingency reserves that are held ready in case of unexpected failures and black start reserves that support system restoration in the event of a power loss. Ancillary services are provided by power plants procured through PPA terms with the pricing governed by Circular 25/2018/VBHT/BCT. To date, the country's hydro assets have largely provided ancillary services and there are currently no storage assets operating on the transmission grid. RE-IPPs are able to participate in ancillary service provision through the terms of the standard PPA, however, it is noted from discussions with NLDC that awareness of the available incentives is low and the incentives have not attracted significant participation. The deployment of energy storage for ancillary service provision is entirely contingent on schemes that compensate project owners for these services (unlike generation assets, which can also sell power). Expanding ancillary service delivery in line with vRE capacity will require modifications to current procurement mechanisms and the potential for separate ancillary services markets as the electricity market further develops. A review of evidence to understand the full cost/benefits of expanding ancillary services across the full range of services types, technologies (generation and dedicated storage assets both distributed and centralised), and ownership models will be required to design a clear strategy for procurement aligned with electricity market development and vRE deployment. Forward looking and inclusive ancillary services procurement can ensure that these changing system needs meet at least cost by allowing all possible solutions among generation, grids and demand to compete on a level playing field.

Some important initial steps have been achieved in enhancing system flexibility; the national grid code which sets out connection rules for the distribution system (Circular No. 25/2016/TT-BCT) and for the transmission system (Circular No. 39/2015/TT-BCT) was revised in 2019 with Circular No. 30/2019/TT-BCT to provide provisions for improved frequency control. A more significant revision of the grid code is also underway to adopt a unified code aligned with international best practice. ERAV is working with the Danish Energy Agency under the Energy Partnership Programme on this work, which commenced at the end of 2020 with a five-year implementation period.

In 2012, the Smart Grid Road Map was introduced in Decision No.1670/QD-TTg to implement measures to automate grid operation and increase reliability. Now, almost all substations and generators over 30 MW have been connected with Supervisory Control and Data Acquisition software system, which enables remote control of equipment. Viet Nam has also taken steps to develop demand response resources with the Demand Response Roadmap and Implementation plan approved in 2019 under Decision No. 175/QD-BCT. This follows from an earlier pilot implemented by Ho Chi Minh City Power Corporation in 2015, which achieved an average of 600 kW of demand side resource availability across 12 participating end users.

The demand response programme is being initially implemented on a voluntary, non-profit basis by engaging enterprises with power consumption over 1 million kWh per year and able to reduce load by 10-20% within 30 minutes of receiving a demand response notice. Without suitable incentives through payments or tariff benefits, though, participation is likely to remain low. ERAV is tasked to develop an appropriate incentive mechanism in co-ordination with the Ministry of Finance but it is understood this work is still at an early stage.

Renewable energy procurement is regulated through a series of ministerial decisions

The support mechanisms and legal framework for procurement of renewable independent power producers (RE-IPPs) have been established by a number of technology-specific decisions and circulars introduced and revised by MOIT since 2008 (Table 3.3). These regulations have introduced tariff support in the form of feed-in tariffs (FITs) or avoided cost tariffs for certain technologies (applicable to biomass power plants and small-scale hydro). They have also introduced standardised power purchase agreements (PPAs) that set mandatory terms between the RE-IPP and EVN as sole power off taker. This has effectively introduced an alternative procurement framework set apart from the country's Public Private Partnership Law, which governed the procurement of large thermal power plants under Build-Operate-Transfer (BOT) arrangements. These renewable support mechanisms have had varying levels of success over the years. Relatively low levels of deployment witnessed, until Decision No. 11/2017/QD-TTg introduced the solar feed-in tariff, beginning of a rapid deployment of solar PV capacity that took off between 2019 to the end of 2020 (see Chapter 5 for a detailed discussion on the design of the feed-in tariffs).

Table 3.3. Timelines and key regulations for renewable energy support

Technology	Regulation	Implementation Guidelines	Expiry
Small Hydro (<30 MW)	Decision No. 18/2008/QD-TTg	Circular No. 32/2014/TT-BCT	none
Wind (onshore & offshore)	Decision No. 37/2011/QD-TTg Decision No. 39/2018/QD-TTg	Circular No. 32/2012/TT-BCT Circular No. 02/2019/TT-BCT	None (replaced) 1 November 2021
Municipal Solid Waste & Landfill Gas	Decision No. 31/2014/QD-TTg	Circular No. 32/2015/TT-BCT	none
Biomass Cogeneration & Power Plants	Decision No. 24/2014/QD-TTg Decision No. 8/2020/QD-TTg	Circular No. 44/2015/TT-BCT	none
Solar Photovoltaic (rooftop, ground-mounted, floating)	Decision No. 11/2017/QD-TTg Decision No. 13/2020/QD-TTg	Circular No. 16/2017/TT-BCT Circular No. 18/2020/TT-BCT	30 June 2019 31 December 2020

Standardised power purchase agreements fall below international bankability standards

To begin construction a developer must execute a PPA with Electricity Vietnam (EVN) according to standardised terms set out in the corresponding circulars issued by MOIT. The PPA is a critical contractual agreement which all other agreements with lenders and equity investors depend as it sets much of the risk profile for the project depending on the certainty or otherwise of revenues from the offtaker. Standard PPA terms simplify the project development process by negating the need for extended negotiation between potential RE-IPPs and EVN as the offtaker. However, to make the investment attractive and to ensure projects are able to raise debt financing, the risk allocations under the PPA must be finely balanced.

Figure 3.9. Simplified structure of agreements for a renewable energy project

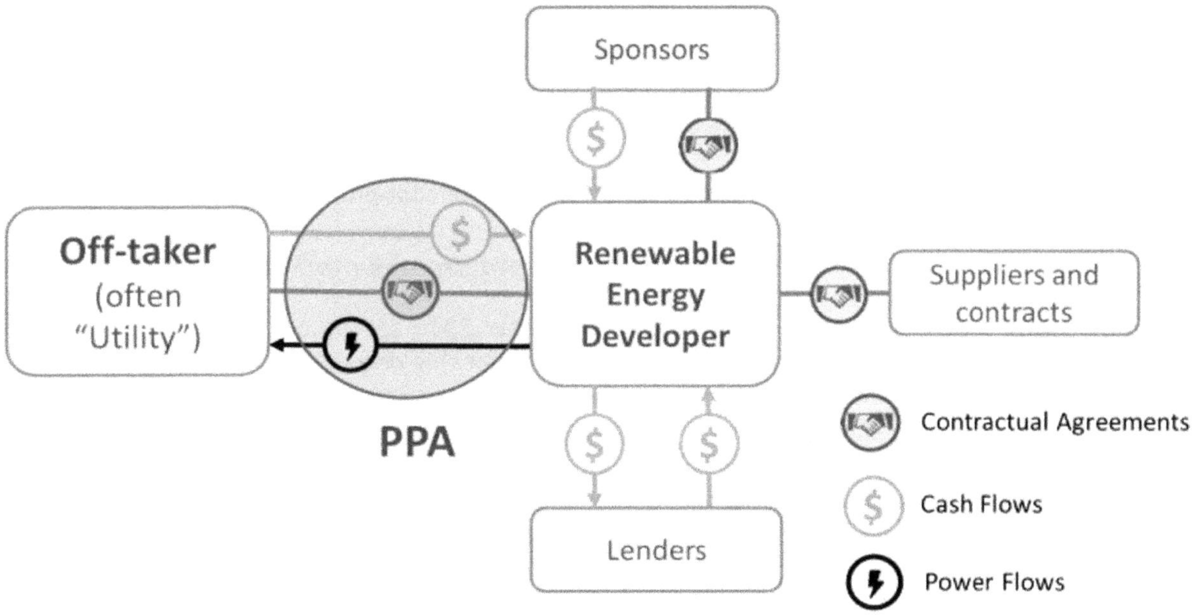

Notes: PPA = Power purchase agreement
Source: (IRENA, 2018[17])

The standardised PPAs in Viet Nam have typically not met international minimum lender requirements for bankability in a few regards and have thus restricted the level of international financing flows from OECD countries into the sector.

- *Curtailment*: the PPA does not impose a clear "take or pay" obligation on EVN and so does not give a guaranteed revenue stream in the event of curtailment events. EVN is obligated to purchase power output only when delivered to the grid. The PPA exempts EVN from the obligation when the grid is under repair, inspection or testing, or breaks down. This effectively leaves projects at risk in the event of curtailment due to grid congestion.
- *Force Majeure*: The PPA does not distinguish between political and natural force majeure events
- *Arbitration:* The governing law of the PPA is Vietnamese law and there is no provision for international arbitration unless agreed by both PPA signatories.
- *Change of Law:* There is no protection for the financial impacts caused by changes in law and/or tax policies after the PPA has been signed.
- *Termination compensation*: Termination compensation is fixed at 1 year's revenue. This has been retained for the latest solar PPA but the latest wind PPA has strengthened this to include all direct losses faced on the remaining contract term.

Low interest rates in OECD markets have driven low costs of debt compared to domestic local currency debt interest rates (4-7% vs. 9-12% nominal[2]), facilitating greater flows of international capital, which has the potential to drive down the prevailing cost of capital in the renewable energy sector. Cost of capital has a large influence on the levelised cost of energy (LCOE) from renewable sources due to higher capital intensity compared to thermal plants. It is estimated that for every 10% reduction in cost of capital there is an LCOE reduction potential of around 6% and that the cost of capital therefore has a greater influence over LCOE than resource quality (Ondraczek, Komendantova and Patt, 2015[18]). OECD consultations with developers and international banks have indicated that to facilitate these flows would require a revision to the PPA terms to give more investor protections particularly over termination and curtailment risks.

The use of non-recourse or limited-recourse financing structures will become increasingly important in Viet Nam's clean energy sector as individual project sizes and total investment requirements increase over the PDP VIII period. Project financing structures allow project sponsors to raise debt financing off balance sheets. This reduces the impact of the project on the developer's debt capacity and cost of debt (World Bank, 2020[19]). The current PPA terms do not provide enough revenue certainty to enable these financing structures and external mitigation options are either unavailable or cost-prohibitive (see chapter 6).

A shift in approach to renewable energy procurement creates market uncertainty

The Prime Minister's Notification No. 402 issued in November 2019 set the course for a transition from FIT-based procurement to competitive auctions. Motivations for this decision include the need for more carefully managed deployment in line with available grid capacity and the desire to harness the cost reduction potential of competitive bidding. The solar FIT (Decision No. 13/2020/QD-TTg) expired on 31 December 2020 and there are no plans to introduce a transitional support scheme for grid-scale solar PV projects. This creates significant regulatory vacuum and uncertainty given the auction system is still at a relatively early design phase and few details are available yet to market participants despite tentative timelines of early 2022. Onshore and offshore wind FITs (Decision No. 39/2018/QD-TTg) are set to expire on 1 November 2021 and no structured transition mechanism is currently being planned with already approved projects in the pipeline expected to be negotiated on a case-by-case basis. The transition to an auction based mechanism will provide opportunities for tariff reduction, but only if sufficient competition is secured for price discovery and conditions are in place to effectively de-risk projects and reduce cost of capital. Abrupt changes or uncertainty to RE policy and support mechanisms can have detrimental stop-and-go effects on industry, local supply chain development, investor confidence and local employment effects. All of which could ultimately disrupt the cost of development of RE projects in the run up to the auctioning programme. These issues are especially critical for (non-nearshore) offshore wind industry, characterised by long lead times for complex supply chain development. A clear roadmap for the envisioned procurement strategy for offshore wind would greatly contribute to creating more certainty for investors and enable realisation of the planned offshore wind capacity on time and in the most cost-effective way.

Current regulations do not provide a specific framework for competitive selection of RE-IPPs and decisions will need to be taken under which law auction-based procurement will be hosted and whether current provisions are conducive to implement an effective auction design (World Bank, 2019[20]). It is understood from consultations that a substation-based bidding framework is favoured by MOIT as it can more effectively synchronise capacity deployment with available grid capacity thereby reducing the risk of curtailment or additional integration costs. Such a system would mean substations across provinces with available interconnection capacity would be identified by MOIT in co-operation with local provincial authorities and EVN NPTC. It is understood that local authorities and local Departments of Industry & Trade (DOITs) will take a lead role in managing the auction process. These details are tentative and no draft documents have yet been released for consultation. A Prime Minister's decision will be required to confirm exact modalities including planning processes, roles and responsibilities, evaluation criteria and the bidding framework itself. It is understood that MOIT is not currently considering a revision to the standardised PPA terms for the launch of the auctioning programme. It will be important to conduct a thorough consultation with industry stakeholders to evaluate the impacts this may have on participation, cost of capital and ultimately the tariff reduction potential. The PPA terms will continue to be problematic for many international developers and lenders including export credit agencies that could play an important role in providing affordable financing and/or de-risking instruments.

Distributed solar has boomed despite issues with administration of net metering

Viet Nam's Rooftop Solar Promotion Program 2019-2025 was launched by MOIT with Decision No. 2023/QD-BCT targeting 1 GW of rooftop solar capacity in the form of 100 000 rooftop systems by the end of 2025. Rooftop solar FITs, along with net metering regulation and standardised PPAs were introduced in 2017 and revised in 2020 to support the achievement of this goal (see chapter 5 for discussion on the feed-in tariff design). The net-metering mechanism was anticipated to regulate payments from EVN to the project owners relying on two-way electricity meters. In a trading cycle, if the amount of electricity generated from a rooftop installation was greater than the consumed amount, the surplus would be carried forward to the next trading cycle. At the end of the year or when the contract was terminated, the surplus amount of energy would then be sold to EVN at the FIT rate. This net metering payment mechanism created administrative difficulties regarding EVN's treatment of taxes and accounting procedures and therefore payments for the majority of installations were delayed pending issuance of further guidelines from MOIT and MOF. To resolve payment delays, on 11 March 2019, MOIT issued Circular No. 05, providing guidelines scrapping the net metering mechanism in favour of a simpler mechanism consisting of two distinct payments between EVN and the installation owner for exported power and consumed power. The promotion of investment in distributed solar was remarkably successful and by end of 2020, 101 996 projects with total capacity of 8.274 GW had been connected before the expiry of the FIT eligibility on 31 December 2020. MOIT is now in the process of designing a follow on support scheme for rooftop solar with initial indications that a tiered FIT design based on capacity is being considered (see chapter 5).

Renewable portfolio standards have been prioritised but are yet to be implemented

Vietnam's Renewable Energy Development Strategy prioritised a number of policy mechanisms for the promotion of renewable energy. This includes the development of a Renewable Energy Portfolio Standard (RPS) that would mandate large power generation companies (with capacity greater than 1000 MW and excluding Build-Own-Transfer plants) and power corporations (Viet Nam's distribution and retail companies) to generate or source an increasing share of renewable energy; not less than 3%, 10% and 20% in 2020, 2030 and 2050 respectively. To date, these provisions have not been implemented. However, as the electricity market reform progresses, RPS could be a valuable mechanism to promote RE sourcing by retail companies. The government of Viet Nam will also be designing a renewable energy certification scheme to support the implementation of a corporate sourcing pilot programme (direct PPAs) set to launch in 2022. Such a certification scheme can also facilitate the implementation of RPS mandates.

References

ADB (2018), *ADB Tariff Appraisal Study: Balancing Sustainability and Efficiency with Inclusive Access*. [3]

Australian Government, M. (2014), *Energy Efficiency Appliance Labelling in Vietnam – Summary of Findings*, https://www.environment.gov.au/system/files/energy/files/energy-efficiency-appliance-labelling-in-vietnam-summary-of-findings.pdf (accessed on 19 May 2021). [8]

CLASP (2019), *Vietnam Room Air Conditioner Market Assessment and Policy Options Analysis*. [9]

Egli, F., B. Steffen and T. Schmidt (2018), "A dynamic analysis of financing conditions for renewable energy technologies", *Nature Energy*, Vol. 3/12, pp. 1084-1092, http://dx.doi.org/10.1038/s41560-018-0277-y. [21]

EVN (2021), *EVN Presentation to OECD Review Team*. [14]

EVN (2021), *EVN: Proposing solutions to operate the power system at high renewable energy load*, https://en.evn.com.vn/d6/news/EVN-Proposing-solutions-to-operate-the-power-system-at-high-renewable-energy-load-66-163-2288.aspx (accessed on 24 May 2021). [15]

IEA (2020), *Variable renewable energy share and phase for selected jurisdictions, 2018*, https://www.iea.org/data-and-statistics/charts/variable-renewable-energy-share-and-phase-for-selected-jurisdictions-2018 (accessed on 24 May 2021). [16]

IEA (2018), *Energy Service Companies (ESCOs)*, https://www.iea.org/reports/energy-service-companies-escos-2 (accessed on 31 May 2021). [12]

IFC (2019), *Greener Buildings Make Better Homes in Vietnam*, https://www.ifc.org/wps/wcm/connect/news_ext_content/ifc_external_corporate_site/news+and+events/news/greener-buildings-make-better-homes-in-vietnam (accessed on 20 May 2021). [13]

IRENA (2018), *Power Purchase Agreements for Variable Renewable Energy*, https://www.irena.org/-/media/Files/IRENA/Agency/Events/2018/Aug/Renewable-Energy-PPAs.pdf?la=en&hash=C365D5D08EBFF26A1F7A29A13D721C5B3C4390D9 (accessed on 18 May 2021). [17]

ISO (2019), *ISO 2019 Survey*. [6]

Lee, A. and F. Gerner (2020), "Learning from Power Sector Reform Experiences The Case of Vietnam", No. 9169, World Bank Group. [4]

Ondraczek, J., N. Komendantova and A. Patt (2015), "WACC the dog: The effect of financing costs on the levelized cost of solar PV power", *Renewable Energy*, Vol. 75, pp. 888-898, http://dx.doi.org/10.1016/j.renene.2014.10.053. [18]

Rock, M. et al. (2013), "Technological Learning, Energy Efficiency, and CO2 Emissions in China's Energy Intensive Industries", *Policy Research Working Paper*, No. 6492, World Bank Group. [5]

Tan, S. and T. Tran (2020), *Impacts of COVID-19 on Firms in Viet Nam, Results from the Business Pulse Survey*, World Bank Group, https://openknowledge.worldbank.org/bitstream/handle/10986/34902/Impacts-of-COVID-19-on-Firms-in-Vietnam-Results-from-the-Second-Round-of-COVID-19-Business-Pulse-Survey.pdf?sequence=1&isAllowed=y (accessed on 19 May 2021). [2]

Tap Chi Tai Chinh Online (2019), *Energy Labeling - Energy Efficiency Solution*, https://tapchitaichinh.vn/nghien-cuu-trao-doi/dan-nhan-nang-luong-giai-phap-tiet-kiem-nang-luong-hieu-qua-306629.html (accessed on 19 May 2021). [7]

Viet Nam News (2020), *Workshop discusses challenges faced by energy service companies market*, https://vietnamnews.vn/economy/803776/workshop-discusses-challenges-faced-by-energy-service-companies-market.html (accessed on 20 May 2021). [10]

World Bank (2020), "Project Finance - Key Concepts", https://ppp.worldbank.org/public-private-partnership/financing/project-finance-concepts (accessed on 21 May 2021). [19]

World Bank (2019), *Viet Nam Solar Competitive Bidding Strategy and Framework*, http://documents1.worldbank.org/curated/en/949491579274083006/pdf/Vietnam-Solar-Competitive-Bidding-Strategy-and-Framework.pdf (accessed on 21 May 2021). [20]

World Bank (2018), *Clean Production & Energy Efficiency Implementation Completion & Results Report*, http://documents1.worldbank.org/curated/en/781731523025593046/pdf/Implementation-Completion-and-Results-Report-ICR-Document-04032018.pdf (accessed on 19 May 2021). [1]

Zhu, X. (2020), "China's Remarkable Success in Developing ESCOs: Current Status, Policy Drivers, and Prospects", in *Incorporating Energy Service Companies in Nationally Determined Contributions - The potential of ESCOs for meeting the climate goals in the Paris Agreement*. [11]

Notes

[1] (i) Document 26/2020/VBHN-BCT (Circular 38/2016/TT-BCT) for plastic; (ii) Document no. 28/2020/VBHN-BCT (Circular 24/2017/TT-BCT) for paper; (iii) Document no. 27/2020/VBHN-BCT (Circular 20/2016/TT-BCT) for steel; (iv) Circular No. 39/2019/TT-BCT for sugar; (v) Document No. 25/2020/VBHN-BCT (Circular 52/2018/TT-BCT) for seafood processing industry; (iv) Circular 19/2016/TT-BCT for beer and beverages; (vii) Circular 02/2014/TT-BCT for chemicals.

[2] Figures based on OECD interviews with foreign and domestic banks and developers.

4 Investment and competition policy

This chapter reviews Viet Nam's investment and competition framework in the context of clean energy. It examines the country's efforts to level the playing field between the national power utility and independent power producers, as well as to create a fair, efficient and transparent procurement process for renewables. It assesses Viet Nam's foreign direct investment regime and other areas to improve the framework for clean energy investment, including how to facilitate land access.

The substantial deployment of renewable energy in Viet Nam has been driven by a wave of private investment under independent power producer (IPP) terms, consequently increasing the share of private ownership of installed capacity from 20 to 30% since 2018. As the renewable energy market matures, Viet Nam will need to continue to support fair competition and equal access between private developers and state owned enterprises, and particularly with the state utility Viet Nam Electricity (EVN), who holds a dominant position across the electricity sector. The upcoming framework for competitive procurement of renewable projects, the full launch of the wholesale market, the continued equitisation of EVN generation companies and the strengthened independence of the National Load Dispatch Centre (NLDC) will be important milestones for creating a level playing field between EVN and renewable IPPs. Viet Nam has been particularly successful in attracting foreign direct investment (FDI) over the last decade and the country's clean energy transition will play an important role in continuing this trend to achieve the government's ambitions to become a leading manufacturing hub in the region.

Assessment and recommendations

Progress is being made towards developing a competitive power market

Viet Nam should be commended on implementing several stages of its electricity market reforms. Since the 1990's the government has worked towards reforming the power sector in order to ensure efficient and affordable power and long-term security of supply. The 2004 Electricity Law was a key milestone and under the reform process, EVN has undergone restructuring into separate entities to enhance operational independence and divestment from non-strategic generation activities. At the end of 2020, EVN accounted for 48% of total installed capacity, down from 58% in 2018 (VIET, 2021[1]). However, the continued participation of SOEs in the generation subsector and EVN's dominant role across all stages of the electricity market remain problematic for the achievement of the ambitious electricity market development agenda prioritised under the 2004 Electricity Law and Resolution 55 orienting the National Energy Development Strategy to 2050. While a majority of renewable projects have been developed by the private sector, it remains important to develop a fair and transparent procurement process in order create a level playing field. The establishment of the wholesale market will be the next milestone, and as more variable renewable capacity is introduced, this market can play a key role in increasing efficiency and driving cost reductions through competition if price signals are effectively harnessed.

Significant transmission upgrades are needed to integrate variable renewable capacity

By 2045, variable renewable electricity could make up more than 44% of Viet Nam's installed capacity (Institute of Energy, 2021[2]). Meeting long-term demand growth and deployment targets for new generating capacity, especially variable renewable generation, will require significant amounts of investment in transmission infrastructure. According to the draft PDP VIII, between 2021 and 2045 Viet Nam requires USD 85 billion in grid investment, or between USD 3.3 and USD 3.4 billion per year, on average. It is essential that this transmission infrastructure be built in a timely manner whilst also keeping costs within a reasonable limit. EVN's role in planning and developing transmission will remain critically important, but Viet Nam should consider the potential role private investors can play in supporting new transmission investments. Under Article 4 of the Electricity Law, the state holds monopoly rights in transmission activities, which includes investment, management and operation. The lack of framework for private participation in the transmission subsector makes it unclear how such investments could be made possible in the future. A review of the Electricity Law is under discussion within the current Socio-Economic Development Strategy (SEDS) cycle. In order to upgrade the transmission system to keep up with current needs, priority should be given to enabling private participation and developing a framework that allows for bankable concession agreements.

Contracting under Public Private Partnership (PPP) laws are underused for clean energy projects

Although power grids and power plants are amongst the five permitted sectors under the new law on Public-Private Partnership (Law No. 64/2020/QH14) (the "PPP Law"), procurement under the PPP law has not been widely used for recent clean energy projects. The recent surge in renewable deployment has been driven by feed-in-tariffs (FIT) established by a separate regulatory framework which introduced standardised power purchase agreements (PPAs) governed under the Law on Investment. As Viet Nam transitions away from the FIT, the PPP law may provide an effective legal framework for larger-scale renewable projects, as more flexibility is permitted to negotiate contract terms.

However, the PPP law does remain unclear on the availability of government guarantee undertakings (GGUs) which are often critical to securing non-recourse project finance debt. The reduction in protection for currency convertibility risk and a requirement for Vietnamese law as the governing law will also prove problematic for many sponsors and lenders. This should be seen as a source of implementation risk for the ambitious deployment plans under the PDP VIII draft, particularly for highly complex and capital intensive integrated liquefied natural gas (LNG) to power projects which have been accelerated under current plans. With respect to energy efficiency, the stipulated minimum project value of VND 200 billion (USD 8.5 million) may create barriers for PPP arrangements, given the typically smaller and fragmented nature of energy efficiency projects (often under USD 1 million). Models for significant project aggregation will be required to achieve the necessary scale to meet these thresholds.

Commitment to clean energy will strengthen its status as an attractive FDI market

Viet Nam is already an attractive location for foreign direct investment, and thanks to its effective management of COVID-19, the country is positioned to benefit from the disruption to established global supply chains caused by the pandemic as well as ongoing trade disputes. This is in line with Viet Nam's ambitions to become a leading industrial hub amongst ASEAN economies, accounting for 40% of GDP by 2030, with 30% attributed to manufacturing and processing industries (Resolution No. 23-NQ/TW). As the pressure increases for multinationals to reduce their overall carbon footprint, and supply chains come under increasing scrutiny, the availability of affordable, secure and clean power for supply chain activities will take increasing importance. Viet Nam's commitment to energy efficiency and low carbon energy will strengthen its attractiveness to foreign investors. Corporate sourcing of renewable electricity is a route for Viet Nam's manufacturing base to rapidly and cost-effectively decarbonise. This is also attractive to multinationals as it provides the opportunity to demonstrate additionality to their stakeholders, in the sense that additional renewable capacity is being developed in Viet Nam by virtue of their PPA. Moreover, with the right pricing structure, a long term corporate PPA can hedge against rising electricity costs. The government must be commended for its willingness to innovate in this area with a much-anticipated pilot direct PPA programme planned to commence this year.

Dispute Resolution should be strengthened in order to boost investor confidence

Under standardised power purchase agreements dispute resolution takes place through mediation before the Electricity and Renewable Energy Authority (EREA), and if unresolved can be escalated to the Electricity Regulatory Authority of Viet Nam (ERAV), with results appealable in Vietnamese courts. In practice, some PPA disputes have gone through local arbitration, notably the Viet Nam International Arbitration Centre, subject to agreement by both parties. As Viet Nam's power system continues to evolve, including, for example, the move away from the feed-in tariff support to competitive auctioning coupled with the increasing share of IPPs, ERAV's dispute resolution role is likely to grow in importance. It is therefore important that ERAV's independence be strengthened, so that the decisions it makes are perceived by market participants as fair, objective and free of political interference. Under the new competitive bidding framework, Viet Nam should provide recourse to arbitration as a standard practice, departing from the current framework which requires EVN's consent on a case-by-case basis.

Coordination around land-use rights remains a challenge for project development

Land access is an important topic for both transmission infrastructure and renewable electricity projects. Land remains in the hands of the state, and individuals and entities are able to purchase the right to use the land through Land Use Right Certificates (LURCs). Foreigners are able to secure LURCs for renewable projects, however the process for obtaining them remains challenging, particularly for developers unfamiliar with the context. There is a need to improve the transparency and co-ordination of various approval processes, as well as co-ordination between governmental and provincial stakeholders, to achieve cost-effective and expedient renewable project development and limit the possibilities for opacity. Future renewable auction mechanisms provide an opportunity for simplified land acquisition and clearance processes. In particular, the People's Provincial Committee can play a larger role in identifying the location for renewable projects, and in taking responsibility for land acquisition and clearance. Moreover, to facilitate better planning, the national and provincial land use master plan should take into consideration land needs for development of renewable projects and transmission infrastructure.

Box 4.1. Main policy recommendations on investment and competition policy

- Ensure that the wholesale market incentivises system-friendly operations by providing accurate and high-resolution (in terms of time and geography) price signals to all appropriate market participants. Exposure to correct price signals can incentivise greater efficiency in operation and capital allocation.
- Strengthen ERAV's independence, so that all market participants view the decisions it makes as fair, objective and free of political interference. Consider providing recourse to arbitration as a standard practice for renewable electricity PPAs.
- Enhance the independence of the NLDC in the near term and consider a timeline for the independence of the transmission company, Viet Nam Electricity National Power Transmission Corporation (EVNNPT), and the separation of distribution and competitive activities such as generation and retail in EVN power corporations.
- Consider revising the legal framework to enable private investment in transmission infrastructure, in order to realise planned upgrades in a timely and cost effective manner. Priority should also be given to developing a framework for competitive bidding and bankable concession agreements, for instance through the new PPP law.
- Establish guidelines for competitive and transparent procurement of renewable projects in order to support a level playing field between private sector and state-owned enterprises (SOEs), both domestic and regional. Ensure that development risks regarding allocation of LURCs are taken into consideration in the design of the bidding framework.

Creating a level playing field between public and private investors in clean energy infrastructure

In the face of constrained public finance and growing energy demand, private investment has been recognised as a key component to ensure long-term security of a power supply, which is accessible and affordable to consumers. Viet Nam has sought to move away from a centrally-planned monopoly towards a power sector with multiple participants and at this time, the market can be labelled as partially competitive, with EVN holding a dominant position. A regulatory authority has been established, and the upcoming auction mechanism will pave the way for competitive bidding and greater transparency. Viet Nam is implementing plans to increase efficiency and competition by privatising shares of SOEs, and in particular the state utility's (EVN) ownership of generation assets through a process known as equitisation, as well as by increasing corporate governance.

More efforts are needed to level the playing field between IPPs and EVN

The electricity market in Viet Nam remains heavily government owned by state utility EVN and its subsidiaries who maintain a monopoly over electricity transmission distribution, wholesale and retail (see chapter 2). Until 2018, 58% of generation remained in the hands of EVN, with a further 13% owned by PetroVietnam and Vinacomin (VIET, 2021[1]). The landscape has been changing with a surge of new private investment since 2019, through renewable projects (Figure 4.1). This has primarily taken the form of greenfield investment in wind and large amounts of solar under independent power producers (IPPs) arrangements. From 2018 to 2020, the share of capacity owned by IPPs jumped from 21% to 31% of total installed capacity (VIET, 2021[1]). By virtue of the integrated structure of the market, renewable project development and operation remains heavily dependent on EVN. For solar, wind, biomass, waste to energy and small hydro projects, IPPs depend on non-negotiable power purchase agreements (PPA) from EVN, the sole offtaker of electricity in Viet Nam (discussed in Chapter 3). Under current legislation there is no framework for industrial and commercial users to directly source renewable electricity from IPPs.

Figure 4.1. Ownership of installed capacity in Viet Nam 2018 and 2020

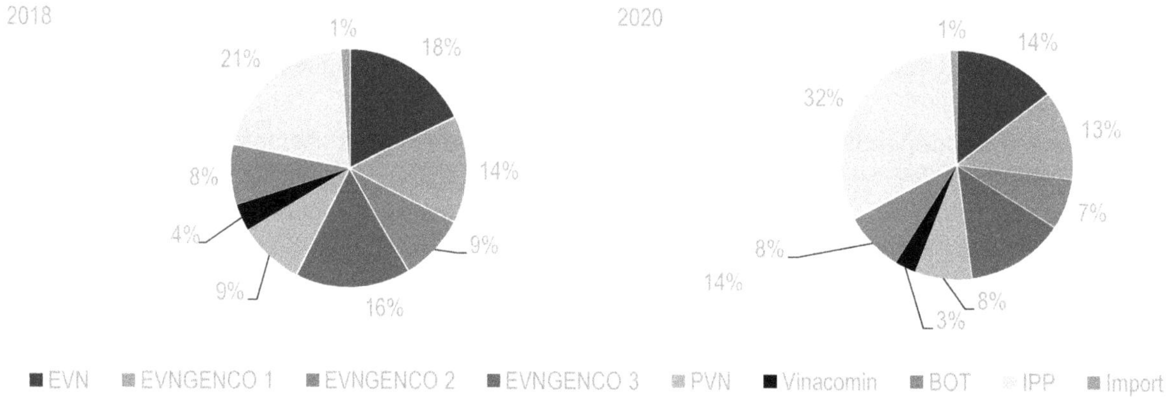

Note: excludes rooftop solar
Source: Viet (2020) State management role in power sector

StatLink https://stat.link/km6wzh

Although a majority of renewable projects have been developed by the private sector, renewable electricity does feature in SOE strategies, albeit modestly. This reinforces the need for a fair and transparent procurement process. The current system could be perceived to favour SOEs from the energy sector who, by virtue of their structural ties with the Ministry of Industry and Trade (MOIT), would be better placed to navigate the project development process, combined with competitive advantages of SOEs in Viet Nam, such as facilitated access to land, and their ability to borrow from state-owned commercial banks on more preferential terms.

To date SOE renewable targets remain modest. For instance, PetroVietnam, Viet Nam's state owned oil firm, only aims to develop 100 MW of renewables capacity by 2025 and 900 MW by 2035 (Renewables Now, 2020[3]). EVN's generation companies (GENCOS) already have 215 MW of solar capacity, with plans to increase capacity in forward looking strategies (VIET, 2021[1]) (EVN, 2019[4]). In an investor conference in January 2021, ahead of its initial public offering (IPO), GENCOS 2 announced that it recently completed 50 megawatt power (MWp) of solar power projects, and had 55 MW of wind power under construction, with plans for eight new power projects of a total capacity of 2 593 MW comprising six solar power plants and two thermal plants (Viet Nam News, 2021[5]). As EVN continues to partially privatise its generation companies, investment in renewable electricity may feature in its strategy to attract investors. However, significant participation in the renewable electricity sector would be problematic for competition. At this stage of the electricity market reforms, EVN's GENCOS have a clear advantage over competitors, through structural ties with EVN subsidiaries across the electricity sector but also through its relationship with MOIT.

Equally, as the wholesale market develops, a level playing field is important to ensure that prices reflect actual system conditions and are free from price distortion. An effective wholesale market can help unlock greater efficiency and system flexibility as exposure to price signals provides incentives for efficient capital allocation and responsive asset operation with view of system needs. Market participation of SOE owned assets that benefit from direct or indirect state aid can harm private participants' ability to compete, at a cost to consumers and public finances. Barriers to efficient market operation can also occur where competition policy and SOE governance regulations allow opportunities for anti-competitive practices such as predatory pricing or other abuses of market power.

Viet Nam has made significant progress with the unbundling EVN and SOE reforms. However, the continued participation of SOEs (albeit reducing over time) in the power market and EVN's dominant role across all stages of the market remain problematic for the achievement of the ambitious electricity market development agenda prioritised under the electricity law and as set out in other sector strategies such as resolution 55.

Currently renewable generators benefiting from FITs have no exposure to market prices as they do not participate in the electricity market. This is common globally as revenue stability and preferential tariffs are needed to stimulate technological progress. However, as renewable generators are integrated into the market at the end of the 20 year FIT period, the market design will need to be adapted to ensure price signals remain conducive to continued asset operation and can incentivise investments. Forward planning for this eventuality will be required as Viet Nam's market development reforms progress, for instance through a gradual exposure to market prices in new assets. Evidence from European markets have shown that high levels of variable renewable generation can lead to declining revenue prospects particularly during times of peak generation (Rövekamp et al., 2021[6]).

There is a need to create a more transparent, clear and predictable procurement process

The main instrument for project procurement is the Power Development Plan (PDP), which lists a pipeline of projects to be developed over the period. A key milestone in the project development process for renewable projects is the project's inclusion in provincial power development plans. For projects under 30 MW, the evaluation is handled by the Provincial People's Committee (PPC), which is the executive arm of government at provincial level, and by MOIT's regional office, the Department of Industry and Trade, which sits under the PPC. Final approval for projects under 30 MW, and both the evaluation and approval for projects over 30 MW, takes place at central level. This procurement framework and particularly project approval has been noted to lack clear guidance, with different procedures applied across provinces.

The current process leave the door open for speculative practices whereby investors without strong technical expertise or financial resources seek to acquire numerous projects, both onshore and offshore, with the view of selling their stakes in project companies to better suited renewable developers. Establishing a transparent procedure will be a key step to ensuring fair competition and selection of the most appropriate investors, as well as streamlining some of the project development processes. This in turn can reduce the perceived risk of project development, helping reduce risk premiums expected in equity returns and cost of debt (VIR, 2020[7]).

Viet Nam has committed to introducing a structured competitive procurement program for renewable projects in the near future, however, additional legal guidance for how this works under the overall legal mechanisms will need to be developed. Unlike PPP contracts, which have a procedural requirement for bidding under the new PPP law, current regulations do not provide an explicit framework for competitive selection of IPPs for new generation, which includes renewable power but also liquefied natural gas (LNG) projects. Competitive procurement across technologies is important in order to provide transparency and predictability to investors and to drive down costs. Guidance would need to clarify whether investor approval falls under the 2021 Investment Law and current bidding regulations. The development of the competitive bidding mechanism for solar power, is supported by the World Bank, with inputs from line ministries, the private sector and development partners (World Bank Group, 2019[8]). The strategy and framework put forward by the World Bank proposes a competitive selection of investors based on a pre-selected project location, either in terms of a substation or a solar park. Bidding would be conducted at the local level by the PPC, who would evaluate the IPP's financial strength and capacity to raise debt, and its experience in construction and operation of utility scale solar photovoltaic (PV), onshore wind or offshore wind installations, as well as some form of pre-feasibility study of the project (see chapter 5 for further discussion).

Strengthening competition should be a priority in the equitisation process

Under the electricity market reform, EVN has undergone restructuring into separate entities to enhance operational independence with the long-term goal of divestment from generation activities, with the exception of strategic multipurpose hydropower. In parallel to other aspects of the market reform, plans to privatise generation assets, known in Viet Nam as the process of "equitisation", have progressed slower than expected. EVN restructured its generation with the view of fully privatising power plant companies, outside of strategic hydropower, by 2014. This was deferred after EVN suffered a financial crisis from 2009-2010, and significant equity injections were required from government (Lee and Gerner, 2020[9]). A new plan to partially "equitise" EVN's generation assets starting from 2018 was approved by the Prime Minister (Decision No. 852/QD-TTg), with EVN retaining at least 51% shareholdings of GENCOS in the first phase. This process has proven to be challenging, and the first IPO of GENCO 3 was far from reaching its target. Only 0.36% of GENCO 3's shares sold, well below the targeted 12.8%, and raising around USD 8 million rather the desired USD 290 million (OECD, 2018[10]). After a second round, in total 2.8% of the company shares sold. EVN is continuing to implement the equitisation of GENCO 2 and GenCo 1, however, a similar lacklustre response from investors was seen for the IPO of GENCO 2 in 2021 (VIR, 2021[11]).

While EVN's current strategy for partially privatising its generation companies creates new opportunities to finance the energy sector, it does not necessarily increase competition in the market. By keeping a majority share, EVN retains control over operation and investment, in effect maintaining or possibly strengthening its position in the market and leaving their private shareholders with limited influence. The weak turnout at IPO's can be in part linked to high valuation of shares and volatility in Viet Nam's stock market, but also because of concerns over highly indebted generation plants and weak corporate governance (Viet Nam News, 2018[12]). Investors must take on shares in a significant amount generation capacity which has varying risk profiles, as all of EVN's generation activities, outside of strategic assets, are organised under these three GENCOS. The division of generation into a few large companies is useful for EVN to group plants in areas with transmission constraints, when there is insufficient competition in the market, and package less efficient plants together with better performing plants. However, this can represent a disadvantage for external investors, as these plants will increase the risk of the overall portfolio. In the context of an evolving electricity market, in terms of progress on market reforms and in particular the upcoming wholesale market, it may be possible to give bidders more flexibility over power plant grouping, for instance targeting subsidiaries of GenCos, or selling plants individually, which would help investors manage risk (Asian Development Bank, 2000[13]).

In the IPO, concerns were also raised around corporate governance. Minority shareholder rights, have in some areas been weak. However, Viet Nam has seen important developments over the last few years. This includes the Law on Enterprises that came into effect in 2021, which lowers the threshold to 5% shareholders down from 10% for minority shareholders to have access to important corporate information, and waivers the former six-month delay before ordinary shareholders could exercise rights. It also allows for shareholders holding preferred dividends, which are non-voting under Vietnamese law, to attend and vote in shareholder meetings where proposed resolutions adversely affect their rights and obligations (OECD, 2018[14])

Increasing the independence of electricity market actors will ensure effective competition and market confidence

A World Bank analysis of privatisation in developing countries notes that the effectiveness of moving from state to private ownership is closely tied to the strength of the regulatory framework and competition in the market, in order to yield economic gains and improve company performance. In the electricity sector, only when privatisation is coupled with the establishment of an independent regulator is it linked to more generating capacity and higher output. Conversely, in situations of weak competition, attempts to improve performance of state-owned enterprises is ineffective without privatisation (Estrin and Pelletier, 2018[15]).

A key step in the reform process has been the establishment of the Electricity Regulatory Authority of Vietnam (ERAV), who handles inspections and dispute resolution in electricity activities. However, as discussed in chapter 2, ERAV remains structurally dependent on MOIT, and as the market develops ERAV's oversight role will need to be strengthened and potentially expanded. ERAV has authority for dispute resolution under model PPAs. This can create concerns amongst private investors that they may not receive fair treatment if situations of conflict were to arise with EVN, due to limitations to ERAV's authority and independence.

The National Load Dispatch Centre (NLDC), which is also the System Operator, holds an essential role for ensuring effective competition which in turn helps attract private sector investment. The NLDC determines short-term operations of generating plants and is the interface with the transmission system. The NLDC is planned to be unbundled between 2025 and 2030, but until that time it remains structurally dependent on EVN, who also owns a significant share of generation capacity. This lack of independence between generation and system operation creates concerns over the objectiveness of dispatch prioritisation. This is particularly the case given oversupply and congestion in transmission networks, which, alongside a lack of take or pay commitment, represents a significant risk to renewable developers. The independence of NLDC, as well as a clear and transparent mechanism for addressing dispatch congestion, will be important steps to provide generators with more confidence and should be prioritised in the near term.

At this time, the ownership, operation and maintenance of the transmission grid remains with EVN under the National Power Transmission Corporation (EVN NPT). EVN NPT's role in granting grid connection agreements could open the door to perceived or real conflicts of interest that affect the ability for competing IPPs and SOEs to access the transmission system on equal terms. There is also little transparency in the way that grid connection is managed, this could be improved through, for example, an enforceable first-come first-served connection queue overseen by ERAV. Further reforms of EVN's organisational structure will also be required in preparation for retail market liberalisation expected under the market reform roadmap in 2021-2023. Currently EVN's Power Corporations (PCs) carry out retailing, distribution and meter data management functions. Effective retail market reforms may require these functions to be separated, initially via ring-fencing and potentially with full legal separation at a later stage. This is important for ensuring equitable treatment of competing retailers and generators and protection of confidential data that would give a competitive advantage (Ricardo Energy & Environment, 2019[16]).

Promoting equal treatment of foreign and domestic investors in clean energy

The regime for foreign investment is generally quite permissive, and Viet Nam has a very low foreign direct investment (FDI) restrictiveness index of 0.01, with 0 being the most open, and sits ahead of its regional peers in this respect (Figure 4.2). The ratification of the EU-Viet Nam Free Trade Agreement (EVFTA) in 2020 and the Comprehensive and Progressive Agreement for Trans-Pacific Partnership (CPTPP) in 2019 further demonstrates the government's commitment to facilitate opportunities for foreign investors. Clean energy represents an opportunity to support Viet Nam's industrial ambitions through attracting FDI from increasingly environmentally conscious multinationals. For clean energy, certain administrative hurdles remain in place, particularly around project development processes, perceptions of risk allocation and dispute resolution mechanisms.

Figure 4.2. Viet Nam's FDI liberalisation compared to regional peers

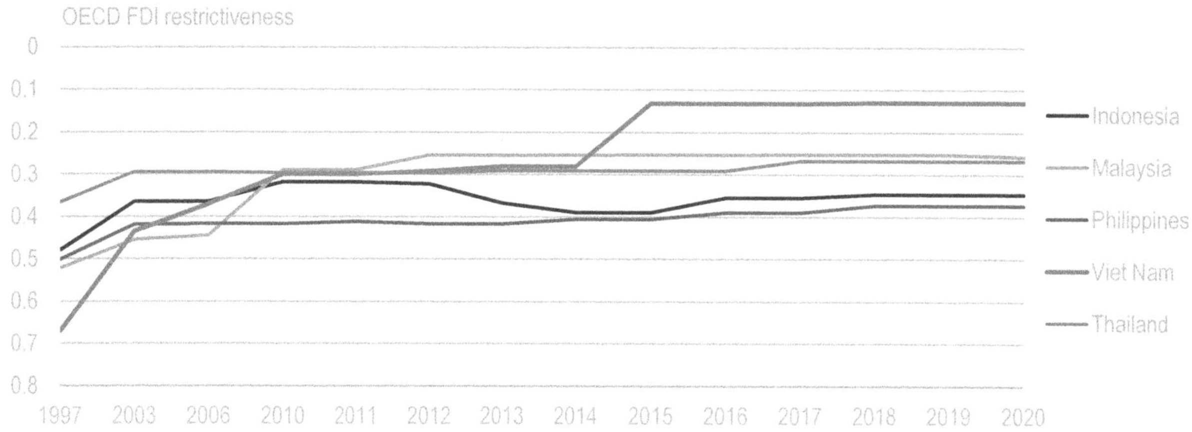

Note: 0 = open, 1 = closed
Source: OECD (2020) FDI restrictiveness (database)

StatLink https://stat.link/14e7oq

Viet Nam boasts an attractive and open environment for FDI

Foreign investors, which are companies where 50% or more of charter capital contribution is foreign owned, are provided with almost equal treatment except those in sectors explicitly named on the "negative list" or "conditional list". Foreign and domestic investment in clean energy is governed by the Law on Investment (No. 67/2014/QH13), which regulates business investment activities in the country, and the Law on Enterprises (No. 59/2020/QH14) which regulates the types of business enterprises permitted in the country and how they operate. The energy sector is amongst permitted sectors and the only additional step that foreign renewable developers must officially take is to apply for an investment registration certificate (IRC), either at central or provincial level (Apricum, 2020[17]). Depending on the size of the project, either the Ministry of Planning and Investment (MPI) or its regional office, the Department of Industry and Trade (DPI), oversees this process. All new enterprises, both domestic and foreign, must also obtain an enterprise registration certificate.

Investors are not compelled to source locally under the investment law. Treaties, such as the WTO Trade Related Investment Measures (TRIMs), and the 2020 EU-Viet Nam Trade and Investment Agreement reinforce this. Other areas of law impose certain local requirements for subcontracting under renewable electricity or energy efficiency investments, which may require capacity building in Viet Nam to ensure local resources are technically able. These include the Law on Bidding and Decree No. 59/2015/ND-CP guiding the Construction Law, which states that a foreign contractor must employ Vietnamese sub-contractors to do construction work in Viet Nam. Current regulations do not expressly require foreign investors to hire local staff, but for certain positions Vietnamese workers are given preference under the 2012 Labour Code. Under the new PPP Law, investors committing to use domestic contractors, goods and materials are eligible for preferential treatment during the bid evaluation process.

Clean energy will be essential to fulfil ambitions of becoming a leading industrial hub

The industrial sector is an engine of growth for Viet Nam's economy and a core part of the country's economic strategy is to attract FDI particularly in manufacturing, with ambitions to become a leading industrial hub amongst ASEAN economies. According to the National Industrial Policy (Resolution No. 23-NQ/TW) government intends for industry to account for 40% of GDP by 2030, with 30% attributed to manufacturing and processing industries. At a time of the disruption to established global supply chains caused by COVID-19 and ongoing trade disputes, and thanks to its effective management of the pandemic, Viet Nam's manufacturing base is well positioned to welcome more FDI. However, industrial environmental performance must continue to improve to ensure the country can capitalise on these trends. Environmental policies of multinationals continue to tighten worldwide and there will be increasing scrutiny on the environmental impact of international supply chains. Energy efficient manufacturing practices and access to renewable electricity should be made a priority in order for Viet Nam to remain an attractive location for FDI. Growing interest amongst domestic and international business has already been highlighted through the medium of Renewable Energy Buyers Alliance (REBA) Viet Nam Working Group (USAID, 2019[18]).

Viet Nam is already aware of this as can be seen by the Pilot Direct Power Purchase Agreement (DPPA) between renewable electricity developers or power generation companies and commercial and industrial consumers (Draft DPPA Decision), submitted to MOIT in 2020. With Draft Decision No. 544, MOIT is proposing a synthetic DPPA mechanisms for off-site renewable electricity projects to be implemented between 2020 and June 2022. The DPPA pilot is proposed to be limited to power consumers for industrial manufacturing and generation would come from grid connected solar and wind generators over 30 MW, already approved under PDP VII-revised.

Complex procedures and unclear risk allocation may limit FDI in renewable projects

Despite low FDI restrictiveness, the first phase of renewable deployment has primarily been developed and financed by leading Vietnamese conglomerates such as BIM Group, Trung Nam Group and Xuan Cau Group as well as major ASEAN developers such as AC Energy from the Philippines and, Super Energy and B Grimm from Thailand. FDI from OECD countries has been low, linked to complicated project development processes, perceptions of risk, and lack of confidence in mechanisms for dispute resolution.

The permitting and licensing process for renewable projects is extensive, requiring a number of administrative procedures and legal documentation relating to investment and enterprise certifications, inclusion in national and provincial planning, grid connection agreements with EVN, land clearance and environmental impact assessment. This has been a relatively complicated process, requiring a number of stakeholders at both central and provincial level. While international investors should appreciate that each market in Asia is different, an additional complexity in Viet Nam is that administrative procedures may vary across provinces. This often requires legal and technical support with expertise in the particular province to prepare documents, as well to navigate the process with relevant provincial authorities, which increases costs. High investment in time and resources in the development process for renewable projects can be a deterrent, as investors will carefully weigh up the risk-return-ratio. Given that there is currently no competitive bidding process in place, this also leaves open the opportunity for inefficient practices, such as local investors unqualified in renewable development but better able to navigate the system, developing projects with the intention of selling shares to foreign investors at a profit.

As discussed in chapter 3, PPA terms leave investors open to certain risk. Model PPA for renewables do not offer take-or-pay obligation or minimum purchase guarantee. This creates contractual uncertainties, given high curtailment risks associated with limitations on transmission capacity that developers are facing. Foreign investors are also exposed to currency inconvertibility risk as the FIT rate is fixed to US dollar value but denominated and paid for in Vietnamese dong. Finally, the terms for compensation upon early termination of the PPA, without fault of the developer, are unclear. Lack of compensation predictability creates uncertainty over future cash flows and debt service capacity, particularly given the current developing status of the renewables market.

Mechanisms for dispute resolution may not be sufficient to reassure foreign investors

Dispute resolution under the model PPA is governed by Vietnamese law with mediation through MOIT's Electricity Renewable Energy Authority (EREA) and, if unresolved, escalation to the Electricity Regulatory Authority of Vietnam. Results are appealable in Vietnamese courts. This could be problematic for investors, as EVN and its subsidiaries are closely tied to MOIT through both legal structure and corporate governance. The government has authority over EVN's investments, appointing the members of its board of directors and its senior management (Lee and Gerner, 2020[9]). Combined with the structural dependence of both EREA and ERAV on MOIT this creates uncertainty over fair treatment if a dispute were to arise.

The model PPA allows the possibility of using another dispute resolution body, if both parties consent to arbitration, which allows EVN the right to refuse. In practice, EVN has agreed to local arbitration for some projects, notably through the Viet Nam International Arbitration Centre, however this decision is made on a case by case basis. In general, international investors in Viet Nam tend to prefer international arbitration for dispute resolution as an alternative to domestic courts and before private arbitration centres such as the Viet Nam International Arbitration Centre. Under the New York Convention on Recognition and Enforcement of Foreign Arbitral Awards 1958, foreign investors are able to negotiate provisions for international arbitration deemed more neutral, such as the Singapore International Arbitration Centre. However, it appears that for renewables projects under PPA terms, EVN may be unwilling to agree to arbitration outside of Viet Nam. Under the framework and strategy put forward for the upcoming competitive bidding mechanism for solar energy, the World Bank also advises that international arbitration is available in the event of early termination of PPA (World Bank Group, 2019[8]).

While Vietnamese law specifically governs renewable electricity projects under the model PPA, FDI in other areas often falls under investment treaties, which have been an important policy tool for creating an attractive investment climate. These treaties protect investors post-establishment, giving covered access to investor state dispute settlement (ISDS) mechanisms (inspired by commercial arbitration systems), which enforces fair and equitable treatment and includes provisions against expropriation without compensation and against discrimination. Between the Vietnamese legal framework and international treaties, different levels of protection are provided to domestic and foreign investors, but also different levels of protection are provided to foreign investors depending on the treaty provisions under which they are covered. Under the PPA terms, these practices do not apply to renewable electricity development but may apply to FDI in other clean energy activities, for instance under PPP arrangements, whereby international treaties can be used as a means to resolve disputes.

Facilitating land access for renewable electricity development

Land access is an important topic for both transmission infrastructure and renewable electricity projects. In Viet Nam, land remains the property of the Vietnamese people and is administered by the government on its behalf. Only the rights to use land known as Land Use Rights Certificates (LURCs) can be bought or sold. Vietnamese nationals can purchase these rights indefinitely, whereas for foreigners and foreign businesses these can only be bought for a 50-year period, which is renewable once. This process is much akin to the land system in other countries such as the UK and is not in itself a constraint to investment. The process of co-ordination for LURC acquisition is relatively complex, requiring a number of stakeholders, which may lead to significant delays for infrastructure development.

Issues around securing land rights play a central role in project development

Land is an important risk in the renewable project development in Viet Nam. Level land covers no more than 20% of the country's geography, which has much more tropical lowlands, hills, and densely forested highlands. Land for renewable project development, and particularly solar, competes with other uses, such as agriculture. Under the former planning cycle, the land use master plan and the power development were not synchronised, which led to challenges around availability and planning of flat land. As discussed in chapter 2, this may pose a risk under the current planning cycle, as the PDP VIII draft has been submitted before the National Master Land Use plan has been finalised. To add to this, are risks around delayed connection to grid and grid congestion leading to curtailment. This means that not only is flat land in high demand, but also suitably situated land is even more sought after.

In order to secure land rights, developers must undertake negotiations for LURC through the People's Provincial Committee, who have decentralised administrative authority over provincial lands, under the 2013 Land Law. An appraisal board headed by the provincial governor decides on land planning and sets the land use fees. Steps include appraisal of land and clearance plans by relevant provincial authorities such as the regional office of MONRE, the Department of Natural Resources and Environment (DONRE), negotiations between multiple parties owning LURCs, agreement of land lease fees, and clearance and compensation of current owners. Before completing the agreement with the PPC, the developer must obtain the environmental impact assessment, the investment registration certificate and an enterprise registration certificate for the project. For renewable project developers this creates a multi-layered process, which can vary across provinces and which is generally a long, costly and complex procedure for IPPs. Until a competitive investor and project evaluation process is in place, this process does not exclude speculative practices, whereby prime locations are secured by investors without the capabilities to develop renewables, with a view to selling licences or shares in the company to experienced renewable developers. In addition to the development of the renewable project, the IPP is responsible for investing, installing and operating power lines and transformers from the renewable plant to the nearest connection point, which depending on the location of the plant relative to the substation, may pass through land with multiples LURC owners. This has the effect of significantly increasing project development risk.

Another essential function of land rights is to secure long-term investment and financing. The renewable plant is considered the main asset which can be used as security for lenders, and the ownership of the plant relies on the IPP having legal rights over the land. Land rights enable project companies or a special purpose vehicle (SPV) to hold the plant over the course of the PPA and financing agreement (World Bank Group, 2019[8]). Under the Law on Land, project developers may take security over land and assets attached to the land, but only with credit institutions operating in Viet Nam (World Bank Group, 2016[19]). This restricts the flows of international debt capital for renewable project development, due to an inability to take security over land for foreign credit institutions. Some transactions have bypassed this by using a local bank as security agent. However, this arrangement is a grey area in the legal sense and has not been tested in the courts. Under the incentives for renewable energy, projects can be exempt or benefit from reduced land-use rental payment, but if they take advantage of this incentive, developers lose the right to take security over land, although they may still mortgage the assets attached to the land, with credit institutions operating in Viet Nam (Hogan Lovells, 2018[20]).

As discussed earlier in the chapter, significant investments are needed to update transmission infrastructure. Within the current legal framework, this falls under the responsibility of EVN given that transmission is a state monopoly activity. Land issues, however, are not exclusively a concern for the private sector. Land clearance is a key issue faced by EVN in the construction of new transmission lines, which often cross long distances. A similar negotiation process is required with LURC owners for those territories. Transmission lines require comprehensive environmental impact assessments and appraisal by relevant ministries, in particular MONRE, due to their passage lines through protected areas, such as forest lands. If Viet Nam is to consider private investment in transmission infrastructure, this will be an important consideration for potential investors and lenders.

Competitive bidding guidelines, floating solar and cities provide new opportunities

Suitable land resources for renewable projects are in limited supply, particularly for those well situated for grid connections and where variable renewable energy (vRE) capacity will not contribute to congestion in the grid. Moreover, under the former master planning, projects often competed against land for agricultural purposes, as provincial land use plans and the PDP VII-revised were synchronised. With these risks in mind, the solar bidding strategy and framework proposed by the World Bank puts forward a competitive selection of investors based on a pre-determined project locations. The two models proposed, substation-based and solar park model, aim to address concerns around transmission grid stability and project development risk (World Bank Group, 2019[8]).

The substation-linked model helps optimise the use of existing transmission capacity and reduces both the potential cost of integrating vRE and the risk of curtailment. EVN NPT would have responsibility for identifying substations across provinces which have available interconnection capacity limits and invite bidding for a specific MW capacity at each substation. In the long term this could also proactively drive grid investments needed for new vRE generation, by planning grid and vRE capacity together. Government would undertake a screening of environmental and social constraints for land around the substation in co-ordination with the provinces, but under this model IPPs are responsible for identifying land for their bid, and will be responsible for land clearance procedures. This means that although curtailment risks are reduced, the land development risks remain with the developer.

Under the solar park model, land identification and clearance is managed by the PPC and EVN, in line with provincial land use plans. They would also undertake investments for the solar park infrastructure. This means that all administrative prerequisites around the land rights steps are obtained before the competitive bidding procedure begins and the winning IPPs gains full ownership of the land without undertaking lengthy negotiations with the PPC. The IPP will be responsible for arranging the financing, construction, and operation of the solar project. The solar park model significantly lowers development risks and can shorten the development timeline for IPPs. Costs savings particularly linked to acquiring land rights, should therefore be reflected by lower PPA tariffs. While lower risks can attract larger more risk adverse investors, this approach is more demanding on the government, who manages the process and who must have sufficient institutional capacity and budget to undertake the selection, clearance and infrastructure work.

In the face of land constraints, floating solar PV facilities are an interesting opportunity, particularly given Viet Nam's existing hydro infrastructure. Viet Nam already boasts the largest installation in South East Asia, Ho Tam Bo and Ho Gia Hoet 1 floating PV facilities, both located on irrigation lakes in the Chau Duc district, connected in 2020 with a generation capacity of 35 MWp each. This is following an Asian Development Bank financed, 47.5 MWp floating solar PV facility on the existing 175 MW Da Mi hydropower plant owned by Da Mi Hydropower Joint Stock Co.

The potential of rooftop solar PV in urban areas has also been recognised as a potential to meet electricity needs. A 2017 study commissioned by the World Bank found a potential of 18 000 GWh in Hồ Chi Minh and 2 300 GWh in Na Dang (Effigis Geo-Solutions, 2018[21]) and under Decision No. 2023/QD-BCT, Viet Nam's Rooftop Solar Promotion Program 2019-2025 targets 1 GW of rooftop solar capacity by 2025. By the end of 2020 101 996 projects with total capacity of 8.274 GW had already been achieved.

Harnessing public procurement and public-private partnerships for clean energy

Public procurement and public-private partnerships are powerful instruments for driving private investment in energy efficiency and renewable electricity. By setting energy related technical standards and output specifications within public procurement and public-private-partnership practices, government can harness private sector efficiency and incentivise innovation and investment in clean energy technologies.

Technical standards in public procurement drive investment in energy efficiency

Central and regional governments could play a key role in driving energy efficiency market development as large energy consumers. This pertains, notably, to improving energy performance of public sector buildings and in public sector utilities such as telecoms and water supply and sanitation. To enable this energy efficiency, performance criteria should be mainstreamed into public procurement practices whether under public private partnerships or under more conventional public procurement limited to design and construction contracting or procurement of products and appliances.

Energy efficiency is not yet systematically integrated into public procurement in Viet Nam. With respect to public sector procurement mandates, current regulation encourages the public sector to prefer arrangements for the supply of specific products, or the provision of services with a defined cost, defined activities and specified equipment. Countries typically encounter issues around budgeting, which make it difficult for public entities to finance energy efficiency investments from savings in energy costs. For example, energy efficiency investments may be financed from investment budget whereas the resulting savings are credited to the operational budget (Gynther, 2016[22]). Prioritising energy in public procurement helps raise awareness and create incentives for the industry to innovate and create business models around energy service provision. Mandatory technical standards have an important role in incentivising these investments, such as the National Energy Efficiency Building Code QCVN 09:2013/ BXD (VEEBC), which sets mandatory technical standards for the design, construction or retrofitting of civil buildings. However, as discussed in Chapter 3, enforcement remains an issue. Viet Nam has already had a few examples of public lighting programmes. For instance, in 2018 a private company won a bid to replace all inefficient lamps with LED in Hoa Binh Authority under an ESCO investment business model, whereby the company operates the city lighting systems with an annual provincial payment, to be transferred back to the authority after nine years. Similar projects for city lighting are being applied in Dac Nong, Can Tho, and Long Xuyen.

PPP can be an effective tool for supporting greater clean energy investment

The new Law on Public-Private Partnership (PPP) (Law No. 64/2020/QH14) codifies provisions relating to PPP projects, reducing previous uncertainties over which legal framework is applicable to PPP projects. But at the same time this law also determines precise projects that can fall into the definition of PPPs which are: transportation; power grids and power plants (except for hydropower plants and state monopolies as prescribed by the Electricity Law); irrigation, clean water supply, water drainage, sewerage and waste treatment; health care and education; and IT infrastructure.

For energy efficiency in particular, the stipulated minimum project value of VND 200 billion (USD 8.5 million) may create certain barriers for PPP arrangements for EE, given the typically smaller and fragmented nature of energy efficiency projects (often under USD 1 million). Models for significant project aggregation will be required to achieve the necessary scale to meet these thresholds. However, another approach is to integrate energy efficiency into PPP contracts as a general practice, by setting technical specifications that define energy performance requirements over the lifetime of the project. The advantage of performance requirement is that it is measurable in the outcomes of the project, and does not set requirements on specific solutions, allowing for innovation and incentivising the private partner to develop an integrated approach to energy efficiency from early in the project design phase (GI Hub, 2019[23]).

Although power grids and power plants are amongst the five permitted sectors under new law, PPPs have not been widely used in renewable projects. Given that the recent surge in renewable electricity has been driven by feed-in tariffs (FIT), projects have generally been implemented through independent power producer investment with terms determined by the power purchase agreements. As Viet Nam transitions away from the FIT, PPP arrangements may prove to be useful instruments for larger or riskier renewable projects, where government incentives and negotiable contract terms can provide additional reassurance to investors. Moreover, EVN and other energy SOEs have noted their interest in developing a long term renewable strategy and PPPs can leverage public funding to have wider impact.

Private participation can play a key role in updating the transmission system

According to PDP VIII, between 2021 and 2045 Viet Nam will need to invest around USD 85 billion in grid infrastructure, or between USD 3.3 and USD 3.4 billion per year, on average. Transmission infrastructure has been an issue for developers, both in terms of delayed connection of plants to the grid and transmission system congestion leading to curtailment. To accommodate current generation needs, between the 2021 to 2025 period alone, 651 substations, 120 projects on 500 kV lines, and 531 projects on 220 kV lines are planned. Given that the PDP VIII does not clearly identify generation sources, EVN is not yet actively planning transmission investment for new generation. Given the urgency of updates, it is critically important that this transmission infrastructure be built in a timely manner, and with a view of the scale of investment required, it will be important to keep costs within a reasonable limit. In other countries, transmission projects have notoriously been delayed and gone over budget, especially when they are built in densely populated or environmentally sensitive areas.

There are various models for private participation in transmission infrastructure, such as long-term concessions, Build, Own, Operate, Transfer (BOOT), Merchant line and financial ownership. While there is no perfect model for private participation, long-term concessions and BOOT models have been the most effective in attracting high levels of private capital to countries across the world (IEA, 2020[24]). Independent Power Transmission (IPT) models with BOOT contracts gives the concessionary responsibilities for building and operating a single transmission line or a package of a few lines in exchange for an annual payment. IPTs are widely used around the world, including Brazil, Chile, Colombia, India, Mexico and Peru (Box 4.2) (ESMAP, 2015[25]) In order to be implemented in Viet Nam, these models would require policy and regulatory changes and will depend on the effective design of bankable contracts and a competitive tender process. Under Article 4 of the Electricity Law, the state holds monopoly rights over activities of transmission, which includes investment, management and operation. While there is no framework for private sector investment, there has already been one exceptional case of a private investor for a large solar power project investing in a 500/220 kV substation and transmission line to EVN's grid (Pham, 2020[26]). The draft PDP VIII proposes an amendment of the Electricity Law towards greater flexibility for private investment in the power sectors including in transmission infrastructure, ensuring that all resources can be mobilised. The review of the Electricity Law is still under discussion, but combined with the new PPP law, effective since 2021, which provides for investments in power plants and power grids, this could serve as a potential avenue for private investment.

Box 4.2. Private investment in transmission – the experience of Brazil

Brazil stands out among other emerging economies for having mobilised over USD 38 billion in private capital for transmission expansion projects since 1999, primarily in the form of long-term concessions. Between 1999 and 2020 alone, Brazil organised 50 tenders of multiple lots resulting in the award of 334 concessions and 96 000 km of transmission lines designed, built and operated by the private sector. With scarce investment capital Brazil favoured the Independent Power Transmission (IPT) model offering 30-year BOOT contracts with annual payments. The contract incentivises the IPT to commission the transmission line on time, to keep costs over the duration of the contract to a minimum and to ensure high availability for the transmission line over the contract term. Although Eletrobras, the government-owned transmission company, continues to own the majority of the transmission grid, new concessionaires have entered the sector. Between 1999 and 2010, nearly 70% of investments in transmission came from private investment, with foreign companies accounting for 30 %, local private companies 39%, and SOEs 31%.

Competitive bidding for companies is based on lowest annual revenue, which is the annual fee the IPT will be paid if successful in the tender. While the outcome of the tender sets the price, the regulator can review during five-year price determinations. Agência Nacional de Energia Elétrica (ANEEL), the Energy Regulatory Agency, runs the tendering process and sets a cap on maximum annual revenue. To be eligible for the tender, a number of technical and financial conditions are required for bidders to participate in tenders, such as proof of contracts with relevant subcontractors, minimum levels of liquidity, equity and capital, and tax compliance, and ANEEL holds the company's bid guarantee of 1% of investment. Winners are selected based on a reverse bidding, which establishes construction deadlines and rules for the regular energy transmission service provision.

To ensure timely delivery, the process provides incentives to meet deadlines and imposes penalties on delays to commissioning. Transmission companies that have previously had delays are banned from the tender for a given period. The ITP contract also mandates access to the transmission network on a consistent and nondiscriminatory basis. A rate of 97% availability of the transmission line is require under which the IPT may be penalised. ITP companies sign contracts with all network users and third parties who may want to access the line, including generation companies, distribution companies and large customers dependent on these lines.

The process of competitive tendering has also reduced transmission costs, with winning bids between 1999 and 2020, on average 25.8 percent lower than annual revenue estimated by ANEEL, and reductions on estimated individual line costs of up to 70.3 percent.

Opening the transmission sector to competition for new projects can help Viet Nam meet its transmission upgrades planned in the PDP VIII draft. The Brazil example highlights that the independent power transmission models can successfully mobilise large amounts of capital for grid upgrades and that having multiple owners to transmission infrastructure does not necessarily compromise transmissions system efficiency or security. This is largely due to the central government transmission planning by the Ministry of Mines and Energy (MME) and the Energy Research Office (EPE) with the National System Operator (ONS), which has effectively co-ordinated transmission projects from design through to system operations, combined with a strong regulatory agency (ANEEL) governing concessionaires. This highlights the importance of strengthening the independence and powers of the electricity regulator, as well as the independence of the power system planning and operation.

Source: ANEEL (2021) Results of auctions website ESMAP (2015) Private Sector Participation in Electricity Transmission and Distribution-Experiences from Brazil, Peru, The Philippines, and Turkey, World Bank (2021) Private Participation in Infrastructure (PPI) (database), IBRD (2017) Linking Up: Public-Private Partnerships in Power Transmission in Africa

References

Apricum (2020), *Vietnam's solar success story and why its solar M&A landscape is about to heat up*, https://www.apricum-group.com/vietnams-solar-success-story-and-why-its-solar-ma-landscape-is-about-to-heat-up/?cn-reloaded=1. [17]

Asian Development Bank (2000), *Developing best practices for promoting private sector investment in infrastructure power*, http://www.adb.org. [13]

Duong, V. (2020), *Patent Landscape on Green Technology in Viet Nam.*, https://www.researchgate.net/publication/342436180_Patent_Landscape_on_Green_Technology_in_Viet_Nam/citation/download. [28]

Effigis Geo-Solutions (2018), *Assessment of rooftop photovoltaic solar energy potential in Vietnam.* [21]

ESMAP (2015), *Private Sector Participation in Electricity Transmission and Distribution-Experiences from Brazil, Peru, The Philippines, and Turkey*, The International Bank for Reconstruction And Development / THE WORLD BANK GROUP, Washington, https://documents1.worldbank.org/curated/en/786091468189572248/pdf/99009-ESMAP-P146042-PUBLIC-Box393185B.pdf (accessed on 2 June 2021). [25]

Estrin, S. and A. Pelletier (2018), *Privatization in Developing Countries: What Are the Lessons of Recent Experience?*, Oxford University Press, https://academic.oup.com/wbro/article/33/1/65/4951686. [15]

EVN (2019), *EVN to focus investment on 5 solar power projects*, https://en.evn.com.vn/d6/news/EVN-to-focus-investment-on-5-solar-power-projects-66-163-1533.aspx. [4]

GI Hub (2019), *Chapter 5. Output specifications | Reference Guide on Output Specifications for Quality Infrastructure.* [23]

Gynther, L. (2016), *Energy Efficiency & Public Sector Policy brief*, https://www.odyssee-mure.eu/publications/policy-brief/public-sector-building-energy-efficiency.html. [22]

Hogan Lovells (2018), *Renewable Energy in Vietnam*, https://www.hoganlovells.com/en/publications/client-briefing-renewable-energy-in-vietnam. [20]

IBRD (2017), *Linking Up: Public-Private Partnerships in Power Transmission in Africa*, World Bank Group, Washington, https://openknowledge.worldbank.org/bitstream/handle/10986/26842/LinkingUp.pdf?sequence=3&isAllowed=y (accessed on 1 June 2021). [30]

IEA (2020), *Attracting private investment to the electricity transmission sector in Southeast Asia.* [24]

Institute of Energy (2021), *Draft Power Development Plan 2021-2030 with a vision to 2045.* [2]

Lee, A. and F. Gerner (2020), *Learning from Power Sector Reform Experiences The Case of Vietnam*, World Bank, http://www.worldbank.org/prwp. [9]

OECD (2018), *OECD Investment Policy Reviews: Viet Nam 2018*, OECD Investment Policy Reviews, OECD Publishing, Paris, https://dx.doi.org/10.1787/9789264282957-en. [14]

OECD (2018), *OECD Investment Policy Reviews: Viet Nam 2018*, OECD Investment Policy Reviews, OECD Publishing, Paris, https://dx.doi.org/10.1787/9789264282957-en. [10]

Pham, L. (2020), *First private-invested 500/220kV transmission line in Vietnam connected*, http://hanoitimes.vn/first-private-invested-500220kv-transmission-line-in-vietnam-connected-314366.html. [26]

Renewables Now (2020), *PetroVietnam to foray into renewables, eyes 900 MW by 2035 - report*, https://renewablesnow.com/news/petrovietnam-to-foray-into-renewables-eyes-900-mw-by-2035-report-706109/. [3]

Ricardo Energy & Environment (2019), *Establishing the Vietnam Wholesale Electricity Market (VWEM)*, https://www.adb.org/sites/default/files/project-documents/48328/48328-001-tacr-en_0.pdf. [16]

Rövekamp, P. et al. (2021), *Renewable electricity business models in a post feed-in tariff era*, Elsevier Ltd. [6]

USAID (2019), *Vietnam Releases Direct Power Purchase Agreement Policy Proposal for Public*, https://www.usaid.gov/vietnam/press-releases/jun-12-2019-vietnam-releases-direct-power-purchase-agreement-policy. [18]

VIET (2021), *State management role in power sector*, Vietnam Initiative for Energy Transition, Hanoi, Vietnam. [1]

Viet Nam News (2021), *EVNGENCO 2 to sell over 581 million shares through IPO*, https://vietnamnews.vn/economy/859677/evngenco-2-to-sell-over-581-million-shares-through-ipo.html. [5]

Viet Nam News (2018), *Doubts remain over the EVN's sub-unit IPOs*, https://vietnamnews.vn/economy/463725/doubts-remain-over-the-evns-sub-unit-ipos.html. [12]

VIR (2021), *Investors give EVN Genco 2 cold shoulder at IPO*, https://www.vir.com.vn/investors-give-evn-genco-2-cold-shoulder-at-ipo-82519.html. [11]

VIR (2020), *FiT revamp vulnerable to speculation*, https://www.vir.com.vn/fit-revamp-vulnerable-to-speculation-76532.html. [7]

World Bank (2019), *Investment Policy and Regulatory Review: Viet Nam*, http://documents1.worldbank.org/curated/en/400351586323809041/pdf/Vietnam-2019-Investment-Policy-and-Regulatory-Review.pdf. [27]

World Bank Group (2021), *Data on Private Participation in Infrastructure (PPI)*, Infrastructure Finance, PPPs & Guarantees, https://ppi.worldbank.org/en/ppidata (accessed on 17 June 2021). [29]

World Bank Group (2019), *Viet Nam Solar Competitive Bidding Strategy and Framework*, http://www.worldbank.org. [8]

World Bank Group (2016), *Project appraisal document on a proposed credit in the amount of sdr 107.00 million (us$150 million equivalent) to the socialist republic of vietnam for the viet Nam improved land governance and database project*. [19]

5 Investment promotion and facilitation

This chapter analyses the use of targeted incentives for energy efficiency and renewable energy development, and provides insights into good practices in other countries. It highlights key measures implemented by the government to improve the business environment for clean energy projects, as well as areas of untapped opportunity to attract further investment. It also examines the role that public procurement of energy efficiency services and corporate sourcing of renewables can further support clean energy market development.

Strong support has been provided by government to facilitate clean energy investment in Viet Nam. The strong action taken to reduce direct fossil fuel subsidies coupled with innovative plans to develop a local carbon market will do much to ensure capital is directed towards projects that support green growth. A favourable tax structure providing corporate income tax holidays to renewable projects and energy efficient equipment manufacturers also provides important incentives to investors. The doing business environment could be improved to further facilitate investment, particularly foreign investors with less familiarity with Viet Nam's legal environment. Due to the decentralised governance structure, project developers must interact with multiple contacts across different agencies whereas implementation of laws and regulations is not always uniform across provinces. Administrative procedures can also be relatively complex as evidenced by tax procedures which take on average twice as long to compared to the regional average (World Bank, 2021[1]).

Assessment and recommendations

Viet Nam has taken strong action to reduce fossil fuel subsidies

The Government of Viet Nam has taken strong actions to reduce fossil fuel subsidies in the energy sector and prioritise market mechanisms for the pricing of energy products. The subsidisation rate for fossil fuel consumption directly by end-users or for electricity generation was estimated at 1% in 2019, down from 4.3% in 2015. This represents only 0.1% of GDP compared to regional peers such as Indonesia at 1.7% and Malaysia at 0.5% (IEA, 2020[2]). In addition to direct subsidies, electricity retail tariff controls have historically accounted for a large source of indirect subsidies. Retail tariff subsidies incentivise over consumption and undermine energy efficiency investment. Since the Electricity Law in 2006, the government has gradually strengthened transparency in the retail tariff setting and moved to market-based pricing. The average retail tariff (ART) was revised upwards 13 times since 2006 to around USD 8 cents/kWh today. Despite this, the ART is estimated to remain below long-term marginal cost to cover operation and maintenance and debt servicing expenses, while providing a return on capital for future investment (estimated at US 12 US cents/kWh). Further sources of indirect subsidy include corporate concessions and tax breaks, improved access to land and access to preferential loan terms from state owned banks; such benefits have been available to state-owned enterprises (SOE) operating or developing fossil fuel assets (Lee and Gerner, 2020[3]).

Planning for a carbon market is underway to strengthen Viet Nam's climate policy

Viet Nam is one of a few countries in the region that has implemented an environmental protection tax (EPT) to promote green growth. Introduced in 2012, it places a levy on the production or importation of products with negative environmental impacts, namely: petroleum, coal, hydro chlorofluorocarbons, plastic bags and chemical pesticides. A proportion of EPT revenues capitalise the Viet Nam Environmental Protection Fund and provides concessional financing for projects with positive environmental benefits. Resolution No. 579 in 2018 increased the tax rate on coal by 50%. An ex-ante assessment concluded that this increase would lead to a reduction in coal-related CO2 emissions of 10.25% (Nong, 2018[4]).

In November 2020, Vietnam's National Assembly adopted a revised Law on Environmental Protection that prioritises the launch of a domestic emissions trading market. The Ministry of Natural Resources and Environment (MONRE) has worked with the World Bank under the Partnership for Market Readiness Programme since 2016 to develop much of the analytical work required to underpin this. This includes the development of a monitoring, reporting and verification system, and greenhouse gas registry. A roadmap is also under development to set key implementation activities and milestones. It is understood that a voluntary market will be targeted for launch by 2027 and mandatory participation by 2029 (Viet Nam Water Portal, 2020[5]). The introduction of a carbon market in Viet Nam can promote investment decisions that deliver environmental protection at the lowest overall economic cost. However, its effectiveness in the energy sector will depend on the interaction with the underlying power market structure and operation. The plan for a carbon market will therefore need to be designed and integrated into the overall roadmap for power market reform to ensure price signals can be effectively passed through to power market participants and drive investment decision making. Its effectiveness will also be dependent on the management of policy alignment across different policy domains, for example, in the case of energy efficiency where tariff cross subsidisation may work against price signals from a carbon market.

Fiscal incentives are in place to promote clean energy investment

Viet Nam investment law defines clean energy as a preferential investment sector and therefore grants eligibility for fiscal incentives. This includes a preferential corporate income tax (CIT) rate, exemption from import tax for eligible components and exemption from land lease charges in certain localities. Manufacturing businesses producing energy efficient equipment are eligible for incentives, however, no demand-side incentives are yet available through the tax structure for companies or individuals investing in energy efficiency or green buildings. Such incentives can be an important policy tool to drive market transformation. Viet Nam's incentive framework for clean energy investment provides significant benefit to clean energy investors but the procedures for granting and administrating these benefits are complex. The OECD's Investment Policy Review 2019 notes that there is a lack of clear guidance to investors and that the application of rules can be inconsistent. Drawn out exchanges with tax authorities is often required for the granting of tax incentives and tax procedures are generally time consuming. The World Bank's Doing Business rankings concludes that 384 hours are required on average each year by businesses on tax administration compared to the average for East Asia and the Pacific of 178.

Renewable energy project approval and permitting processes can be streamlined

The process for approval and permitting for renewable energy projects requires sponsors to liaise with a number of different public agencies whereas it has been noted that applicable laws and regulations are not always uniformly applied across different provincial authorities. This creates the perception of complexity for clean energy investors that may discourage new market entrants and increase development costs. The experience of operational wind power projects suggests that development times lay between three to five years which is roughly comparable to the EU average for onshore projects of 3.5 years (MOIT/GIZ, 2016[6]). With the plan to transition to an auction system it will be important to ensure that the processes for permitting and site preparation are streamlined for potential bidders. Hidden costs related to administrative processes and approvals can make it difficult for bidders to estimate costs accurately. If there is uncertainty or a high-risk perception it may lead to bids with higher contingencies priced in. Alternatively, where unexpected additional costs are incurred it may risk approved projects not being realised or winning bidders requesting renegotiation of terms.

Public retrofitting schemes can accelerate the energy efficiency market development

Public energy retrofitting programs can be an effective driver of energy efficiency market development due to the large quantity of project pipelines that can be unlocked. Public sector programs can also facilitate wider adoption in the commercial and industrial sectors by demonstrating scalable financing models such as energy performance contracting. Energy services company (ESCO) markets in the United States, Canada, and the European Union developed largely as a result of government initiatives to promote public sector programs (World Bank, 2016[7]). There has been isolated examples of public programs in Viet Nam but they have not been widely replicated beyond their implementation periods. Provinces and municipalities, rather than central government, play a central role in facilitating public energy efficiency programs due to the high degree of fiscal decentralisation in Viet Nam. This creates challenges for project aggregation – an important requirement for energy efficiency investment due to the low capital costs of individual projects. Viet Nam has no agency that can coordinate aggregation and support provincial procurement at a central level to achieve economies of scale, ensure high quality project design, standardisation, and monitoring and verification.

Box 5.1.Main policy recommendations on clean energy investment promotion and facilitation

- A clear roadmap to move to full cost recovery levels in the tariff structure should be developed to provide consumers sufficient long-term visibility to adapt to tariff uplifts and to provide a market signal for the promotion of energy efficiency investment.
- The plan for a carbon market should be designed and integrated into the overall roadmap for power market reform to ensure price signals can be effectively passed through to power market participants and drive investment decision-making.
- The government of Viet Nam should prioritise the development of demand-side tax incentives for companies and individuals that invest in the highest energy efficient equipment. Such incentives can be structured by the energy performance thresholds enshrined in Viet Nam's energy labelling regulations and tax reductions provided at point of purchase or through rebates.
- Project approval and permitting processes should be streamlined to reduce administrative costs and timelines for renewable energy project development. This could be achieved by establishing a nodal agency (or one-stop shop) that provides a single point of contact for clean energy project developers.
- The government of Viet Nam should consider establishing a centralised agency (for example a variant on the Super ESCO model) that is mandated to support provincial authorities to develop, procure, finance, and monitor and verify the savings for public energy efficiency programmes. The agency would provide a key facilitation role to aggregate high-quality projects for contracting to private sector ESCOs. The agency could also provide intermediary services to promote greater market confidence in energy performance contracting in the private sector.

Fossil fuel subsidy reform and carbon pricing

Viet Nam has taken strong action to reduce fossil fuel subsidies

The Government of Viet Nam has taken strong action to reduce direct subsidies in the energy sector and prioritising market mechanisms for the pricing of energy products. There are currently almost no direct subsidies for energy products apart from small subsidies targeting poverty reduction in certain subsectors, including modest electricity subsidies for impoverished households and smallholder farmers, and diesel subsidies for households involved in artisanal fishing. Decision No. 69/2013/QD-TTg sets the regulatory priority for electricity pricing to follow market mechanisms, while Circular No. 83/2014/NĐ-CP dated on 3 September 2014 sets the priority for oil, gas and petroleum products to follow market mechanisms. The Green Growth Strategy and Climate Change Strategy both set targets of phasing out subsidies by 2020. The subsidisation rate in the electricity sector now sits at 1% down from 4.3% in 2015. This represents only 0.1% of GDP compared to Indonesia at 1.7% and Malaysia at 0.5% (IEA, 2020[2]). Although direct fossil fuel subsidies have been restricted, tariff price controls account for a large source of indirect subsidies and have historically placed pressure on state budgets. Corporate concessions and tax breaks, discounted resources and land, and access to preferential loans from state owned banking institutions have also historically been widely available for SOEs including those operating or developing fossil fuel assets.

Figure 5.1. Fossil fuel subsidies in selected countries 2020

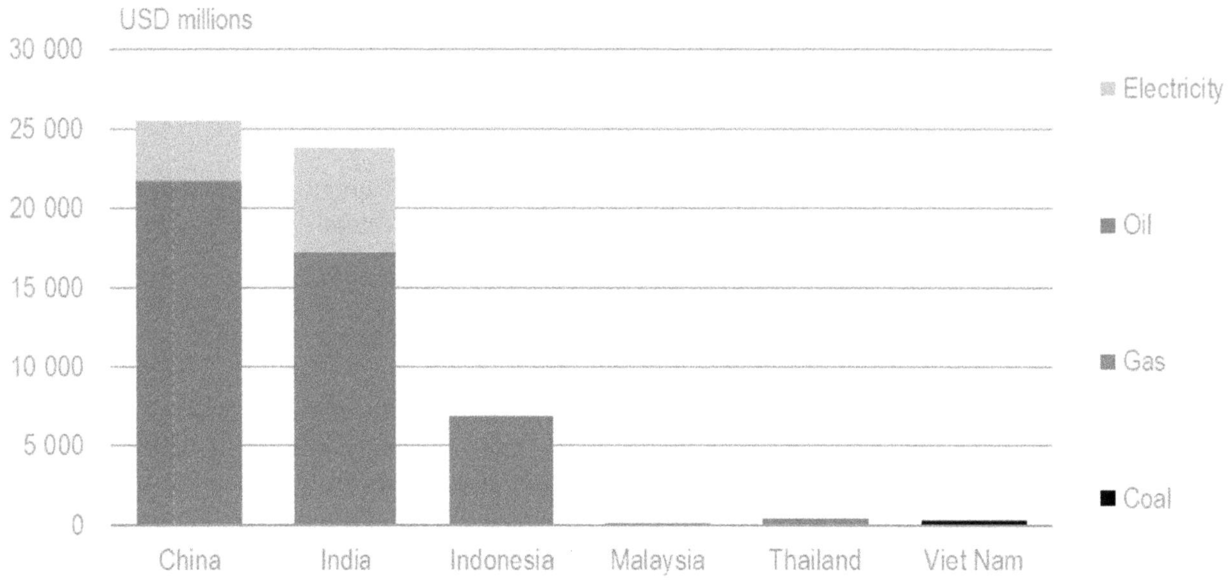

Source: IEA fossil fuel subsidies database 2021

StatLink https://stat.link/dzypv0

The Government of Viet Nam has made modest progress reforming retail electricity tariffs, which have historically been administratively set below cost recovery levels. Tariff subsidies incentivise overconsumption, undermine the investment case for energy efficiency and negatively affect the profitability of utilities. Since the Electricity Law in 2006, the average retail tariff (ART) has been revised upwards 13 times to around USD 8 cents/kWh today. These tariff uplifts have been important but have largely remained in line with inflation rates, as an example, ARTs increased by 53% from January 2010 to January 2015 compared to cumulative inflation for the same period of around 56%. The ART today remains below estimated long-term marginal cost to cover operation, maintenance and debt servicing expenses, while providing a return on capital for future investment (estimated at USD 12-14 cents/kWh) (Lee and Gerner, 2020[3]). Viet Nam Electricity (EVN), the state-owned utility, has the delegated authority under Decision No. 24/2017/QD-TTg to adjust retail tariffs by a maximum of 5% every six months subject to macroeconomic conditions, whereas adjustments between 5-10% fall to the Ministry of Industry and Trade (MOIT), and above 10% requires prime ministerial approval. Decision 24 provides greater transparency and clarity on the process and methodology for tariff uplifts however there is little clarity on timelines and targets. Having a strong position in this regard will help to signal to energy users to adapt their behaviours and plan investments to optimise their energy usage while supporting EVN's profitability.

As single buyer for renewable energy independent power producers, the financial strength and outlook of EVN is of increasingly critical importance for facilitating investment since the availability of sovereign-backed payment guarantees to cover off-taker risk has been restricted due to public debt management laws implemented by Resolution No. 25/2016/QH14. Supported in part by tariff uplifts, EVN has remained a marginally profitable enterprise over recent years with net profit margins increasing from 1.5% in 2015 to 2.5% in 2019 (compared to a global average of 9.5% for the utility sector) (CSI Market, 2020[8]). EVN received its first credit rating in 2018 with an Issuer Default Rating (IDR) of BB with a Stable Outlook in line with Viet Nam's sovereign rating. The capacity to raise tariffs is a critical metric in a rating agency's evaluation of a power company's creditworthiness. Two successive increases of effective tariffs totalling 12.6% in 2018 and 2019 boosted total revenues by VND 59.4 trillion (USD 2.5 billion) (Brown and Vu,

2020[9]). To maintain EVN's financial performance, uplifts of the tariff will likely be required due to emerging risks including increasing hydrology variability that could affect hydro power plant output and increase fuel expenses, exposure to currency risks (dollar denominated debt accounts for 73% of EVN's borrowings), and reduced access to concessional sources of financing (Fitch Ratings, 2020[10]).

Planning for a carbon market is underway to strengthen Viet Nam's climate policy

Viet Nam is one of a few countries in the region that has implemented an environmental protection tax (EPT) to promote green growth. Introduced in 2012 with the Environmental Protection Law it places a levy on the production or importation of products with negative environmental impacts, namely: petroleum, coal, hydro chlorofluorocarbons, plastic bags and chemical pesticides. A proportion of EPT revenues capitalise the Viet Nam Environmental Protection Fund (VEPF) and provides concessional financing for projects with positive environmental benefits. The EPT also offsets a proportion of additional costs incurred due to Viet Nam's FIT policies. Resolution No. 579 in 2018 increased the tax rate on coal by 50% with an ex-ante assessment concluding that this increase would lead to a reduction in coal-related CO2 emissions of 10.25% (Nong, 2018[4]).

In November 2020, Vietnam's National Assembly adopted a revised Law on Environmental Protection that established the mandate for the Ministry of Natural Resources and Environment (MONRE) to design a domestic emissions trading market. MONRE has worked with the World Bank under the Partnership for Market Readiness Programme since 2016 to develop much of the analytical work required to underpin the programme. This includes the development of a monitoring, reporting and verification system, and greenhouse gas registry. A roadmap is also under development to define activities and implementation milestones. It is understood that a voluntary market will be targeted for launch by 2027 and mandatory participation regulated by 2029 (Viet Nam Water Portal, 2020[5]). The introduction of a carbon market in Viet Nam can promote investment decisions that deliver environmental protection at the lowest overall economic cost. However, its effectiveness in the energy sector will depend on the interaction with the underlying power market structure and operation. The plan for a carbon market will therefore need to be designed and integrated into the overall roadmap for power market reform to ensure price signals can be effectively passed through to power market participants and drive investment decision making. Its effectiveness will also be dependent on the management of policy alignment across different policy domains for example in the case of energy efficiency where tariff structures may work against price signals from a carbon market.

Targeted incentives and funds for energy efficiency investment

Improved demand-side incentives can play an important role in market transformation

Viet Nam's investment law defines clean energy as a preferential investment sector and therefore grants eligibility for fiscal incentives. The incentive takes the form of a tax holiday providing complete exemption from corporate income tax (CIT) for two years after the enterprise first makes profits, followed by a further four years in which CIT is charged at 50% of the applicable rate. Such businesses also benefit from a preferential CIT rate of 17% for the first 10 years. Exemption from import taxes for eligible components, and exemption from land lease charges are also applied in certain localities. These incentives are likely to have been a key investment facilitator and supported the development of the clean energy sector; however, their cost-effectiveness and exact contribution to meeting clean energy policy goals, and wider economic benefits are unclear. It is the OECD's understanding that no comprehensive cost-benefit analysis has been undertaken to date (OECD, 2018[11]).

Manufacturing businesses producing energy efficient equipment are eligible for incentives, however, no demand-side incentives are yet available through the tax structure for companies or individuals investing in energy efficiency or green buildings. International experience shows that such incentives play an important part in driving market transformation.

Structuring and implementation of such an incentive scheme is simplified by the established energy labelling regulations and appliance-testing infrastructure. Such incentives can come in the form of tax credits, enhanced capital allowances, or VAT reductions that reduce CIT, personal income tax, or VAT. For example, the Italian government created an incentive programme in 2010 offering a 50% tax deduction for the replacement of household appliances such as refrigerators, washers, dryers, ovens and freezers with more efficient new units. Mexico similarly provided government-funded subsidies to consumers to cover a portion of the purchase of new, energy-efficient refrigerators and air conditioners. Other examples, such as the Carbon Cashbag programme in Korea, which created credits for energy-efficient and low-carbon products that could then be used for things like discounts on public transportation, have been used to incentivise energy efficiency uptake (de la Rue du Can et al., 2014[12]), while more innovative approaches include examples such as the on-wage financing scheme launched by Ghana to improve the accessibility and affordability of energy-efficient appliances in line with the countries new energy efficiency standards and labelling regulations (U4E, 2020[13]).

Viet Nam's incentive framework for clean energy investment provides significant benefit to clean energy investors but the procedures for granting and administrating these benefits are complex. The OECD's Investment Policy Review 2018 notes that there is a lack of clear guidance to investors and that the application of rules can be inconsistent. Drawn out exchanges with tax authorities is often required for the granting of tax incentives and tax procedures are generally time consuming. The World Bank's Doing Business ranking concludes that 384 hours are required on average each year by businesses on tax administration compared to the average for East Asia and Pacific of 178.

Financing conditions for energy efficiency remain challenging

Energy efficiency investment in the industrial sector has increased over the course of Viet Nam Energy Efficiency Programme (VNEEP) I & II with overall investment in key energy intensive industries estimated at about USD 800 million between 2010-2015. Despite this progress the sum falls short of the estimated overall investment needs of about USD 1.7 billion when considering economic potential (UNDP & MPI, 2017[14]). The government must be commended for its achievements in establishing a regulatory framework to promote energy efficiency, including energy audit and energy management obligations, and the introduction of mandatory specific energy consumption targets (chapter 3). To date, the implementation and compliance rate for these regulations are thought to be low but improvements in this area prioritised for the VNEEP III period will do much to promote the mainstreaming of energy efficiency in industry operation and investment planning. Improving access to affordable financing on reasonable terms for industry and energy service companies (ESCOs) will be key to realising the economic benefits of these regulations, an issue highlighted as a significant market barrier.

Banks are the main source of financing in Viet Nam with credit most commonly extended based on a track record of existing corporate relationships with interest rates of 10-12% and collateral requirements covering 80-120% of total credit amount (see chapter 6 for more discussion on the banking sector). Such financing conditions pose a challenge for energy efficiency as they erode project economics (particularly given the low energy tariffs prevalent) and lead businesses to commit their remaining debt capacity to core business investments. It poses particular challenges for the uptake of third party financing and energy performance contracting models offered by ESCOs (a key market facilitator for energy efficiency investment) as they tend to be under-capitalised companies lacking the existing banking relationships and balance sheets to allow them to raise debt. Despite the early actions taken by the government of Viet Nam to minimise the economic impacts of the COVID-19 pandemic, the profitability of many businesses have been impacted. A World Bank business survey found that on average, firm sales are about 36% lower than the same period last year whereas 51% of businesses have seen decreased orders (Tan and Tran, 2020[15]). This will cause additional hurdles to overcome to facilitate energy efficiency investment over the recovery period.

Figure 5.2. Firm experience of reduced demand during COVID-19 period

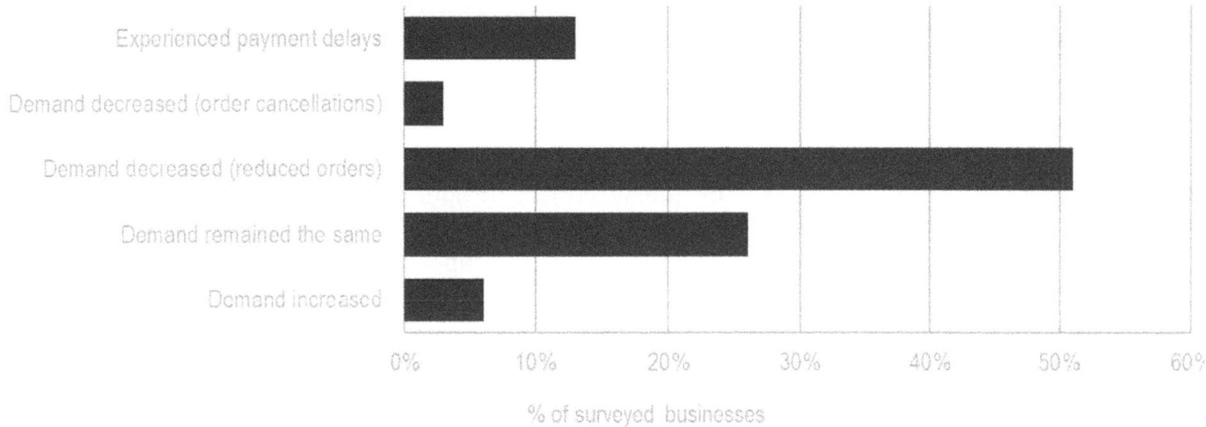

Note: The survey collected responses from 501 firms through a mix of phone and in-person interviews. The firms are located across 15 provinces, representative at three different firm size categories and four broad sectors - agriculture, manufacturing, wholesale and retail, and other services.
Source: (Tan and Tran, 2020[15])

StatLink https://stat.link/iuqb65

Improving access to finance for energy efficiency investment is a multifaceted challenge. On the one side, it requires support to facilitate the development of sizable, high quality and bankable project pipelines. On the other, it requires support for the banking sector to access long-term, dedicated capital (ideally on preferential terms) to build the human resources able to undertake project due diligence and to provide options for credit enhancement to reduce collateral requirements. The World Bank's Vietnam Energy Efficiency for Industrial Enterprises (VEEIE) project which began implementation in 2018 and will run to 2022 has provided a USD 100 million credit line on lent by the Ministry of Finance to participating financial institutions for energy efficiency projects in industry. By May 2020, USD 23.34 million, accounting for 23.34% of the total credit line, had been disbursed across 13 subprojects (compared to the 60 subprojects targeted for 2022) (World Bank, 2020[16]). The World Bank, with co-funding from the Green Climate Fund, is following up with the Scaling Up Energy Efficiency for Industrial Enterprises in Vietnam programme which will set up a risk sharing facility (RSF) to further support access to commercial financing for energy efficiency projects. The RSF will provide partial credit guarantees to participating financial institutions to cover potential defaults on loans to industrial enterprises and energy service companies (ESCOs). The programme is targeting the mobilisation of USD 250 million of commercial financing for energy efficiency projects by 2025.

Investment in public programmes can drive energy efficiency market development

Public energy retrofitting programmes can be an effective driver of energy efficiency market development due to the large quantity of pipeline that can be unlocked if sufficient resources are committed and enabling conditions are in place. Public sector programmes can also promote wider adoption in the commercial and industrial sectors of scalable financing models such as energy performance contracting. ESCO markets in the United States, Canada, and the European Union developed largely as a result of government initiatives to promote public sector programs (World Bank, 2016[7]). There has been limited activity in this area in Viet Nam to date apart from small-scale pilot projects that have not been widely replicated beyond their implementation periods.

Provinces and municipalities rather than central government must play a central role in facilitating public energy efficiency programmes due to the high degree of fiscal decentralisation in Viet Nam. Since the State Budget Law 2002, local governments have borrowing and expenditure authority in their jurisdictions. They also retain all revenues from taxes and fees related to administrative charges while also sharing revenues from value added tax, corporate income tax, personal income tax and excise tax on domestic goods (Morgan and Trinh, 2016[17]). In 2017, provincial expenditure made up 54% of total public expenditure and 60% of total capital investment (Asian Development Bank, 2017[18]).

This decentralised fiscal structure creates challenges for project aggregation across provinces, an important facilitator for energy efficiency investment due to the low capital costs of individual projects. Viet Nam has no agency that can coordinate aggregation and procurement processes at a central level to achieve economies of scale, ensure high quality project design, standardisation, and monitoring and verification. In addition, the decentralised fiscal structure creates challenges for investment planning which is often unaligned with strategic priorities and leads to public capital allocations that are spread too thinly. A Ministry of Planning and Investment (MPI) portfolio review of 2013-15 concluded that public resources could accommodate less than half of total investment needs from both central and local governments for already approved projects and that there were 40 000 public projects ongoing with the majority managed at the local government level (World Bank, 2018[19]).

Local governments have a variety of financing options available to them, including the domestic capital market, commercial loans, and on-lending from the central government of external funds. Borrowing is monitored closely by the Ministry of Finance due to borrowing ceilings imposed under the Law on State Budget Management (chapter 6). Currently the level of commercial bank lending to local governments for public infrastructure is low. Banks are reluctant to extend credit due to past policies of "directed lending" that led to a misallocation of private capital to poorly performing public projects. The assumption of implicit guarantees from central government meant appropriate project due diligence was rarely carried out causing high rates of non-performing public loans (World Bank, 2018[19]). Issuance of subnational bonds is another option but may be limited to the most prosperous provinces due to the lack of credit enhancement and technical competencies. Unlike the corporate bond market where credit enhancement is available through the Credit Guarantee and Investment Facility, no such facility exists for subnational issuers. Two small green bonds have been issued at the subnational level by Ho Chi Minh City and Ba Ria Vung Tau province in 2016 but have not been replicated by other provinces (see chapter 6).

Despite the options available to raise private financing for local sustainable infrastructure the financing experience of most provincial authorities is limited to the management of overseas development aid and concessional loans, which have typically been fully on-granted to them by the central government (World Bank, 2013[20]). Such resources will become increasingly scarce in future and state resources insufficient for the level of investment required. Increasing access to private financing at the provincial level is therefore becoming more critical and the enabling conditions should be strengthened to reflect this. There is a need for a new legal and regulatory framework to govern the full range of rights and obligations of lenders and borrowers in the event of a default. Without the certainty of a clear recourse mechanism enshrined in law, commercial lenders will remain hesitant to extend credit particularly given the difficulties faced with assessing subnational credit risk. A 2018 study found data provided by provincial governments to be out-dated, unreliable and sometimes conflicting, with annual deviations of up to 50% of actual expenditure commonly found (Campanaro and Duc Dang, 2018[21]). Financial management practices including planning, budgeting, accounting, reporting and auditing will need to be improved to overcome these informational barriers to facilitate investment. State resources should also be used more strategically to focus on leveraging commercial co-financing by covering key project risks rather than full investment capital. Institutional structures such as Colombia's FINDETER may provide a good model for Viet Nam in this area.

Box 5.2. Case Study: Colombia's Financiera de Desarrollo Territorial (FINDETER) fund

Following constitutional reforms that introduced fiscal decentralisation in Colombia in the 1980s many municipalities and provincial authorities faced challenges accessing commercial finance for infrastructure projects, having had little or no previous experience borrowing long-term debt on commercial terms. Lenders on the other hand were hesitant to extend credit to local governments as they lacked any precedent to judge credit risk. Financiera de Desarrollo Territorial (FINDETER) was established as a financial intermediary to address these financing constraints. FINDETER functions as a second-tier lender providing discounted loans to commercial banks that finance local infrastructure projects. FINDETER was initially set up with equity provided by the Government of Colombia and loans from the World Bank and the Inter-American Development Bank. Thanks to its good credit rating, it borrows at better rates than commercial banks and provides long-term capital for on-lending, while commercial banks retain 100% of the credit risk of local government borrowers (World Bank, 2016[22]).

Figure 5.3. FINDETER Financing structure

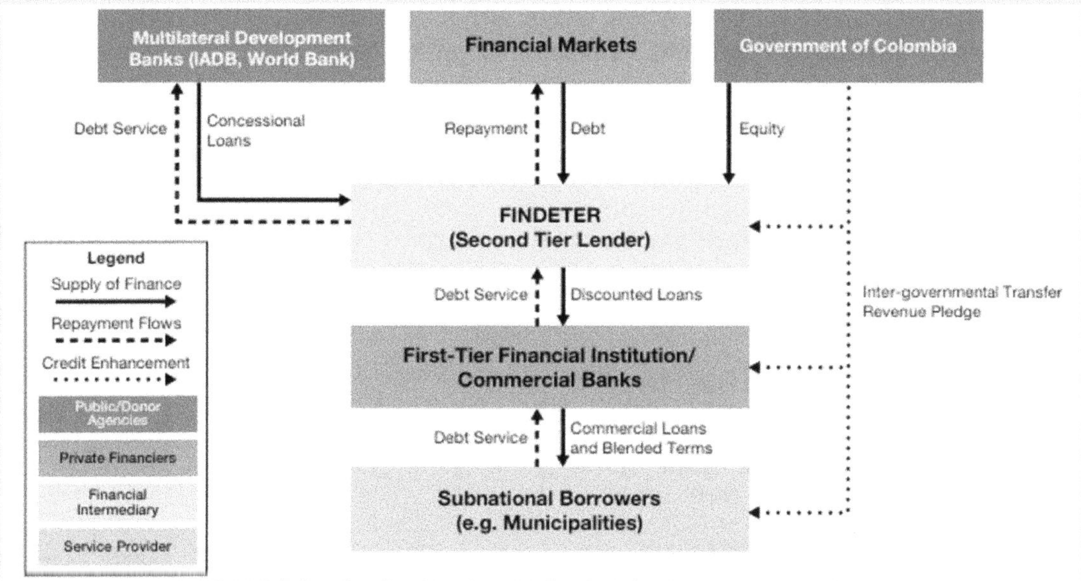

Source: (World Bank, 2016[22])

A crucial component of the financial structure is an intercept provision, which allows second tier lenders to intercept revenues from a special account if loan payments are not made, and in turn, to repay these to FINDETER. This structure also allows FINDETER to collect payments directly from the bank's local borrowers if a bank becomes insolvent. The intercept provision has maintained a low percentage of non-performing loans and reinforced FINDETER's credit rating. FINDETER offers maturities of up to 15 years, which is notable, as loans to local governments without the involvement of FINDETER would normally not exceed five years (World Bank, 2016[22]).

With a similar decentralised fiscal structure and challenges faced by some provincial governments to access long-term capital for energy efficient technical infrastructure and retrofitting programmes, the government of Viet Nam could consider such a funding structure to overcome financing constraints and leverage private sources of capital.

Targeted incentives and funds for renewable electricity

Feed-in tariffs have facilitated a rush of renewable investment but with mixed results across technologies

Targeted tariff incentives for renewable energy procurement have been in place since 2008 when Decree No. 18/2008/QD-TTg introduced an avoided cost tariff for small generators below 30 MW along with a dedicated procurement framework for renewable IPPs (see chapter 3 for discussion on the standardised power purchase agreements). The tariff is benchmarked to the marginal cost of the most costly generator on the system and updated yearly by the Electricity Regulatory Authority of Viet Nam (ERAV). This avoided cost tariff was initially technology neutral but later revised in 2014 to apply to only those technologies without targeted feed-in tariffs (FITs) following the introduction of the first dedicated wind FIT in 2011. The avoided cost tariff scheme was the precursor for the country's FIT incentives that were introduced in a series of decisions and implementing circulars from 2011 onwards (Table 5.1). The FIT rates are provided to eligible generators at a fixed rate for a period of 20 years from commercial operation date. The FITs are paid in Vietnamese dong (VND) but the tariff is indexed yearly to the VND/USD exchange rate set by the State Bank of Viet Nam. This provision is designed to reduce currency exchange risk for international investors financing a greater proportion of investment capital with hard currency but with revenues in local currency. In practice, this has benefited domestic investors to a greater degree due to the appreciation of the dollar against the dong providing increasing returns for sponsors with local currency financing costs. The FITs for solar and wind have a time-based expiry and capacity limits are controlled through the planning process rather than through a capacity quota or degression mechanism in the FIT design (see chapter 2).

Table 5.1. Details of renewable energy tariff support mechanisms

<table>
<tr><th>Technology Class</th><th>Tariff</th><th>Tariff period</th><th>Tariff Indexing</th><th>Time limits / capacity quota</th></tr>
<tr><td>Small Hydropower</td><td>Avoided cost tariff benchmarked yearly to the highest marginal cost generator on the system</td><td rowspan="9">20 years</td><td rowspan="2">none</td><td rowspan="4">none</td></tr>
<tr><td>Municipal solid waste & landfill gas</td><td>Waste – 2 114 VND/kWh (USD 9.1 cents)
Landfill gas – 1 532 VND/kWh (USD 6.6 cents)</td></tr>
<tr><td>Biomass Power Plants</td><td>Avoided cost tariff benchmarked yearly to the marginal cost of coal generation using imported fuel later scrapped in 2020 for a simple FIT set at 1 968 VND/kWh (USD 8.5 cents)</td><td rowspan="7">Paid in VND but indexed to USD/VND exchange rate
No indexing for inflation</td></tr>
<tr><td>Biomass Combined Heat & Power</td><td>1 220 VND/kWh (USD 5.2 cents) later increased to VND 1 634 (USD 7 cents) in 2020</td></tr>
<tr><td rowspan="3">Solar PV</td><td>Ground mounted – 2 086 VND/kWh (USD 9.1 cents) reduced to 1 644 VND in 2020 (USD 7.1 cents)</td><td rowspan="3">COD of 30 June 2019 extended to 31 Dec 2020 with no further extension for grid-scale projects. Rooftop FIT will be redesigned and extended pending official approval</td></tr>
<tr><td>Rooftop – 2 086 VND/kWh (USD 9.1 cents) reduced to 1 943 VND in 2020 (USD 8.4 cents)</td></tr>
<tr><td>Floating – introduced in 2020 at 1 783 VND/kWh (USD 7.7 cents)</td></tr>
<tr><td rowspan="2">Wind</td><td>Onshore – 1 614 VND/kWh (USD 7 cents) increased to 1 928 VND in 2018 (USD 8.4 cents)</td><td rowspan="2">COD of 1 Nov 2021 with no extension planned after this date</td></tr>
<tr><td>Offshore (inter-tidal) – 2 223 VND/kWh (USD 9.6 USD) (introduced in 2018)</td></tr>
</table>

Note: COD = Commercial operation date. USD rates calculated based on VND/USD rate of 0,000043
Source: Ministry of Industry and Trade

Viet Nam's FITs have seen mixed results in terms of facilitating investment across the different technologies covered. The most eye-catching achievements were witnessed in the solar sector where the FIT drove rapid, large-scale investments due in part to the higher tariff (USD 9.1 cents for ground-mounted installation compared to the 2011 wind FIT of USD 7.1 cents). From 2017 when the solar FIT was introduced to the end of 2020, 5.7 GW of ground mounted solar was connected to the grid which catapulted Viet Nam's solar market to become the largest in the ASEAN region. A similar investment boom was witnessed in the distributed solar market where, by the end of 2020, rooftop solar installations grew from a few hundred MWs to 9.7 GW spread across 102 000 individual systems (EVN, 2020[23]). More distributed solar capacity came online in a single year in Viet Nam than the total capacity installed in India at the time (3 GW by August 2020) (IEA, 2020[24]). Such rapid development of variable renewable generation has led to challenges with grid integration and management of reverse flows in the distribution network. Some projects have experienced power curtailment particularly in provinces with high levels of solar deployment such as Ninh Thuan province where 10 out of 25 solar project owners reported having to operate at 30-40% capacity resulting in losses of USD 21.7 million (ASEAN ACE, 2020[25]) (see chapter 3 for discussion on actions being taken to increase system flexibility).

Facilitating the rapid build out of solar capacity with an attractive FIT was in part driven by necessity due to delays experienced in the construction of large thermal power plant projects procured under the Public Private Partnership (PPP) laws. During the 2016-2020 period, only 58% of planned coal-fired capacity was actually realised, compared to 118% in hydropower and 205% in non-hydro renewables (IEEFA, 2020[26]). These delays led to a tightening supply margin prior to the COVID-19 period and forecasted power shortages of 400 million kWh in 2021, peaking at 13.3 billion kWh in 2023[1]. EVN has done admirably well to manage connections and adapt system operation in the face of such a fundamental shift in system architecture over such a short period. To avoid barriers to facilitating investment in line with increased PDP VIII targets, it will be important to continue to take actions to mitigate the risk of curtailment for both greenfield and operating assets. Widespread curtailment without protections in the power purchase agreement (PPA) can erode investor and lender confidence leading to higher financing costs and restricted foreign direct investment (FDI).

Large investments in grid infrastructure will be required over the PDP VIII period at levels beyond the financing capacity of EVN. To overcome this investment gap MOIT are increasingly prioritising the facilitation of private participation in the transmission sector. The country's first privately invested 500/220kV substation and transmission line was constructed in 2020 under a stand-alone pilot agreement. To replicate this model will require the development of a revised legal framework including the amendment of the Investment Law and Electricity Law that were designed to protect EVN's monopoly in the transmission sector. It will also require the implementation of a bankable concession model that can ensure the required investment protection and returns for investors while ensuring appropriate regulations and operational guidelines are in place to ensure coordination with EVN (See chapter 4 for a discussion on this topic).

FITs have been less successful at facilitating investment flows for non-solar renewable technologies. This is evident in the wind sector where a fraction of the capacity has been deployed despite high resource quality. By the end of 2020, 472 MW of wind capacity was in operation, falling short of the 800 MW targeted in the revised PDP VII. In part this is due to the legacy issue of the first wind FIT introduced in 2011 which was set too low to provide sufficient risk-adjusted returns on investment. MOIT revised the FIT upwards in late 2018 (and introduced an offshore inter-tidal specific FIT) with an eligibility deadline of November 2021, setting challenging development timelines for projects to reach commercial operation before the expiry. The disruption caused by the COVID-19 pandemic caused development delays and it is thought that up to 1.3 GW of the 2.9 GW of wind projects with signed PPAs are now at risk of missing the November 2021 FIT expiry (GWEC, 2020[27]).

In June 2020, the Prime Minister issued Document No. 693/TTg-CN calling for MOIT to streamline the approval of additional wind projects and to consider facilitating this with an extension of the FIT to run until

December 2023. A total of 11.6 GW of wind capacity was included in the Power Development Plan by December 2020, in which 8.7 GW were described by MOIT as being very unlikely to reach commercial operation date before the FIT cut off[2]. In October 2020, MOIT issued official Letter No. 8159/BCT-DL which contained a proposal for a wind FIT extension until 2023 but with step-down reductions to the tariff. It is understood that this proposal is no longer being considered and that wind capacity procurement will be managed through an auction system without a transitional FIT period. It is unclear how projects currently in the pipeline with approved PPAs but missing the FIT expiry will be supported.

An avoided cost tariff for biomass power plants and a FIT for biomass combined heat and power (CHP) was introduced in 2014 with Decision No. 24/QD-TTg. For biomass plants, this set the tariff for eligible generators at the average marginal price of a coal power plant utilising imported fuel. Decision No. 942/QD-BCT in 2017 later introduced a regional uplift to the avoided cost calculation methodology. Since its introduction, no investments in biomass power plants have been realised. Biomass CHPs received a 20 year fixed FIT at 1 220 VND/kWh (USD 5.2 cents) this was less than half the tariff offered to similar technologies in Thailand (USD 13 cents) and the Philippines (USD 12.4 cents) (GGGI, 2018[28]). There are currently 38 sugar mills in Viet Nam that have invested in biomass CHP with a total capacity of around 352 MW but with only eight plants exporting to the grid. Analysis undertaken by Global Green Growth Institute concluded that up to 737 MW of total biomass CHP capacity could be developed in the sugar industry alone given improved investment incentives. In recognition of the slow development of the biomass market the government approved Decision No. 8/QD-TTg in 2020 which saw the scrapping of the avoided cost tariff for biomass power plants in favour of a fixed FIT set at 1 968 VND/kWh (USD 8.5 cents) and an uplifted biomass CHP FIT of 1 634 VND/kWh (USD 7 cents).

The support mechanism for offshore wind procurement is still uncertain

With a stated target of 2-3 GW offshore wind in 2030 going up to 11 GW in 2035 in the high scenario, the draft PDP VIII sets a relatively cautious phase-in of offshore wind in the energy generation mix. Even with these more modest volumes, a number of important policy choices need to be made in the near term to create a stable framework for the development of (non-nearshore) offshore wind industry and cost-effective realisation of projects. International experience indicates that economy of scale for offshore wind projects is quickly approaching 1 GW and larger projects are more conducive to deliver lowest possible levelised cost of energy (LCOE).

The challenges regarding long-term visibility regarding the regulatory framework of RE technologies is especially critical for (non-nearshore) offshore wind industry, characterised by long lead times for complex supply chain development. Lack of clarity regarding the key regulatory and support scheme prospects can cause significant delays and cost increases due to higher risk perception. At the point of developing this report, an analysis with the aim of establishing clear definitions, evaluating and selecting a support scheme and its critical parameters is still under way. A clear roadmap for the envisioned framework development of the offshore wind would greatly contribute to creating more certainty for the investors and enable realisation of the planned offshore wind capacity on time and in the most cost-effective way. An approach that has yielded positive results e.g. in Denmark has been consulting with developers and the supply chain in a proactive way[3] to establish a common understanding of the key opportunities and challenges in e.g. the specifics of a particular regulation or the development of offshore wind more generally.

Whilst many critical elements pertaining to the offshore wind regulatory framework are still in development (including the Marine Spatial Plan, offshore vs nearshore wind site definition, support scheme design etc.), international examples of best practice could be considered to ensure timely and cost-effective capacity build-out, for example, ensuring sufficient area reservations in the form of unallocated capacity for offshore wind sites are available to be included in later auctions, incorporating qualification / eligibility criteria to prospective developers as well as progress criteria and timeline to be met in the project development phase. Similarly, the trade-offs between opting for the FIT support scheme to kick-start and mature the market, before transitioning to an auction scheme should be considered. The majority of mature offshore wind markets, as well as regional emerging offshore markets, have resorted to the more stable and less risk-bearing FIT scheme in the initial phases of industry development.

Infrastructure development should be co-ordinated with the planning for offshore wind capacity build-out. A plan for construction and upgrade of seaports to timely serve the needs of forthcoming offshore wind projects should be included in PDP VIII and integrated with seaport planning in the National Energy Master Plan. Due to unparalleled size and weight of offshore wind equipment, existing seaports in Vietnam with suitable locations should be upgraded to meet requirements for transportation, installation, operation and maintenance. The progress of seaport upgrading should be in line with the development timeline of the offshore wind projects to provide adequate infrastructure and ensure financial feasibility.

Finally, a streamlined and transparent permitting process for offshore wind would be greatly advantageous. The one-stop shop model introduced in Denmark, with the Danish Energy Agency assuming the single focal point for all offshore wind development-related interfaces, has contributed to cost-effective and successful development of offshore wind industry in Denmark.

Feed-in tariff support for distributed solar is set to continue

Viet Nam's support mechanism for distributed solar expired at the end of 2020. This marked the end of the solar FIT established by Decision No. 13/2020/QD-TTg which extended the first solar FIT (Decision No. 11/2017/QD-TTg) originally set for expiry on June 30 2019. Decision 13 also marked the first time a non-EVN offtaker was permitted under the law. This was an important development as it opened the market to third-party ownership business models for on-site solar installations under 1 MW. Whereas solar asset owners were previously only permitted to self-consume or sell power to EVN, Decision 18 allowed a third party to invest, own and operate generation assets and sell power to a corporate customer for on-site consumption with the flexibility to negotiate the commercial terms and tariff directly. This provision also paves the way for corporate PPAs whereby offsite generation projects can enter into supply contracts with corporate customers and pay to deliver power through EVN's grid.

The additional regulatory developments required to realise this model is being piloted in 2021 (discussed further below). The Government of Viet Nam is set to continue support for the distributed solar market with an updated FIT mechanism expected to be developed in the coming year. Early indications suggest that MOIT favours a tiered tariff structure dependent on system capacity with larger installations receiving a lower tariff. Another important design element being considered is the requirement for larger installations to install control systems that enable improved monitoring and system control by the National Load Dispatch Centre (NLDC). Given the high levels of variable renewable energy already integrated to the grid this would be an important development that would enable NLDC to better utilise distributed energy resources for system balancing. MOIT is also considering building in greater flexibility to enable quicker tariff adjustments to control deployment rates.

Pilot corporate power purchase agreements will provide new routes to market

The Government of Viet Nam with support from the United States Agency for International Development (USAID) is currently designing a pilot direct PPA programme which is set to launch in 2021 pending the Prime Minister's approval of proposal No. 544/TTr-BCT. The contract will likely take the form of a "synthetic PPA" which will enable qualifying generators to develop offsite renewable installations while signing PPAs with a corporate "synthetic-offtaker". The generator will export power to the national grid at wholesale spot prices while also signing a contract for difference with an agreed strike price with the corporate off-taker. Under these terms, if the wholesale price is lower than the strike price the corporate off-taker will make payments to the generator for the difference and vice versa if the wholesale price is higher than the strike price. Renewable generation certificates will also be exchanged from the generator to the off-taker

(Figure 5.4) The pilot will target up to 1 GW of renewable capacity with eligibility limited to wind or solar power projects above 30 MW that have already been approved for inclusion in the Power Development Plan. The inclusion of direct PPAs in Vietnam's regulatory framework will be an important step to continue to facilitate increasing foreign direct investment into the country's manufacturing sector (see chapter 4). Direct PPAs also provide an opportunity for developers to diversify offtaker risks with an alternative to EVN as a sole contract counterparty.

Figure 5.4. Synthetic direct power purchase agreement structure

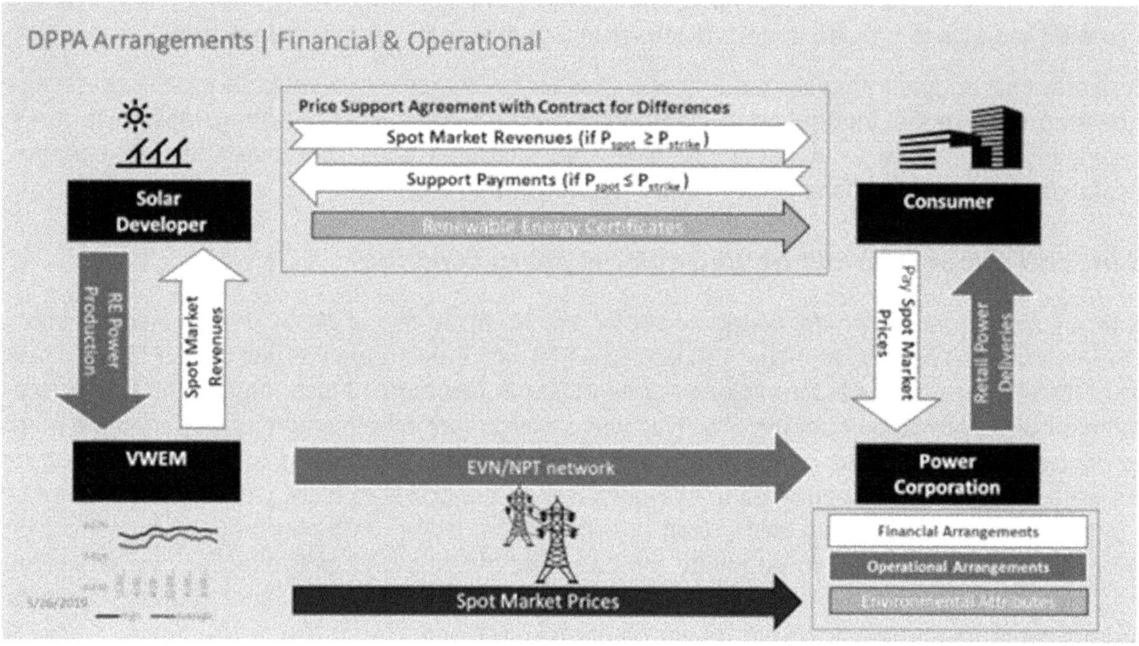

Source: USAID Viet Nam Low Emissions Energy Programme

References

ASEAN ACE (2020), "Vietnam: Six Ways to Keep Up the Renewable Energy Investment Success", *Policy Brief*, No. 13, http://dx.doi.org/10.13140/RG.2.2.11479.50081. [25]

Asian Development Bank (2017), *Managing Fiscal Risks of Subnational Borrowing in Viet Nam: Improving Public Expenditure Quality Program*, http://dx.doi.org/10.22617/BRF179112-2. [18]

Baker Mckenzie (2021), *Vietnam: New draft decision on the future Solar Auction Program.* [35]

Bank, W. (2018), *Public Investment in Viet Nam: Assessment and Reform Priorities for Overcoming the Bottlenecks.* [30]

Brown, M. and T. Vu (2020), "Vietnam's EVN Faces the Future: Time To Get Renewables Right", Institute for Energy Economics and Financial Analysis. [9]

BVG Associates (2015), *Approaches to cost-reduction in offshore wind A report for the Committee on Climate Change*, https://bvgassociates.com/cases/approaches-cost-reduction-offshore-wind/ (accessed on 16 February 2021). [33]

Campanaro, A. and C. Duc Dang (2018), *Mobilizing Finance for Local Infrastructure Development in Vietnam: A City Infrastructure Financing Facility*, http://dx.doi.org/10.1596/978-1-4648-1287-3. [21]

CSI Market (2020), *Utilities Sector Profitability*, https://csimarket.com/Industry/industry_Profitability_Ratios.php?s=1200 (accessed on 25 May 2021). [8]

de la Rue du Can, S. et al. (2014), "Design of incentive programs for accelerating penetration of energy-efficient appliances", *Energy Policy*, Vol. 72, http://dx.doi.org/10.1016/j.enpol.2014.04.035. [12]

Egli, F., B. Steffen and T. Schmidt (2018), "A dynamic analysis of financing conditions for renewable energy technologies", *Nature Energy*, Vol. 3/12, pp. 1084-1092, http://dx.doi.org/10.1038/s41560-018-0277-y. [29]

EVN (2020), *Press release on rooftop solar PV development after 31 December 2020.* [23]

Fitch Ratings (2020), *Fitch Affirms Vietnam Electricity at 'BB'; Outlook Stable*, https://www.fitchratings.com/research/corporate-finance/fitch-affirms-vietnam-electricity-at-bb-outlook-stable-15-09-2020 (accessed on 25 May 2021). [10]

GGGI (2018), *Sweetening the Deal for Biomass Energy in Viet Nam's Sugar Industry.* [28]

GWEC (2020), *Proposed Feed-in-Tariff reduction could "seriously damage" growth of wind power in Vietnam*, https://gwec.net/gwec-proposed-feed-in-tariff-reduction-could-seriously-damage-growth-of-wind-power-in-vietnam/ (accessed on 15 February 2021). [27]

IEA (2020), *IEA Energy Subsidies Database.* [2]

IEA (2020), *Unlocking the economic potential of rooftop solar in India*, https://www.iea.org/events/unlocking-the-economic-potential-of-rooftop-solar-in-india (accessed on 16 February 2021). [24]

IEEFA (2020), *New Regulations Threaten Vietnam's Remaining Coal Pipeline*, https://ieefa.org/wp-content/uploads/2020/10/New-Regulations-Threaten-Vietnams-Remaining-Coal-Pipeline_November-2020.pdf (accessed on 21 February 2021). [26]

Lee, A. and F. Gerner (2020), "Learning from Power Sector Reform Experiences The Case of Vietnam", No. 9169, World Bank Group. [3]

MOIT/GIZ (2016), *Wind Power Investment Guidelines Volume 1: Project Development*. [6]

Morgan, P. and L. Trinh (2016), "Fiscal Decentralisation and Local Budget Deficits in Viet Nam: An Empirical Analysis", No. 613, Asian Development Bank Institute, https://www.adb.org/publications/fiscal-decentralization-local-budget-. [17]

Nong, D. (2018), "General equilibrium economy-wide impacts of the increased energy taxes in Vietnam", *Energy Policy*, Vol. 123, http://dx.doi.org/10.1016/j.enpol.2018.09.023. [4]

OECD (2018), *OECD Investment Policy Reviews: Viet Nam 2018*. [11]

Ondraczek, J., N. Komendantova and A. Patt (2015), "WACC the dog: The effect of financing costs on the levelized cost of solar PV power", *Renewable Energy*, Vol. 75, pp. 888-898, http://dx.doi.org/10.1016/j.renene.2014.10.053. [34]

Tan, S. and T. Tran (2020), *Impacts of COVID-19 on Firms in Viet Nam, Results from the Business Pulse Survey*, World Bank Group, https://openknowledge.worldbank.org/bitstream/handle/10986/34902/Impacts-of-COVID-19-on-Firms-in-Vietnam-Results-from-the-Second-Round-of-COVID-19-Business-Pulse-Survey.pdf?sequence=1&isAllowed=y (accessed on 19 May 2021). [15]

THANH, S. and N. CANH (2020), "FISCAL DECENTRALIZATION AND ECONOMIC GROWTH OF VIETNAMESE PROVINCES: THE ROLE OF LOCAL PUBLIC GOVERNANCE", *Annals of Public and Cooperative Economics*, Vol. 91/1, http://dx.doi.org/10.1111/apce.12255. [31]

U4E (2020), *ECOFRIDGES GREEN ON-WAGE FINANCIAL MECHANISM LAUNCHED IN GHANA BY THE ENERGY COMMISSION, UNEP AND BASE TO MAKE ENVIRONMENTALLY FRIENDLY COOLING PRODUCTS MORE AFFORDABLE*, https://united4efficiency.org/ecofridges-green-on-wage-financial-mechanism-launched-in-ghana-by-the-energy-commission-unep-and-base-to-make-environmentally-friendly-cooling-products-more-affordable/ (accessed on 25 May 2021). [13]

UNDP & MPI (2017), *Private Climate Expenditure and Investment Review Viet Nam*, https://ledsgp.org/wp-content/uploads/2017/10/Vietnam_private-climate-expenditure_FINAL.pdf (accessed on 15 February 2021). [14]

UNESCAP (2017), *Infrastructure Financing Strategies for Sustainable Development in Viet Nam*, https://www.unescap.org/sites/default/files/20170915%20National%20Study%20-%20Infrastructure%20Financing%20-%20Viet%20%20Nam.pdf (accessed on 11 February 2021). [32]

Viet Nam Water Portal (2020), *Vietnam on road to development of carbon market*, https://www.vietnamwaterportal.com/news/vietnam-on-road-to-development-of-carbon-market.html (accessed on 25 May 2021). [5]

World Bank (2021), *World Bank Doing Business*. [1]

World Bank (2020), *Vietnam Energy Efficiency for Industrial Enterprises: Implementation Status and Results*. [16]

World Bank (2018), *PUBLIC INVESTMENT MANAGEMENT IN VIETNAM Assessment and Reform Priorities for Overcoming the Bottlenecks*, https://openknowledge.worldbank.org/bitstream/handle/10986/31762/Public-Investment-Management-in-Vietnam-Assessment-and-Reform-Priorities-for-Overcoming-the-Bottlenecks.pdf?sequence=1&isAllowed=y (accessed on 11 February 2021). [19]

World Bank (2016), *Fostering the Development of ESCO Markets for Energy Efficiency*, https://openknowledge.worldbank.org/bitstream/handle/10986/23949/Fostering0the00or0energy0efficiency.pdf?sequence=5&amp%3BisAllowed=y (accessed on 12 February 2021). [7]

World Bank (2016), *Institutional Blending via Second-Tier Lender FINDETER in Colombia*, https://documents1.worldbank.org/curated/en/546961472031531475/pdf/107973-Colombia.pdf (accessed on 1 June 2021). [22]

World Bank (2013), *Assessment of the financing framework for municipal infrastructure in Vietnam*, http://www.copyright.com/. [20]

Notes

[1] Official Dispatch No. 7200/BCT-DL dated September 25, 2020 on Opinions regarding the Prime Minister's Decision on the pilot program for determination of solar power purchase prices.

[2] Figures set out in MOIT Official Letter No.8159/BCT-DL.

[3] https://ens.dk/en/press/material-market-dialogue-conditions-call-tender-thor-offshore-wind-farm.

6 Financial market policy

This chapter examines the current status and future requirements of clean energy finance in Viet Nam. It reviews the current state of financial markets and highlights the need to deepen capital market development. It highlights financial market regulation, including the role of sustainable finance policies and targeted green finance instruments in mobilising finance for clean energy projects. The chapter also examines the role of development finance in mobilising private capital and opportunities for institutional innovation to catalyse private sector finance and investment.

A major scale up in financing will be needed to meet Viet Nam's clean energy transition goals that will require both domestic and international public and private sources of finance. Creating a clean energy finance ecosystem that has reach across governments, financial markets, industry and development co-operation can support this goal. The green banking policies led by the State Bank of Viet Nam (SBV) are commendable and have played an important role in facilitating domestic finance for clean energy projects. This chapter looks at the current status and future requirement of clean energy finance in Viet Nam; green banking regulation and opportunities to develop capital markets and targeted green finance instruments; and the role of development finance and opportunities for institutional innovation to catalyse private sector finance and investment.

Assessment and recommendations

Rapid solar expansion financed mainly through domestic and regional banks

The impressive solar expansion in Viet Nam that has seen installed capacity reach 8.85 GW of utility scale solar and 9.7 GW of rooftop solar at the end of 2020, was financed to a large degree through domestic banks and added mainly in the last two years (OECD, 2020[1]). Regional developers and financial institutions have also contributed significantly to renewables development in Viet Nam. This signals positive momentum among domestic and regional financial institutions on the attractiveness of renewable energy projects and a recognition of the need to integrate environmental considerations into the finance sector. A growing number of financial institutions around the world have adopted policies to stop financing coal fired power plants making it increasingly difficult to raise capital for coal and helping to accelerate its eventual phase out. Growing difficulty in financing coal both domestically and internationally combined with a strong outlook for electricity demand has helped to increase the attractiveness of financing renewables in Viet Nam.

Regulation has guided the development of green finance frameworks that facilitated domestic lending

The State Bank of Viet Nam should be commended for strong policy direction that has helped to guide the greening of the finance sector by requiring banks to integrate environmental and social (E&S) risk management into their lending practices. Two key policy interventions released in 2015 include the Financial Sector Green Growth Action Plan to 2020 and Directive No. 03 / CT-NHNN on promoting green credit and managing environmental and social risks in credit activities. The 2018 Directive No. 1604/QD-NHNN approves the Green Banking Development Scheme in Viet Nam that encourages banks to increase the weighting of lending portfolios to priority sectors listed on SBV's green projects portfolio. This directive also requires that all banks integrate internal procedures for E&S risk and credit risk evaluation by 2025[1]. While some domestic banks have been active in financing clean energy projects, others still lack sufficient technical capacity to undertake project due diligence and additional support is required to further develop domestic capacity and reduce perceived risks among local financial institutions.

Refinancing of operational projects could create opportunities for new investors

Mechanisms will be needed to recycle capital from operational projects to support those that are at the development or construction phase. This can allow new financial institutions to gain valuable experience and exposure to clean energy projects and drive more private capital (both domestic and international) into the sector.

Lack of access to long term debt capital remains a major barrier to future developments

While there is good appetite to finance clean energy projects, a lack of access to long term debt capital has meant that typical debt tenors of 5 to 7 years are well below that of OECD and some major emerging economies where tenors are often above 15 to 20 years or more. The absence of non-recourse project finance in Viet Nam, which is the norm for renewable energy projects in OECD and other major economies, restricts the funding capacity of individual developers with limited equity capital and prevents efficient risk allocation and market development. High collateral requirements also pose a particular challenge for smaller developers, including energy service companies that are implementing energy efficiency projects as their limited capital is often used up after just one or two projects.

Viet Nam will need to access international capital to meet future financing needs

Development finance institutions have played a key role in financing hydropower, transmission and distribution network expansion and industrial energy efficiency in Viet Nam, but have only played a limited role in financing solar and wind projects as the domestic finance sector has so far had sufficient financing capacity. Liquidity issues may become a constraint as Viet Nam looks to develop its offshore wind resources which require funding above USD 2-3 billion in a single project. This is beyond the capacity of the domestic market and will require an international consortium of development and private finance institutions to address the unique risk characteristics of such large projects. International lenders have also maintained that the current power purchase agreement (PPA) conditions are not bankable due to high perceived risks related to arbitration and risks of curtailment. PPA contracts in Viet Nam are also not as comprehensive as those in Europe or other OECD countries, leaving uncertainty which is difficult for financial institutions to manage.

Box 6.1. Main policy recommendations on financial market policy:

- Implement regulation that includes a clearly defined green bond framework including definitions for eligibility, reporting and verification protocols. Support the development of green bond issuances for sovereign, sub-sovereign and corporate issuers. Such a framework should be consistent with the ASEAN green bond standard and aligned with other green bond standards to allow for a broad investor base. Green bonds offer an attractive opportunity to refinance existing projects and provide a source of much needed long-term capital.
- Develop solutions that can facilitate on-lending schemes or other financing mechanisms that can facilitate access to long-term capital by domestic finance institutions and take advantage of low cost capital from multilateral and bilateral development banks. Such schemes could be designed to target energy efficiency and smaller renewable energy projects where project developers struggle to access financing due to limited equity capital. This could require a re-evaluation of development finance mandates to shift from sovereign lending to be able to facilitate more direct lending to financial institutions without a sovereign mandate.
- Consider the creation of a clean energy fund that can support the use of blended finance structures to mobilise financing from the private sector for renewable energy and energy efficiency projects. This includes the use of de-risking instruments such as guarantees and insurance products as well as support for project preparation and financial structuring. Such mechanisms could be used to attract financing from both domestic and international investors.
- Develop a sustainable finance roadmap that outlines key requirements for financial institutions to develop action plans and regular reporting on alignment of portfolios to sustainable development criteria and exposure to climate change impacts. This should be accompanied by capacity building and information campaigns to build expertise among financial market actors to support sustainable infrastructure finance and in particular the clean energy transition. A further step would include the development of green finance definitions or a sustainable finance taxonomy to support the development of green finance products and overcome concerns of green washing.
- Improve the availability of clean energy finance and investment data through the development of monitoring and evaluation tools. The creation of a clean energy finance and investment database can help to identify funding gaps and help to track climate finance flows. It can also support the development of targeted policy interventions and the design of financing mechanisms to help mobilise private capital for clean energy projects. Increasing the availability of project level data would also help to build investor confidence and reduce perceived risks that could potentially lower the cost of finance, as financial institutions are better able to evaluate various risk return profiles.

Strengthening and deepening local financial markets

Banking sector dominates the financial markets

Viet Nam's financial sector is dominated by banks that account for about 70% of the capital provided in the market (World Bank, 2019[2]). The country's economic growth has been fuelled by high lending rates with one of the highest credit to GDP shares in the region at levels similar to some OECD countries (Figure 6.1). Over the last 25 years, banking credit rose rapidly from just 17% of GDP to over 130% in 2018 (World

Bank, 2019[2]). Much of this credit growth has been directed towards lending to state-owned enterprises and more recently towards real estate and housing with small and medium enterprises struggling to access credit (World Bank, 2019[2]). About 80% of the banks' capital is held in short-term accounts limiting the availability of long-term credit that is needed to finance infrastructure projects (World Bank, 2019[2]).

Figure 6.1. Viet Nam's economic growth has been accompanied by rising debt levels

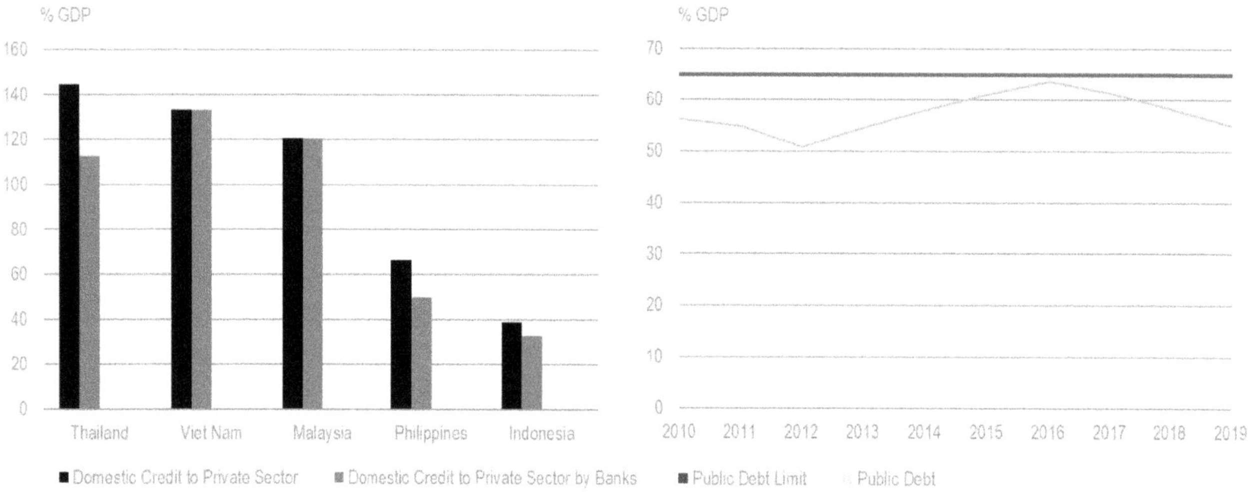

Source: World Bank 2020, Development Indicators

StatLink https://stat.link/nsqfwx

Public sector debt levels have risen significantly, as the government invested in critical infrastructure to support the growing economy and attract foreign direct investment. Overall public debt is constrained by a legal lending limit of 65% of GDP. After reaching nearly this limit in 2016, public debt has fallen, as a result of government efforts to tighten fiscal policy. The government is increasingly relying on the private sector to fund infrastructure development to maintain public debt well below the legal limit.

The rapid growth of the credit market in Viet Nam has raised some concerns around its sustainability particularly given the slower than anticipated implementation of Basel II capital adequacy requirements. The State Bank of Viet Nam (SBV) had initially set a deadline of 1 January 2020 for the country's 17 leading banks to comply with Basel II requirements. Despite some progress with 10 of the 17 banks fulfilling the capital requirements by December 2019, SBV decided to extend the deadline to 2023 to allow the remaining banks more time to meet the requirement as many struggled to raise sufficient additional capital. The current restriction on foreign ownership of 30% and nonperforming loans left from the 2012 banking crisis have led to slow progress among smaller banks (Denimal, 2020[3]).

According to the Global Infrastructure Outlook, Viet Nam will need to invest a total of USD 605 billion from 2016 – 2040 to meet the country's infrastructure needs (GIH, 2021[4]). These investments are required in the energy, telecommunications, transport and water sectors with energy accounting for the largest share at 42% of total investment needs in infrastructure. Based on current investment trends, the country is on its way to reaching infrastructure investments of about USD 503 billion with an investment gap of about USD 102 billion. Filling this gap will require an improvement in the overall investment environment for infrastructure to attract foreign investors and expand private participation in infrastructure development.

Development of capital markets could unlock additional financing for clean energy

Meeting the investment needs of the infrastructure sector will require an increase in the availability of long-term capital and further development of Viet Nam's capital markets. The country's stock and bond markets are both significantly less developed than some of its regional peers (Figure 6.2) and represents an opportunity to shift savings from short-term deposits towards longer-term investments in bonds and equity. With significant investment needs in infrastructure development, a deepening of the capital markets is needed to attract long-term capital to finance these long-lived assets. Diversification of the bond market to stimulate more corporate bond issuances could help to widen the bond market that is currently made up almost exclusively of government bonds, with corporate bonds representing just 8% of the market. In 2018, the government issued Decree 163, which is the first corporate bond framework to support corporate bond issuances. Regional neighbours such as Malaysia, Thailand and to a lesser degree the Philippines have issued corporate bonds to support financing needs of the private sector.

Figure 6.2. Further expansion of capital markets needed to increase access to long term capital

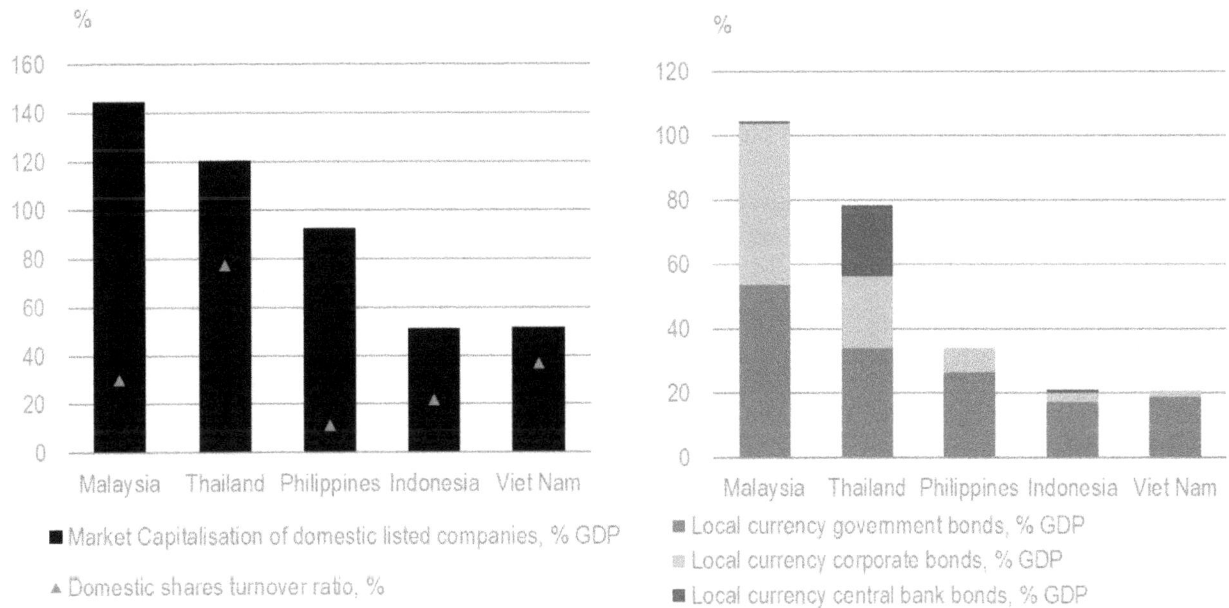

Source: World Bank (2020), development Indicators

StatLink https://stat.link/ozbp2v

Regulatory barriers have created obstacles to the creation of a liquid corporate bond market as issuances via private placement are much easier and less costly, making the public bond market less attractive. Private placements require less disclosure to investors and are quicker than those of a public offering and hence corporates have tended to issue corporate bonds via private placements. Decree 163 also prohibits the resale of corporate bonds issued via private placements for one year. With limited disclosure requirements for private placements, concerns have risen that these bonds could come to the market without sufficient information that would provide for retail and public investor protection.

Equity markets in Viet Nam have performed well with the Ho Chi Minh Stock Index rising 240% since 2015 compared to the FTSE ASEAN All-Share Index falling 7% over the same period. Viet Nam's stock market as a share of GDP reached over 50% in 2019, similar to Indonesia, but well below other regional peers such as Malaysia, Thailand and the Philippines where the stock market capitalisation is near or well above 100% of GDP (Figure 6.2). Although total capitalisation is comparatively low, the secondary market is relatively active and behind just Thailand in terms of domestic share turnover.

Growth of Viet Nam's capital markets and banking sector will need to be accompanied by improvements in reporting and disclosure that are in line with international standards. While most major markets have adopted International Financial Reporting Standards, Viet Nam has yet to adopt such requirements. Lack of transparency and comparability in reporting practices poses additional risks to investors and will limit the potential growth of the market and can lead to higher financing costs.

Access and status of finance for clean energy

Unprecedented growth in rooftop solar in 2020 makes Viet Nam the 3rd largest solar market and 8th largest renewable market

Whereas other countries have struggled to meet roof top solar targets, Viet Nam in 2020 added an astounding 9.3 GW of rooftop solar capacity which boosted total investments in renewable electricity capacity to USD 7.4 billion, just ahead of France, making it the 8th largest renewable market last year (Bloomberg, 2021[5]). Two-thirds of this capacity (6 GW) was added in December, as developers rushed to complete projects to meet the deadline for the solar rooftop feed-in-tariff that expired at the end of 2020. The vast majority of financing for these projects have come from domestic banks (both state-owned and private commercial banks) with limited concessional investment made available from public sources (although some funds have been channelled into the sector through the Viet Nam Environmental Protection Fund and the Viet Nam Development Bank).

Table 6.2 Top renewable energy markets by capacity investments in 2020

Country	2020 Renewable energy capacity investment (USD billions)	Change from 2019
China	83.6	-12%
United States	49.3	-20%
Japan	19.3	10%
United Kingdom	16.2	177%
Netherlands	14.3	221%
Spain	10.0	16%
Brazil	8.7	23%
Viet Nam	7.4	89%
France	7.3	38%
Germany	7.1	14%
India	6.2	-36%
Total	303.5	2%

Source: BNEF (2021)

Viet Nam's rise to one of the largest renewable energy markets in just a short time frame demonstrates the role that incentives and in particular, feed-in tariffs (FITs) can play in establishing renewable energy markets but requires good planning to facilitate licensing and to ensure adequate grid development. The time bound nature of the ground mounted and solar roof top FITs created strong incentives for developers to accelerate project development to benefit from the attractive FITs and sent a strong signal to the market on the key role solar and renewables will play in the Vietnamese power sector. This however has created a solar boom that if not carefully managed could lead to a repeat of the boom and bust cycles seen in

Europe as a result of changes to FITs. Viet Nam's plans to shift to competitive auctions will need to be carefully designed and the country could learn from experiences in other countries (see chapter 5).

Many of the leading Vietnamese conglomerates such as BIM Group, Trung Nam Group and Xuan Cau Group as well as major ASEAN developers such as AC Energy (from the Philippines), Super Energy and B Grimm (from Thailand) have been among the leading developers of the solar market in Viet Nam. Financing of these projects has benefitted from strong balance sheets of project developers and existing relationships with local and regional commercial banks. Viet Nam's top down central planning has also facilitated co-ordination between its economic development strategy and that of its financial market strategy, with the benefit of preparing financial institutions on the need to integrate climate risks and support for environmental solutions including clean energy as part of lending practices. Further details on the greening of the banking sector and integration of sustainable finance regulations are outlined in the following section.

Attracting private sector investment and finance key to meeting future electricity needs

According to the draft power development plan (PDP) VIII released for consultation in early 2021, the Ministry of Industry and Trade (MOIT) estimates that cumulative investments in the power sector between 2021 and 2030 will need to reach an estimated USD 128 billon, of which USD 95 billion will be required for new generation capacity and USD 33 billion for grid expansion (Baker McKenzie, 2021[6]). Investment needs in the power sector over the 2031 to 2045 period rise to an estimated USD 192 billion (USD 140 billion for generation capacity and USD 52 billion grid development). These estimates do not include investments that will also be required in energy efficiency to help control overall electricity demand growth and thereby future power sector investment needs.

Under the draft PDP VIII, MOIT estimates that annual investment needs in electricity infrastructure for the next decade will reach an average of USD 12.8 billion per year, rising to USD 19.2 billion after 2030. In comparison, a World Bank study estimates that the government of Viet Nam has the capacity to finance about USD 15 to 18 billion in annual infrastructure spending out of a total demand for infrastructure investment of USD 25 to 30 billion (World Bank, 2020[7]). The government's capacity to finance infrastructure is limited due to the legal public debt ceiling of 65% of GDP. Viet Nam was close to reaching this limit in 2016 but a tightening of fiscal management in recent years has effectively brought this down to 55% in 2019 (Figure 6.1).

This highlights the need to attract more finance from the private sector to meet Viet Nam's growing demand for infrastructure and in particularly electricity infrastructure that will account for roughly half of total infrastructure spending. Private sources of finance have a bigger role to play in the financing of electricity generation and in particular renewable generation projects in Viet Nam (IEA, 2019[8]). The government is also exploring options to attract private investments in transmission given high capital expansion needs over the next decades. Despite the critical role for private capital in the electricity sector the government must also carefully consider the continued role of public finance, particularly for early phase technology deployment, with offshore wind a case in point, and for critical enabling infrastructure such as storage assets and network strengthening. Transmission network expansion and strengthening, as an example, has benefited greatly from the availability of overseas development assistance, particularly from Japan. This financing is contingent on government guarantees which are now rarely provided.

Viet Nam Electricity (EVN), the state-owned utility, has struggled to keep up with investments in grid expansion under the recent solar boom that has left a surplus of power in the central and southern region and insufficient network capacity to transmit power to the northern region where there is a shortage of power supply. In 2018, EVN received a standalone credit profile rating of BB by Fitch, equivalent to Viet Nam's sovereign rating. The rating helps to facilitate future fund raising needs via the domestic and international capital markets to help ease public sector borrowing (including reducing the need for government guarantees). The outlook for EVN's rating was recently upgraded from stable to positive, in line with the revision in Viet Nam's sovereign outlook.

Domestic and regional banks have been the main source of financing for the rapid solar expansion in Viet Nam. International banks together with international developers, have played a relatively limited role, given international bankability concerns related to the power purchase agreements (PPAs) that domestic (and some regional) banks are more willing to accept. Consultations with financial institutions confirmed the willingness of domestic banks to increase lending to solar and onshore wind projects and interest in building capacity to evaluate offshore wind and energy storage projects with a view to potential financing of these projects in the future. De-risking mechanisms will be needed to support the first offshore wind and energy storage projects to help banks build experience and technical capacity. The scale and high capital costs of offshore wind projects will require a consortium approach to financing, with both domestic and international finance institutions from the public and private sector working together to address different risks in order to finance these projects.

Developing project finance structures could help to lower financing costs and increase capital availability

While liquidity in the financial market for solar and onshore wind is reasonably good, the cost of financing that is often above 10% is very high compared to OECD and other major economies where interest rates for renewable projects are closer to 5-6% (Coleman, n.d.[9]) (Steffen, 2020[10]). Projects have almost been exclusively financed through corporate finance with significant collateral requirements. This limits the capacity of project developer's to raise adequate finance as firms are limited by equity availability. In more mature financial markets, non-recourse project finance with long tenures (15-20 years) is considered the norm and these attractive financing conditions have dramatically lowered renewable energy costs in these markets.

Project finance structures allow for a larger share of debt financing for projects that can lower the overall financing costs for projects. However, strong cash flow certainty is necessary and some risks can be difficult to mitigate unless covered by power purchase agreements that can address risks such as curtailment through take or pay structures or other guarantee mechanisms. Large project finance transactions in the energy sector have happened for the large build-operate-transfer (BOT) thermal power plants but these have been led by syndications with large international bank involvement. This has been made possible due to flexibility in negotiating PPA terms under the PPP laws and availability of government guarantee undertakings.

Vietnamese banks lack experience in structuring non-recourse project finance and underwriting based on renewable project fundamentals rather than on balance sheets. Regulation (Circular 22) also sets limits on long-term lending using short-term deposits, highlighting the need to improve access to long-term sources of capital. In addition, the high credit risk rating (SBV Circular 41) applied to project finance loans of 160% regardless of the underlying structure of projects creates a major barrier for non or limited recourse project financing. Standard Basel II guidelines applied in other countries provides for a project by project evaluation that allows for a lower risk weighting for projects demonstrating high certainty on project cash flows that are often provided through long term PPAs.

Energy efficiency projects developed by energy service companies (ESCOs) tend to be developed by relatively small firms with limited balance sheets and experience in financial structuring of projects. With little or no credit history, ESCOs often face additional challenges accessing finance including high collateral requirements from commercial banks that can exceed the value of the project and are often beyond the firms' means. Support is needed through guarantee schemes aimed at de-risking projects or via dedicated energy efficiency funds. These funds should target projects with good replicability structures that address risks which the market currently is not able to adequately evaluate so that in the future, as these projects demonstrate their financial viability, the market can take over without the need for de-risking.

Improving data availability on energy efficiency loan performance and support to build technical capacity for energy efficiency project due diligence is also needed to better evaluate underlying project cash flows and savings. The development of standardised energy performance contracts can also facilitate project replication and aggregation as well as leasing business models that can help to improve project scale to levels that can increase the attractiveness of such projects for financial institutions.

Sustainable finance regulation, green banking and green bonds

Viet Nam's sustainable finance policies are rooted in the National Action Plan for Green Growth (2014-2020)[2] and the National Strategy for Green Growth (2011-2020) that calls for the mainstreaming of green growth objectives within the financial sector and the development of green financial products. This strategy outlines the need to formulate mechanisms and policies to stimulate green practices among financial institutions and corporations. It identifies the need to use financial, credit and market-based instruments to encourage the development of a green economy and also signals the development of a greenhouses gas (GHG) emissions trading system as well as a carbon tax. The strategy also highlights the use of green credit, overseas development assistance and technical assistance to support the implementation of the country's green growth strategy. The various regulations governing Viet Nam's green banking policies are summarised in the timeline below (Figure 6.3).

Figure 6.3. Summary of Viet Nam's Green Banking regulation

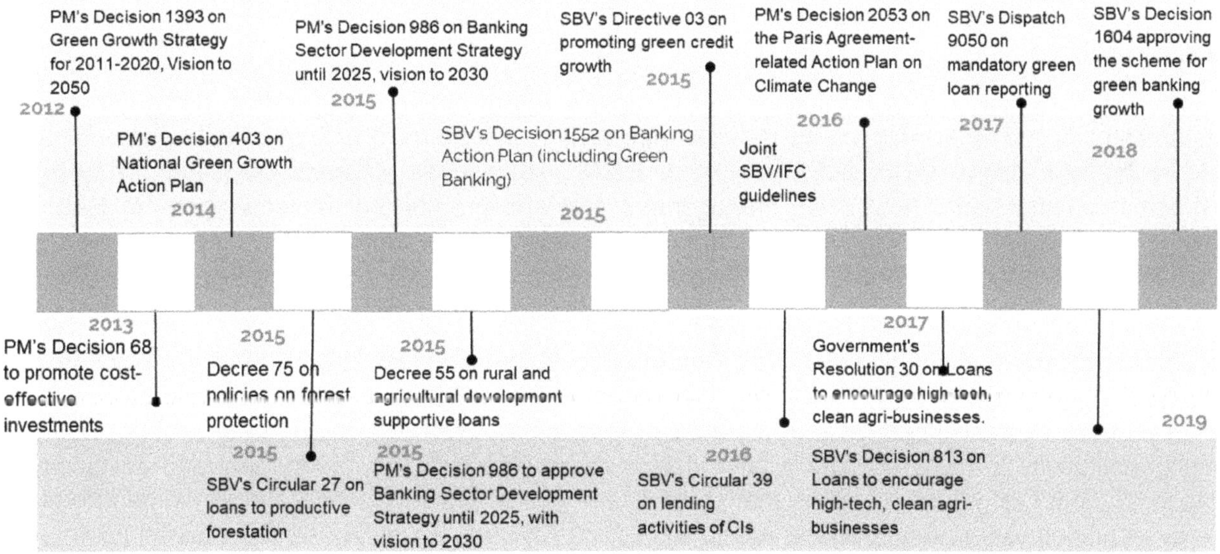

Source: ADB 2021

The State Bank of Vietnam (SBV) has issued a number of sustainable finance regulations and policies to promote the availability of green credit and integrate environmental and social risks within lending activities of finance institutions. These include Directive No. 3 from 2015 that encourages the banking sector to consider a number of sustainable development issues within its lending practices such as environmental protection, energy efficiency, human health and improving environmental quality. The directive calls for an increase in lending towards activities that contribute to green growth and sustainable development objectives, including designing green lending policies for sectors such as energy efficiency and renewable energy.

Viet Nam's green banking action plan

Decision No. 1552 from 2015 sets out an action plan for the banking sector to implement Viet Nam's green growth strategy and has helped to raise awareness and build capacity among domestic financial institutions on green credit development and banking products. SBV Decision No.1604 GD-NHNN introduced in August 2018 approved a scheme for green bank development in Viet Nam. This scheme aimed to accelerate awareness and corporate responsibility within the banking sector to increase the credit available for environmentally sustainable projects including energy efficiency and renewable energy and aims to ensure that all banks will have developed internal procedures that support green banking. This includes building a strategic framework for green banking; establishing a comprehensive ESG risk management strategy; and developing an action plan to expand green banking activities.

Directive No 3. issued by SBV requires credit institutions to provide quarterly reports on green credit issuances and undertake environmental and social risk assessments and Circular No. 9050/NHNN-TD provides further implementation guidelines. The reporting framework covers 12 including clean energy and renewable energy. However, data is reported for the sector as a whole without details at the technology or sub-sector level. The State Bank of Viet Nam should consider further developing the reporting frameworks to include this level of detail and working with banks to improve green tagging. This is particularly critical for credit extended for energy efficiency which is commonly not distinguished from general corporate loans. Additional clarity is needed on definitions for green projects that align with international and ASEAN standards and hence a revision of the current green credit reporting format should be considered. The Ministry of Natural Resources and Environment (MONRE) has also been tasked with helping to lead the development of a green finance taxonomy to provide clearer definitions on qualifying green projects and close co-ordination with SBV and MOIT will be needed to ensure alignment with sectoral plans and policies.

Reports submitted by finance institutions to SBV, show a total of VND 46.6 trillion (USD 2 billion) in outstanding credit to renewable energy projects representing a mere 0.5% of loan portfolios among banks which submitted reports (ADB, 2021[11]). The directive also requires all credit institutions to formalise environmental and social (E&S) risk management and encourages the implementation of E&S risk management systems for lending activities that also includes regular monitoring of borrowers' own E&S risk management processes and quarterly disclosures.

To improve confidence and help facilitate project due diligence for clean energy projects among financial institutions, additional monitoring and evaluation tools could be developed to facilitate the development of a comprehensive clean energy finance and investment database. Such a database would help to lower perceived risks by providing details on project performance that can reduce financing costs by allowing finance institutions to more accurately price risk. It would also help the government and development partners to better target interventions that could help mobilise private finance and investment to clean energy technologies that might require additional support. To start, the database could collect information on financing volumes, cost of capital and participants to help improve market transparency.

Viet Nam is committed to supporting the development of sustainable finance practices in the country and has implemented a comprehensive set of regulations targeted at ESG risk management practices. As a member of the Sustainable Banking Network, Viet Nam is engaging with financial regulators and banking associations in other countries to improve ESG risk evaluation practices and share international good practices on sustainable finance development.

Status of Green Banking in Viet Nam

Viet Nam has made impressive progress in establishing the country's green banking framework and this has helped to increase domestic lending for clean energy projects by improving awareness among the banking sector and encouraged the development of targeted green lending products that has helped to facilitate access to domestic funding for clean energy projects. At the end of 2020, 36 domestic credit institutions held VND 333 trillion (USD 14.5 billion) in outstanding debt for green projects, mainly in agriculture and renewable energy projects (SBV, 2021[12]).

Data from the end of June 2019 shows that clean energy projects accounted for approximately 15% of the green lending portfolio in Viet Nam, the second largest after green agriculture which accounts for nearly half of all outstanding green credit (Figure 6.4). While lending to green projects has more than quadrupled between 2015 and June 2019, green credit still represents a very small share of total credit availability in Viet Nam reaching just over 4% in June 2019.

Figure 6 4. Green lending development in Viet Nam and breakdown by sector

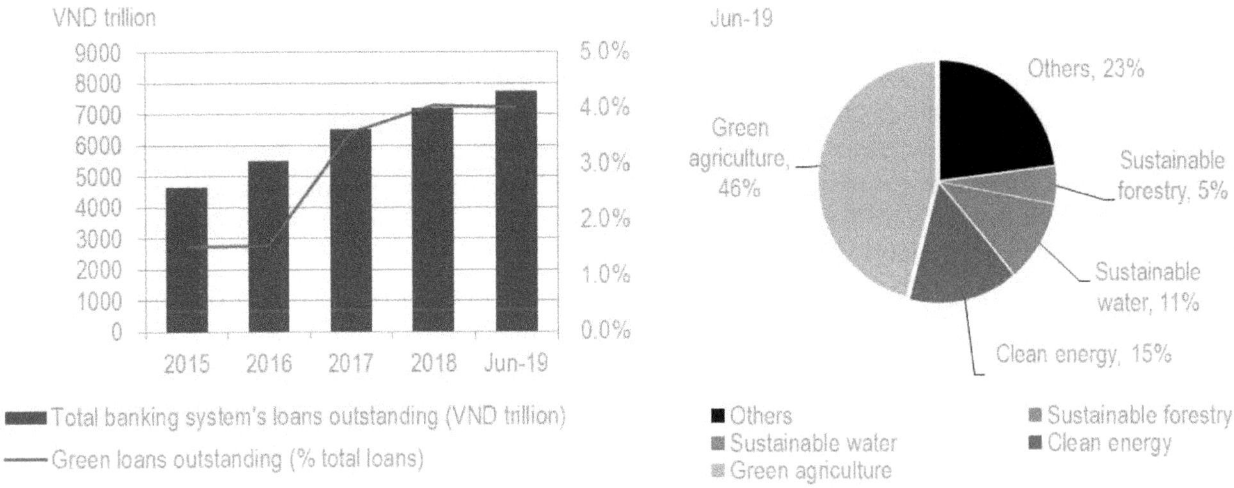

Source: SBV

StatLink https://stat.link/q9lpkm

Early success of SBV's efforts to green the banking sector are demonstrated in the country's impressive solar market development that was led by domestic developers and financed locally with regional developers and financing institutions also playing an important role. Ensuring sustained momentum for renewable energy investments and accelerating energy efficiency deployment will require continued efforts to promote green banking in the finance sector and awareness to overcome potential barriers created by efforts to improve and implement prudential regulation.

The roadmap outlined in SBV Circular 22 to delay the implementation of a lower maximum short-term to medium to long-term loans has been delayed by one year, as a result of the need to ease lending capacity to improve credit availability for firms to manage COVID-19 related business challenges. The gradual reduction from 40% to 30% by October 2023 outlined in the circular will effectively reduce the capacity of banks to provide medium and long-term credit and reduce credit liquidity in the domestic market. These prudential regulations are a necessary step to ensure financial sustainability of the banking system, but create additional challenges for financing clean energy projects and put pressure on banks to raise additional sources of capital to be able to increase financing.

The development of capital market vehicles, such as green bonds, and facilitating securitisation to refinance operational projects is one option to addressing liquidity issues. Financial market regulation will need to be developed to provide for a comprehensive green bond framework (green bond development is discussed below) and to also permit securitisation of existing loans. To date, refinancing remains limited and has mainly occurred through development banks such as the 2021 refinancing of the 240 MW Dau Tieng 2 solar power project [3]and via state owned banks such as Vietcombank, BIDV and Agribank that have refinanced participating banks at lower interest rates.

Green bonds offer an attractive opportunity to raise long term capital at scale

Viet Nam's green bond market remains relatively untapped with just two small municipal green bonds issued in 2016 by Ho Chi Minh City and Vung Tau. Listed on the Ha Noi Stock Exchange, these two pilot issuances raised USD 25 million and USD 4 million, respectively, to finance water infrastructure. Since then no other green bonds have been issued. A survey of commercial banks in Viet Nam undertaken by the Global Green Growth Institute (GGGI) in 2020, highlights the absence of a green bond framework as the main challenge in accelerating the green bond market in Viet Nam (GGGI, 2020[13]). This survey also highlighted the lack of internal procedures for green bond investments as well as insufficient project pipelines (green bond issuers) as other major obstacles.

Decree 163 released by the government in 2018 is the first legal framework for corporate bond issuances and supports Viet Nam's 2017-2020 roadmap for the development of the bond market. While it encourages the use of corporate bonds for green projects, the decree lacks sufficient clarity on standardised definitions for green projects. Development of a comprehensive green bond framework will be a priority to establish the green bond market in Viet Nam and in addition to standardised definitions, should also include guidelines for issuances, a reporting framework and standards for disclosure.

The ASEAN Capital Markets Forum, has released Green, Social and Sustainability Bond Standards based on the ICMA's Green, Social and Sustainability Bond Principles. As a member of this forum, Viet Nam should align any future green bond policies and definitions with this international standard. Many ASEAN member economies including Indonesia, Malaysia, Thailand and the Philippines have already raised billions in international financing via green bonds and Viet Nam should evaluate the potential of meeting the country's long-term capital requirements via green bonds.

Green bond and loan issuances globally reached USD 258 billion in 2019, up over 50% compared to 2018. In ASEAN, 2019 also saw a big increase in green bond and loan issuances reaching USD 8.1 billion, a near doubling of 2018 levels (Climate Bonds Initiative, 2020[14]). Between 2016 and 2019, the region completed a total of 39 green bond/loan/sukuk issuances with a total cumulative value of USD 13.4 billion (Figure 6.5). The buildings and energy sectors accounted for two-thirds of all funds raised in ASEAN from green bonds and loans. In 2019, financial corporate issuances accounted for the largest share of funds raised at more than 29%, followed by non-financial corporates representing 27% and sovereign issuances at 15% of funds raised.

Figure 6.5. Corporates lead green bond and loan issuances in ASEAN

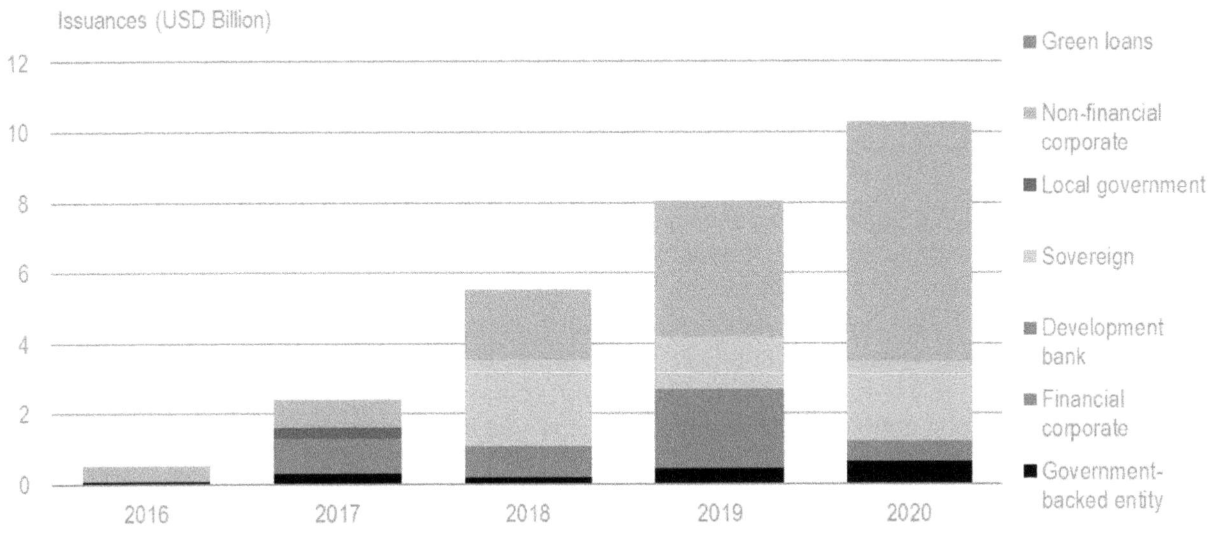

Source: Climate Bond Initiative 2021

StatLink https://stat.link/zy9x3d

The development finance community could play an important role in helping Viet Nam to access long term capital via the international green bond market. This could be achieved through the provision of technical assistance for establishing a suitable green bond framework, preparation of issuances, capacity building for potential issuers, de-risking instruments (guarantees or debt subordination) to increase the attractiveness of issuances for international investors and through directly investing in the green bonds (OECD, 2021[15]). A number of development partners and multilateral development banks such as Asian Development Bank (ADB), World Bank (WB), GGGI in Germany and the UK are currently providing technical assistance to Viet Nam to support the development of the green bond market. ADB's technical assistance is targeted at supporting Viet Nam in the development of its domestic green bond market which shows significant potential for growth and a good source of local currency finance.

In other markets, development finance institutions have played a key role in kick-starting the green bond market. Private investors new to a market are attracted by co-investing with DFIs as they often have strong political influence in the issuing country that can lower perceived risks. To attract the trillions held by international institutional investors will require significant scale (typically issuances of USD 500 million and above) and bonds denominated in hard currency. While Viet Nam's clean energy sector represents a very attractive market for international investors looking for green investment opportunities, liquidity and hard currency requirements are challenging for most corporates and sub-sovereign issuers in the Vietnamese clean energy sector and may require involvement from the central government.

Indonesia's green bond market has been driven by large sovereign issuances which have supported investments in clean energy projects among other green projects. To date the country has raised a total of USD 3.2 billion of green sukuk issuances, comprised of USD 2.75 billion from the three global issuances and USD 490 million (IDR 6.88 trillion) from the two domestic issuances. In addition to the above mentioned sovereign issuances, three financial institutions have also issued corporate green bonds. In November 2019, the government of Indonesia also issued the world's first retail sovereign green sukuk raising IDR 1.46 trillion (USD 150 million) in the local market from retail investors. This success was followed by the second retail green sukuk issuance in December 2020, raising IDR 5.4 trillion (USD 557 million) that achieved the highest purchase volume and attracted the largest number of investors in the history of Savings Sukuk issuance. Millennials also accounted for more than half (56.7%) of the new investors attracted from this issuance. Indonesia's experience developing its green bond market could provide useful lessons for Viet Nam as it considers developing this market (Box 6.2).

Box 6.2. Lessons from developing Indonesia's green bond market

To support the implementation of Indonesia's sustainable finance regulation and facilitate a shift towards sustainable finance products, Indonesia's financial services authority (OJK) issued Regulation No. 60/2017 that outlines the conditions for green bond issuances in the domestic market. The regulation defines 11 eligible sectors (including renewable energy and energy efficiency) that qualify as a green project and is in line with both the Green Bond Principles and the ASEAN Green Bond Standards issued by the International Capital Market Association. Issuers are also required to report on the use of proceeds and environmental benefits from the projects must be reported and verified by an independent third party.

Indonesia was the first country to issue a sovereign green sukuk in 2018 raising USD 1.25 billion in the foreign bond market. While a green bond needs to meet certain environmental thresholds, a green sukuk must also comply with Sharia investment principles that go beyond environmental considerations to include other sustainability and well-being considerations as well as precluding certain investments that are not permitted under Sharia law. This first issuance was followed by subsequent issuances in 2019 and 2020 that raised a further USD 1.5 billion to fund green projects including energy efficiency and renewable energy projects. The 2020 Green Sukuk Issuance in the global market has made notable achievements including obtaining the lowest coupon rate for a 5 year tenor, oversubscription by 7.4 times and attracting a greater share of Green Investors (34% vs. 29% compared to the two previous issuances).

Indonesia has so far raised a total of USD 3.2 billion of green sukuk issuances, comprises USD 2.75 billion from the three global issuances and USD 490 million (IDR 6.88 trillion) from the two domestic issuances. In addition to the above mentioned sovereign issuances, a number of financial institutions have also issued corporate green bonds. In November 2019, the government of Indonesia also issued the world's first retail sovereign green sukuk raising IDR 1.46 trillion (USD 150 million) in the local market from retail investors. This success is followed by the second retail green sukuk issuance in December 2020, raising IDR 5.4 trillion – which achieved the highest purchase volume and attracted the largest number of investors in the history of savings sukuk issuance.

Millennials also accounted for more than half (56.7%) of the new investors attracted from this issuance. While the amount was relatively small and the tenor short at just 2 years, it represents a number of important milestones in the transition towards more sustainable finance. First, it demonstrated that there is appetite for green bonds among retail investors and allows for a diversification of the investor base, particularly millennial investors who were the primary audience for this issuance; secondly, the issuance was completely done online using a platform developed in-house by the Ministry of Finance which paves the way for further issuances at relatively low costs demonstrating the capacity fintech can play in helping to reduce financings costs as well as to increase financial inclusion; and thirdly, it helped to raise awareness of the importance of investing in solutions to address climate change and the role individuals can plan in being part of the solution as minimum subscriptions to the bond were fixed at just IDR 1 million (USD 70) making the bond widely accessible to a significant portion of the population.

Role of development finance

Development finance institutions have been active in supporting Viet Nam in the development of its clean energy sector both in terms of providing technical assistance and financing energy efficiency and renewable energy projects. Multilateral development banks such as the World Bank and the ADB have been working closely with the government to provide technical assistance to policy makers, project developers and the financial sector to help strengthen the country's clean energy ecosystem. A number of bilateral development banks including KfW (Kreditanstalt für Wiederaufbau), AFD (Agence Française de Dévelopement) and JBIC (Japan Bank for International Co-operation) among many others are also financing clean energy projects and an overview of some of the major development finance programmes are highlighted in Table 6.3 below.

In 2017 the government of Viet Nam and international development partners created the Viet Nam Energy Partnership Group (VEPG) to strengthen co-operation and exchange of expertise and knowledge on the energy sector. The objective of the VEPG is to facilitate more effective international support to help Viet Nam achieve its sustainable energy objectives. This is achieved by providing a platform for high level policy dialogues, a platform to align ODA with Viet Nam's energy and climate objectives, a platform to coordinate technical assistance and through information sharing with partners. VEPG activities are undertaken through 5 thematic technical working groups covering renewable energy, energy efficiency, energy sector reform, energy access and energy data and statistics. Each group is headed up by two co-chairs representing MOIT and one of the development partners, which allows for more effective coordination and support among various partners to help meet clean energy priorities through targeted technical and financial assistance.

Table 6.3. Selected clean energy programmes with DFI support

	Selected programmes
ADB	USD 100 million loan to finance municipal waste to energy project USD 37 million loan to finance 47.5 MW Da Mi floating solar project USD 116 million loan (of a total USD 173 million syndication) to finance 144MW of onshore wind Viet Nam's first certified green loan of USD 27.9 million (of a total USD 186 million syndication) to finance 257MW solar project USD 24.5 million loan (of a total USD 160.5 million syndication) for refinancing 240MW Dau Tieng 2 Tay Ninh solar power project
AFD	€ 24 million loan to EVN to finance the Se San 4 solar pant and other planned loans to EVN for expansion of Laly hydro plant and grid strengthening
IFC	USD 57 million loan for onshore wind projects Phu Lac 2 and Loi Hai 2
JBIC	USD 200 million credit line to Vietcombank for on lending to renewable energy projects
EU	€ 100 m grant for energy sector policy support and financing for energy access, renewables, energy efficiency and energy data
EU	Sustainable Energy Transitions programme - €142 m grant to support improved energy efficiency, increase the renewable energy mix and improve the energy information system
KfW	€14.5 million grant to provide a top up for solar and wind IPPs
WB	A number of grants covering renewable energy mapping, roof top solar PV development, solar auction design and implementation, and a USD 411 million mix grant/loan to support the Trung Son Hydropower project. the WB will also support the development of a commercial financing market for industrial energy efficiency investments with a USD 11.3 million grant in coordination with a USD 75 Million Green climate Fund guarantee to establish a risk sharing facility to scale-up commercial energy efficiency loans.

Source: VEPG 2020 Project partner survey[4] and (World Bank, 2021[16]).

Between 2001 and 2017, development finance institutions supported nearly USD 2 billion in renewable energy projects with hydropower accounting for the largest share of funding over this period (Figure 6.5). As the bulk of the hydro potential in the country has now been developed, financing has shifted more recently to other renewable technologies such as solar and biomass. Solar in particular stands out in 2016 as receiving the bulk of DFI funding for renewable electricity generation. These early investments have helped to demonstrate solar power projects and increase confidence among domestic banks to lend to solar projects. In addition to the values shown below, DFIs have been a major source of financing for the expansion of the country's transmission and distribution infrastructure.

Figure.6 6. Renewable energy financing by development finance institutions

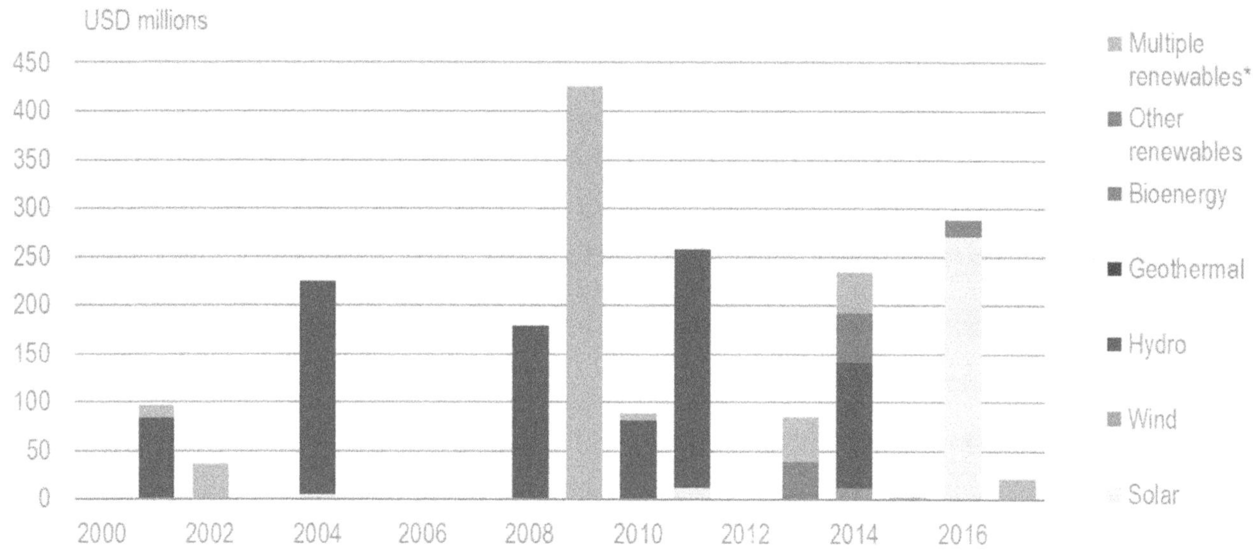

Source: IRENA (2020) Renewable Energy Finance Flows

StatLink https://stat.link/qu8nyh

As Viet Nam's economy developed and attained lower-middle income status, ODA support for clean energy has shifted from grants and concessional lending to non-concessional loans and technical assistance. The recent expansion of the utility scale and roof top solar markets benefited from the availability of domestic and regional credit, with interventions from development finance institutions playing a role in a either very large projects such as the 275 MW solar project in Phu Yen Province or helping to demonstrate new technologies such as the 47.5 MW floating solar project in Binh Tuan Province. Both projects attracted international banks and also benefited from financing from ADB and by Leading Asia's Private Infrastructure Fund, a special fund set up by ADB to provide co-financing for non-sovereign infrastructure projects and supported by development partners such as JICA.

Current clean energy development assistance programmes are relatively concentrated on renewable energy programmes with fewer programmes targeted at energy efficiency and less direct funding targeted at energy efficiency projects. While development finance institutions have been active in supporting energy efficiency, particularly industrial energy efficiency the current overall share of funding and number of individual projects is significantly less than for renewable energy projects. The small scale of the average energy efficiency project and diversity of actors makes it more challenging and the usual requirement for government involvement to access development funding also creates limitations. Options to overcome these challenges include dedicated on-lending programmes through domestic banks, government procurement for energy efficiency and financial support for energy service companies.

Viet Nam has offshore wind targets of about 3-5 GW of capacity to be added from 2030. With individual projects requiring investment capital of USD 2-3 billion, financing these projects will be beyond the capacity of domestic financing institutions (DFIs). Financing offshore wind will require a consortium of domestic and international banks with development finance institutions and export credit agencies supporting through the provision of guarantees to help de-risk the first projects. Other emerging clean energy technologies such as energy storage and waste to energy projects will also need support from DFIs as domestic finance institutions lack sufficient technical capacity and experience to finance such projects.

Although domestic banks have so far been very active in financing solar and wind projects, many have highlighted the lack of long-term capital as a major obstacle. Prudential regulation around short-term capital to medium and long-term debt, currently set at 30% will limit the sector's ability to continuing meeting future clean energy financing needs unless the sector can raise long term capital. A number of DFIs are keen to support Viet Nam's clean energy development and take advantage of their low cost capital to help finance projects through on-lending programmes to domestic banks. However, the reduction in issuance of sovereign guarantees due to the public debt management law has prevented wider use of on-lending of concessional debt to state-owned banks whereas on-lending to private commercial banks is often restricted to near commercial rates. This has so far limited the use of on-lending programmes as a way to increase long-term capital for clean energy projects.

Blended finance to unlock private capital

Blended finance mechanisms that use development funds to help catalyse private finance through various de-risking instruments including first loss and partial risk guarantees, co-investments and subordination among others has not been widely used in the clean energy sector in Viet Nam, although there is good experience for financing water infrastructure in the country[5]. Other blended finance mechanisms include grants for project preparation and project structuring. Development finance institutions could work with the government to develop a multi-donor blended finance platform, similar to the Sustainable Development Goas (SDG) One Indonesia Fund which has received commitments of about USD 3 billion.

The SDG One Indonesia fund is designed to use strategic development finance to crowd in private capital. One notable example for renewable energy includes the use of a grant from AFD to set up a first loss mechanism covering a maximum of 15% of the loan value for a mini-hydro plant that helped to de-risk and encourage other commercial banks to fund the project. The SDG One Indonesia Fund is implemented by PT SMI, a state-owned enterprise responsible for financing infrastructure projects. In the clean energy sector, PT SMI is developing a financing facility with funding from AFD to set up a dedicated USD 150 million loan facility that also includes an additional grant component (EUR 5.6 million) for technical assistance to support project preparation (AFD, 2020[17]).

For blended finance facilities to have the largest benefits, projects should focus on those with good catalytic potential that can help create markets. In particular, where there is opportunity for replicability and standardisation to help prove market viability and demonstrate new business and financing models for renewable energy or energy efficiency technologies that have yet to be established. As reflected in the OECD blended finance principles, blended finance should be deployed with a view to exit concessional finance and exit public development finance overall (OECD, 2018[18]).

In Viet Nam, blended finance funds could be targeted to support the creation of early markets for less mature clean energy technologies such as waste to energy, energy storage, energy efficiency in commercial buildings, low emission high efficiency cooling projects, among others. For energy efficiency projects, on-lending schemes have worked well in other countries such as Mongolia where the Mongolia Green Finance Corporation (MGFC) was set up under a green bank model with funds from the Green Climate Fund, the Government of Mongolia and a consortium of commercial banks. MGFC provides concessional funds for on-lending by banks and other non-bank financial institutions to blend with commercial funding for financing energy efficiency projects in the residential sector and for small and medium enterprises (MGFC, 2020[19]).

Dedicated finance facilities and institutional innovation to promote clean energy

The Viet Nam Environment Protection Fund (VEPF), under the Ministry of Natural Resources and Environment is a state-owned financing institution created to provide financial support for projects that support environmental protection and biodiversity. This includes the deployment of environmentally-friendly technologies including energy efficiency and renewable energy. VEPF was set up with a capital of VND 1 trillion (USD 43 million) and receives its funding from the state budget and through environmental taxes. There are also discussions underway to allow VEPF to receiving funding from domestic and international institutions that could be an option for the setup of a dedicated blended finance facility as highlighted above.

VEPF provides concessional loans for environmental projects for a tenure of up to 10-years at a fixed rate of 2.6% per year for up to 70% of the total investment capital of a project with a limit that does not exceed more than 50% of the chartered capital of the fund. This equates to a maximum loan of about USD 22 million for any single project. VEPF can also co-finance projects, but has yet to do so. When initially established, VEPF's mandate included the provision of guarantees to projects, although no guarantee structures were ever implemented and the prime minister's decision outlining the fund's operational mandate removed this option. Should the government and donors decide to set up a blended finance structure through VEPF, the ability to implement guarantee mechanisms should be reconsidered as this has been shown as one of the main advantages of blended finance in catalysing private capital.

The renewable energy sector, and solar rooftop projects in particular, is one of the largest sectors to receive VEPF funding with a total of VND 210 billion provided in 2019 and 2020 across 14 solar rooftop projects. In the future, VEPF plans to support rooftop solar, waste to energy and wind projects. While energy efficiency projects qualify for VEPF funding, none have yet been financed and should be considered as a priority in the future. The existing funding limit on individual projects poses challenges for reaching scale given the current sole financing model applied by VEPF and means that financing has so far been limited to small distributed renewable projects. A shift towards more co-financing and provision of de-risking could allow VEPF to be more active in the financing of utility scale renewable energy projects.

Other public financing institutions that can support clean energy projects include the Viet Nam Development Bank (VDB) which has a re-lending programme with funds provided by the European Investment Bank for climate mitigation in Viet Nam and also provides on-lending of ODA loans. Currently, these funds are only provided to state-owned enterprises and not available to support financing of private sector projects, which limits its potential to help scale renewable energy generation as the government has left the expansion of generation to the private sector and also for private investments in energy efficiency.

Green finance facility could help to unlock long term capital and build local capacity

A green finance facility could play an important role in overcoming barriers to raising commercial finance for clean energy projects by using public funds to crowd in private finance. The green finance facility (or green bank) model is designed to address market constraints in finance for climate investments. It uses concessional funding to blend public funds with private capital to build investor confidence and help lower financing costs for new technologies that offer climate mitigation or adaptation solutions. Financial instruments used by countries with green banks or green finance facilities include the provision of debt and equity finance, investing in green bonds, investment and creation of funds to co-deliver projects, concessional finance, on-lending facilities, credit enhancement via first loss or subordinated funding and tenor extension, reimbursable grants to help smaller project developers meet collateral requirements and green mortgages.

Green banks or green finance facilities typically establish products for repeatable financing of a target market and their objective is to mobilise finance from domestic finance institutions. They should focus funding towards commercial or near commercial projects (although some do support promising new technologies to overcome “valley of death” constraints related to technology deployment and reaching scale) that have a strong demonstration impact or potential for replicability to help build investor confidence and develop knowledge and expertise among local financiers. Finance should focus on additionally and pull in commercial finance which would otherwise not have funded a project.

Operational independence from the government can protect against political uncertainty that often comes with changes in government. Such independence can be achieved through the legal frameworks set up in the creation of the facility or institution. Through a programmatic approach, such a facility could also help address capacity gaps (lack of clean energy expertise) within the financial sector including for financial structuring that could also be supported with risk mitigation measures.

Where grants or concessional funding is used, such projects should have significant social impacts and benefits of low interest rates should be passed on directly to the project developer. Once a sector has reached maturity, the facility should phase out financing such projects and shift funding towards other promising sectors that are not able to access commercial funding. A detailed assessment of market needs should be undertaken to ensure that any new facility is well targeted and measures are designed to address suitable risks. Financing challenges linked to regulatory or policy barriers (such as land permitting or PPA terms) cannot be overcome by such a facility and should not be used in such situations.

There is potential to design such a facility to facilitate financing vehicles that could use targeted funding from development finance institutions that can help attract long term capital from international institutional investors either directly for large scale clean energy projects or via on-lending schemes through domestic finance institutions. The current high cost of debt in Viet Nam is an area where a green finance facility might help to lower financing costs through blended finance mechanisms that can use lower cost development finance to increase access to more affordable long term capital sources.

Many domestic banks in Viet Nam are already active in the utility scale and solar roof top market as well as onshore wind market. Such a facility could however help to build experience and capacity for emerging clean energy technologies such as energy storage, waste to energy and offshore wind projects where high individual project costs will require de-risking to be able to raise sufficient capital as well as for energy efficiency projects where project aggregation and standardisation could help facilitate financing.

References

ADB (2021), *Regional Technical Assistance Program on Green, Social and sustainable Bond Market Development*. [11]

ADB (2020), *Projects and Tenders*, https://www.adb.org/projects (accessed on 22 December 2020). [23]

AFD (2020), *Promoting renewable energy and climate investments through a green credit line to PT SMI, a key public financial institution of Indonesia*, https://www.afd.fr/en/carte-des-projets/promoting-renewable-energy-and-climate-investments-through-green-credit-line-pt-smi-key-public-financial-institution-indonesia (accessed on 22 December 2020). [17]

Baker McKenzie (2021), *Vietnam: Key highlights of new draft of national power development plan (Draft PDP8)*. [6]

Bloomberg (2021), *What Does $500 Billion for Clean Energy Mean for Climate Change?*, https://www.bloomberg.com/news/articles/2021-01-21/what-does-500-billion-for-clean-energy-mean-for-climate-change (accessed on 1 April 2021). [5]

Bold Magvan (2020), *Mongolia Green Finance Corporation*, https://www.slideshare.net/OECD_ENV/bold-magvan-mgfc-mongolia-green-finance-corporation (accessed on 18 December 2020). [28]

Climate Bonds Initiative (2020), *ASEAN Green Finance: State of the Market*, https://www.climatebonds.net/files/reports/cbi_asean_sotm_2019_final.pdf (accessed on 6 April 2021). [14]

Coleman, B. (n.d.), "Assessment of a Social Discount Rate and Financial Hurdle Rates for Energy System modelling in Viet Nam", OECD. [9]

Denimal, F. (2020), *Radical Steps Needed from Vietnam Banking Sector*, https://www.regulationasia.com/radical-steps-needed-from-vietnam-banking-sector/ (accessed on 5 April 2021). [3]

GGGI (2020), *Potential of Green Bond in Viet Nam*. [13]

GIH (2021), *Vietnam - Global Infrastructure Outlook*, https://outlook.gihub.org/countries/Vietnam (accessed on 5 April 2021). [4]

HSBC, C. (2020), *ASEAN Green Finance Report 2019: HSBC & Climate Bonds launch major analysis of green investment and policy directions in SE Asia | Climate Bonds Initiative*, https://www.climatebonds.net/2020/04/asean-green-finance-report-2019-hsbc-climate-bonds-launch-major-analysis-green-investment (accessed on 6 April 2021). [20]

IEA (2019), *Southeast Asia Energy Outlook 2019*, https://www.iea.org/reports/southeast-asia-energy-outlook-2019 (accessed on 12 April 2021). [8]

JBIC (2014), *Project Financing and Political Risk Guarantee for Sarulla Geothermal Power Plant Project in Indonesia*, https://www.jbic.go.jp/en/information/press/press-2013/0331-19526.html (accessed on 22 December 2020). [25]

Keuangan, I. (ed.) (2009), *Economic and fiscal policy strategies for climate change mitigation in Indonesia : Ministry of Finance green paper*, Ministry of Finance, Republic of Indonesia : Australia Indonesia Partnership. [22]

MGFC (2020), *Presentation by Bold Magvan, Mongolia Green Finance Corporation at OECD Focus Group Discussion on developing a green finance facility to catalyse private investment*, https://www.slideshare.net/OECD_ENV/bold-magvan-mgfc-mongolia-green-finance-corporation (accessed on 1 July 2021). [19]

Ministry of Finance, I. (2020), *Green Sukuk: Allocation and Impact Report*, https://www.djppr.kemenkeu.go.id/page/loadViewer?idViewer=9468&action=download (accessed on 8 March 2021). [21]

Muhammed Sayed (2020), *Climate Finance Facility*, Development Bank of Southern Africa, https://www.slideshare.net/OECD_ENV/muhammed-sayed-dbsa-climate-finance-facility (accessed on 18 December 2020). [26]

OECD (2021), *De-risking institutional investment in green infrastructure: 2021 progress update | en | OECD*, https://www.oecd.org/environment/de-risking-institutional-investment-in-green-infrastructure-357c027e-en.htm (accessed on 5 July 2021). [15]

OECD (2020), *Multi-dimensional Review of Viet Nam: Towards an Integrated, Transparent and Sustainable Economy*, OECD Development Pathways, OECD Publishing, Paris, https://dx.doi.org/10.1787/367b585c-en. [1]

OECD (2018), *Making Blended Finance Work for the Sustainable Development Goals*, OECD Publishing, Paris, https://dx.doi.org/10.1787/9789264288768-en. [18]

SBV (2021), "Presentation on bank credit policy contributing to the implementation of green growth". [12]

Steffen, B. (2020), "Estimating the cost of capital for renewable energy projects", http://dx.doi.org/10.1016/j.eneco.2020.104783. [10]

Sylvester, B. (2020), *About the Clean Energy Finance Corporation*, Clean Energy Finance Corporation, https://www.slideshare.net/OECD_ENV/bianca-sylvester-cefc-about-the-cefc-experience-setting-up-a-green-finance-facililty-in-australia (accessed on 18 December 2020). [27]

US International Development Finance Corporation (2019), *Information Summary for the Public PT Energi Bayu Jeneponto*. [24]

World Bank (2021), *Green Climate Fund provide Vietnam with US$86.3 million to spur energy efficiency investments*, https://www.worldbank.org/en/news/press-release/2021/03/08/wb-gcf-provide-vietnam-with-us863-million-to-spur-energy-efficiency-investments (accessed on 7 May 2021). [16]

World Bank (2020), *Vibrant Vietnam Forging the Foundation of a High-Income Economy Main Report*, https://www.mendeley.com/reference-manager/reader/6ed9f731-3ca4-3612-aa71-6e44bbfd64c8/62e8a610-2cba-9619-5bc4-e9e19d214633 (accessed on 12 April 2021). [7]

World Bank (2019), *Unlocking capital markets for Vietnam's future development FINANCE IN TRANSITION*. [2]

Notes

[1] Decision 1604/QD-NHNN (2018) on approval of the green banking development project in Vietnam. https://www.vir.com.vn/green-banking-aims-push-forward-63006.html.

[2] https://www.giz.de/en/downloads/Decision_403-2014-TTg_EN.pdf.

[3] https://www.adb.org/projects/54013-001/main#project-pds

[4] A full list of development partner programmes is available VEPG website.

[5] OECD Progress update on Approaches to Mobilising Institutional investment for Sustainable Infrastructure.

7 Cross-cutting issues

This chapter examines cross-cutting issues that can improve Viet Nam's clean energy finance and investment framework. It reviews efforts to improve regional grid integration with a view to facilitating the expansion of renewable electricity, as well as to promote innovation, research and development for clean energy, which can help bring down the cost of clean energy technologies and support the domestic clean energy industry's development. The chapter also examines training and education programmes that are essential to develop skills for clean energy finance and investment as well as efforts to promote gender equality in the clean energy sector.

The rapid development of Viet Nam's renewable energy market raises several opportunities and challenges of a cross-cutting nature. Without careful, long term planning, the potential for mismanagement of end of life solar photovoltaic (PV) waste can have negative environmental effects and deteriorate public confidence in the energy transition. As Viet Nam moves into a new phase of deployment under Power Development Plan VIII it will be important to begin developing the enabling environment to avoid these negative impacts and to extract maximum economic value from the management and recycling of raw materials. Regional initiatives for grid integration holds great promise as a cost effective method for variable renewable energy integration. Progress has been slow to date but renewed focus on overcoming the challenges to establish multilateral trading should be prioritised. The significant investment in clean energy infrastructure over the coming decade and the reshaping of Viet Nam's energy system this will bring offers opportunities to drive regional economic and social development. On the other hand, it also brings challenges for communities whose livelihoods are reliant on declining industries. Long-term planning will be needed to understand the social dimension of the energy transition and to formulate appropriate policies to support vulnerable communities.

Assessment and recommendations

Regional power system and financial services integration has seen modest progress

The Association of Southeast Asian Nations (ASEAN) Power Grid (APG) has the potential to be a key flexibility resource to allow the integration of higher shares of variable renewable energy generation. So far, the development of the APG has been mainly bilateral, and elements that could support variable renewable energy (vRE) integration, such as harmonised grid codes and a regional market, are still in very early stages. Most ASEAN member states have interconnections of some kind, with trade arrangements mostly limited to unidirectional power trades under power purchase agreements or bidirectional trading of electricity without financial compensation. Cross-border interconnectors with multilateral, multidirectional power trading in ASEAN can promote effective asset utilisation and resource sharing that benefits member states and the region as a whole. Viet Nam's participation could help strengthen the APG's ongoing development, whilst also supporting the integration of an increasing share of renewables over the Power Development Plan (PDP) VIII, particularly solar and wind, in a cost-effective, reliable and environmentally sustainable manner.

Financial services integration under the ASEAN Economic Community has seen modest progress to date. As Vietnamese banks move to BASEL II standards, there will be opportunities to capture the benefit from enhanced integration through the ASEAN Bank Integration Framework. Opening the sector to greater competition once Vietnamese banks are sufficiently strong can promote greater sector efficiency, technology and expertise transfer, inward investment and a diversification of the customer deposit base.

Innovation in the clean energy sector will benefit from the strong legal structure developed over the last decade and can be accelerated with targeted support

Viet Nam has made significant progress over the last decade in developing the legal framework and business environment to support innovation most notably with the alignment of intellectual property (IP) rights to international norms and participation in a number of international conventions and treaties. Innovation in the clean energy sector can be particularly important where local conditions necessitate localised technical solutions. In Southeast Asia, the offshore wind industry is facing new challenges due to earthquakes, tsunamis, typhoons and different ground conditions than those in Europe where offshore wind innovation has mostly been centred. As the industry progresses, there may be opportunities where government support for research and development (R&D) can reduce the cost of energy and create local value through commercialised technical solutions or more efficient processes and techniques[1]. Innovation across other areas of the clean energy sector can also be beneficial, notably in scaling up innovative pilot programmes led by EVN to support variable renewable energy integration. This includes the energy services company (ESCO) pilot project and demand side reduction pilot which have both been successfully demonstrated. Innovative solutions for integrating solar photovoltaic waste streams into the existing recycling value chain will also be another important area that would benefit from long-term planning and a targeted enabling framework.

Ensuring a just and inclusive clean energy transition should be a priority

In order to enable an inclusive clean energy transition, priority should be given to ensuring that local communities also benefit from clean energy investments in their areas. The link between renewable energy deployment and research and development driven economic development, job creation and rural empowerment should not be taken for granted. A targeted policy framework and long term strategy are essential to enable communities to derive benefits from the clean energy transition (Clausen and Rudolph, 2020[1]). Priority should be given to setting a policy roadmap for a just energy transition, including maximising co-benefits from vRE, developing green industry and jobs, supporting women-led entrepreneurs in clean energy investments and expanding access to clean energy. Viet Nam could also consider including mechanisms in the procurement framework for utility scale renewable projects which target local socio-economic benefits, such as community engagement practices (DIIS, 2021[2]).

Although power generation will rely on coal for the next decades in Viet Nam, it is important for government to already consider how regions which are heavily dependent on the coal industry will transition after its decline. Restructuring the industry of a region is a long-term process which can take decades. By developing a long term vision for transitioning the economy and reskilling affected workers, Viet Nam can find solutions which can help local communities whilst also supporting growing areas of economic activity, such as value chains for energy efficiency and renewable energy.

Supporting women entrepreneurs can help drive more investment in clean energy

To support a gender inclusive energy transition, steps will need to be taken to mainstream gender in mitigation efforts. Increasing the gender diversity of leadership teams improves the quality of innovation and financial performance of businesses, and ultimately helps economies tap into more innovative potential to drive the clean energy transition. Whilst Viet Nam has one of the most open business environments for women amongst peer countries, there are still many challenges for female entrepreneurs to access credit and networks. Collecting gender-disaggregated data is a first step towards recognising issues and identifying new opportunities. Viet Nam should be commended on establishing the National Statistical Indicators on gender development but this should be taken a step further with indicators on women's participation in mitigation efforts and on lending practices to women-led businesses. Gender diversity should also be prioritised in clean energy finance and investment practices, by supporting more gender lens investing which makes gender diversity a priority in investment decisions and by using gender specific lending strategies within banks. Viet Nam has already seen a number of successful associations supporting women led businesses through networking, mentoring and training opportunities. This could be further enhanced by supporting networks for women working in clean energy technologies.

Expanded green finance and technical skills development programmes will promote clean energy investment and localise green jobs

Just as in OECD economies, sustainable finance is an emerging area with best practices evolving and markets adapting to develop the skills and expertise required. Ongoing capacity development will be required to support banks to integrate environmental and social management systems particularly in the use of quantitative tools for environmental risk analysis. Non-recourse or limited recourse project financing structures are rarely utilised in Viet Nam's clean energy sector to date. Greater use of such structures will support higher levels of domestic investment in clean energy. Project finance requires specialised teams and underwriting processes to undertake due diligence on underlying projects, evaluate cash-flow risks, and structure and de-risk transactions. The government should consider supporting skills development through targeted training programmes in this area. Technical and vocational training is also a key area where activities are already being implemented in co-operation with various development partners. With the speed of development of the green economy, particularly in the clean energy sector, there is a risk that a mismatch could develop in the labour market that could hold back market development. A piecemeal approach to green skills development with fragmented programmes can increase this risk. Viet Nam currently does not have a green skills development strategy which would help to evaluate skills development needs and structure activities with a more integrated approach and over a long-term horizon in line with sector plans.

Box 7.1. Main policy recommendations on cross-cutting issues

- Accelerate regional power grid integration with the aim of multilateral power trading under the ASEAN Power Grid initiative. This can play a crucial role in providing the flexibility needs required for increasing shares of variable renewable energy generation over the PDP VIII period.
- Provide targeted support for innovation in the clean energy sector to reduce energy costs and support local value. This could be particularly relevant in the offshore sector where innovative technical solutions may be required to adapt to local environmental conditions.
- Begin planning for and implementing the enabling framework for the development of a domestic solar photovoltaic recycling industry drawing from the experiences of the EU and other mature markets.
- Collect gender-disaggregated data on women's participation in the clean energy sector in order to mainstream gender in mitigation efforts and tap into more innovative potential to drive the clean energy transition. Develop tools for gender lens investing and gender specific lending strategies to support female entrepreneurs in taking an active role in clean energy investments.
- Develop an integrated strategy for technical and vocational education and training for the clean energy sector or for the green economy as a whole to guide investment and programme development.
- Expand skills development programmes in the banking sector for the development and integration of environmental and social management systems and non-recourse or limited recourse project financing.

Regional integration

Regional power trading can support cost-effective variable renewable energy integration

Strengthening regional power market integration offers several notable opportunities for Viet Nam and for neighbouring countries in the region. Cross border power trade enables complementary utilisation of each country's resource endowments and power system assets, and supports cost effective and secure system integration of variable renewable energy (vRE). In Viet Nam it can allow export of excess renewable energy generation during periods of oversupply while also enabling access to greater flexible generation resources, in particular hydropower, in other countries to support system balancing. Regional power trade has been one of the key enablers for maintaining power quality and energy security in power systems with increasingly high shares of vRE. This has been particularly evident in the EU with multilateral power trading established under Nord Pool. The government of Viet Nam is involved in two long-standing regional initiatives to support power market integration including the ASEAN Power Grid (APG) which aims to connect the energy markets of ASEAN's 10-member nations, and the Greater Mekong Subregion (GMS) programme which also includes Cambodia, the People's Republic of China, Lao PDR, Myanmar and Thailand.

Both the GMS and APG are still at nascent stages, with most trading remaining bilateral and unidirectional, with little coordination between the two regional initiatives, which cater to different stakeholders. Viet Nam trades power bilaterally with its neighbours under long-term power purchase agreements with two categories of cross-border interconnectors: firstly, those transporting power from specific power plants at high voltage. This includes two interconnectors with Lao PDR importing power from the Xekaman 1 & 3 hydro power plants (290 & 250 MW respectively) majority financed by Viet Nam. Viet Nam is planning two further hydro power projects in co-operation with Lao PDR (Xekaman 4 and Nam Mo) in the coming years with a memorandum of co-operation signed in 2016 confirming the ambition for further "co-operation and development of hydropower projects, interconnecting the power systems and purchase of electricity" (EVN, 2017[3]). The second category of interconnectors are those that import export grid power across neighbouring power systems. Viet Nam has two high voltage connections with China in the north of the country with capacities of 300 MW and 200 MW and a high voltage interconnector with Cambodia with a capacity of 200 MW.

Bilateral power trading across either the APG or GMS regions provides an important initial foundation for greater power market integration but the move to multilateral trading arrangements will go further to fully realise the cost efficiency and energy security benefits that can be delivered. Achieving multilateral power trading has significant challenges of a political, technical, and institutional nature. Power markets in the region are at different stages of development and have varying regulatory structures (including on power trading, pricing and support mechanisms) and technical requirements (such as operating voltage and frequency) that require harmonisation. There is also a requirement to come to agreement on data and information sharing that is of a highly political nature and involving sensitive critical infrastructure (Figure 7.1). Given their early and somewhat fragmented stages of development, Viet Nam's participation in these initiatives could help strengthen their ongoing development and potentially support their greater alignment.

Figure 7.1. Prerequisites for development of multilateral power trading

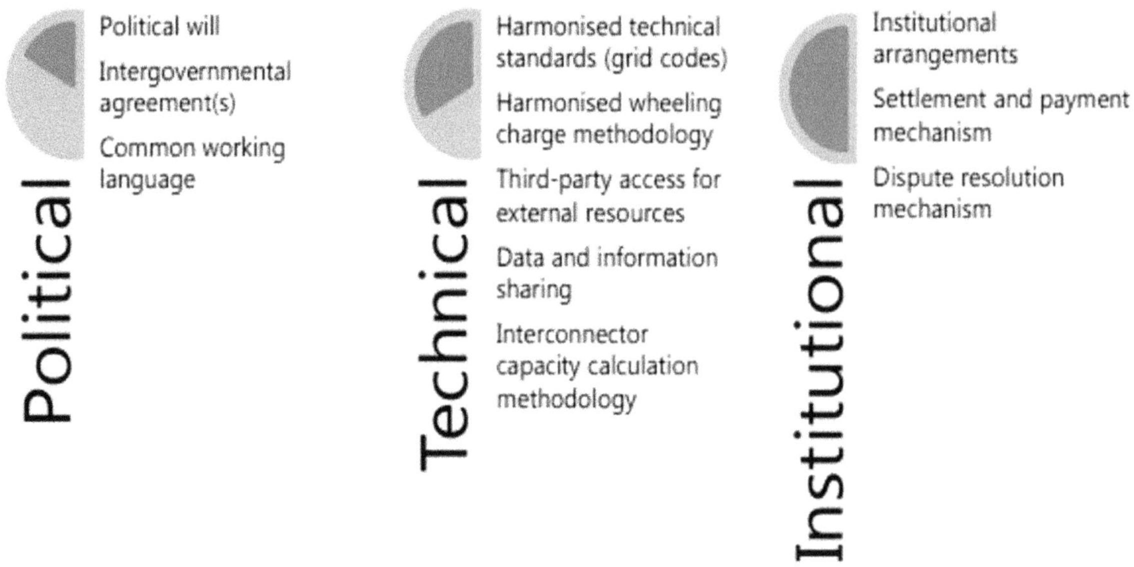

Source: (IEA, 2019[4])

There has been some progress to date under the GMS and APG frameworks. The GMS programme led to the development of draft harmonised grid codes and a draft wheeling methodology. While these have not been formally implemented, the development process included five of the ten ASEAN member states, suggesting that these could provide a good starting point to developing a more general set of harmonised grid codes for the ASEAN region as a whole (IEA, 2019[4]). Viet Nam is also pushing forward on its power market liberalisation and development plans with a firm timeline of activities over coming years to move to fully liberalised wholesale and retail power markets (see chapter 3). Establishment of a strong and efficient national electricity market is a prerequisite for enabling broader regional market integration. The joint Laos PDR, Thailand, Malaysia, Singapore Power Integration Project (LTMS-PIP) has potential to act as a platform to pave the way for accelerated power market integration. As it stands today, the LTMS–PIP involves the sale of electricity from Lao PDR to Malaysia, with Thailand acting as a transit, or wheeling, but will be extended over a two year period (2022-2024) to include Singapore, who confirmed involvement in 2020. At this time Thailand is the main "host" for the platform, however, the work already undertaken under LTMS–PIP, for example its development of a wheeling charge methodology, and the negotiations to be undertaken over the coming two years can forge a path for establishing a more generalised foundation for multilateral trading in the region that Viet Nam could benefit from over the medium to long term.

Stepwise regional financial integration can lead to greater efficiency and capital flows

Since 2003 ASEAN member states including Viet Nam committed to broadening and strengthening regional economic cooperation through the vision of an ASEAN Economic Community (AEC) that would by 2015 "transform ASEAN into a region with free movement of goods, services, investment, skilled labour and freer flows of capital". The pathway to achieving the AEC vision was set out in the AEC Blueprint and the steps for financial market integration further elaborated under the Roadmap for Monetary and Financial Integration of ASEAN (RIA-FIN). RIA-FIN activities were arranged around the three themes of financial services liberalisation, capital market development and capital account liberalisation (removal of capital controls and restrictions to flow of capital).

By the end of 2015 ASEAN member states had completed 87% of all measures under the AEC Blueprint and the AEC was formally established (Rillo, 2018[5]). Despite these achievements financial integration across the region, not just between Viet Nam and ASEAN neighbours, remained fragmented particularly when compared to the significant progress made on trade liberalisation (Thanh, 2015[6]). This may reflect a level of cautiousness influenced by the experience of the Asian financial crisis in the late 1990s and the need for a long-term stepwise approach due to the disparity in institutional and regulatory development across member states. Enhanced financial integration has the potential to benefit Viet Nam in a number of ways including promoting greater capital flows into the country, improving capital allocation efficiency and financing costs through greater competition, greater macroeconomic resilience, and transfer of technology and managerial expertise. However there are also risks if integration proceeds before the financial market and the institutions and governance arrangements are sufficiently developed. In this case market interlinkages may work against macroeconomic stability as external shocks are more easily spread through the region particularly where risk diversification options are limited (Stiglitz, 2010[7]). This may hold true for Viet Nam over the shorter term as capital markets continue to develop and the banking sector fully recovers from the debt crisis which peaked in 2012.

Continued focus on enhancing financial integration beyond 2015 was reaffirmed in an updated AEC Blueprint covering the period to 2025 which prioritises, among other areas of economic integration, measures to achieve an "increased role of ASEAN indigenous banks, more integrated insurance markets and more connected capital markets". Increasing the number of qualified ASEAN banks (QABs) is a key target. The QAB concept was introduced by the ASEAN Banking Integration Framework (ABIF) approved in 2014. Depending on the negotiation of bilateral agreements between member states banks that are able to meet certain pre-requisites including metrics related to majority ASEAN ownership, capital adequacy, and corporate governance standards are able to hold QAB status and receive preferential treatment under regulatory frameworks on par with domestic banks. Flexibility was built into the ABIF to recognise the varying readiness levels of member states and the need to proceed on a stepwise bilateral basis rather than multilaterally. Despite a target under the ABIF for establishment of a bilateral agreement by 2020, Viet Nam to date has not entered into such an agreement with another ASEAN member state and therefore has no QABs. It is also telling that the Development Strategy of the Vietnam Banking Sector to 2025 has no specific objectives directly related to regional integration or for QABs more specifically. As Viet Nam's banks strengthen and move toward BASEL II standards regional integration could support Viet Nam's most developed banks to further strengthen through QAB status particularly as clean energy and other infrastructure investment needs continue to expand and the banking sector remains the primary source of financing.

Research and Development and Innovation

Intellectual property rights have been strengthened but enforcement can be improved

Substantial improvements to protect intellectual property (IP) rights have been made over the past two decades, with recognition within government of its importance in shaping an attractive business climate to promote technology transfer through foreign direct investment (FDI) and licensing, and greater commercialisation of indigenous research and development. The OECD has found that the strength of a country's patent rights is positively correlated to inward FDI with every 1% increase in patent protection correlating to a 2.8% increase in FDI (Park and Lippoldt, 2008[8]). There is also evidence that strong IP rights supports technology transfers through increased licensing. It is important to note that evidence suggests such benefits also depend on wider enabling factors such as government effectiveness, contract enforcement and corruption levels (Arora, 2007[9]).

The legal regime in Viet Nam comprises of several pieces of legislation, including the 2005 Civil Code, the Criminal Code, the 2005 Intellectual Property Law amended in 2009, and their implementing regulations. In 2019, the Government of Viet Nam issued a National Strategy on Intellectual Property with a Vision to 2030, to act as a guideline for ministries, sectors and state agencies to further develop IP rights. Viet Nam's domestic IP laws are generally aligned with international norms and is a signatory of the Paris Convention for the Protection of Industrial Property, the WTO Trade-Related Aspects of Intellectual Property Rights (WTO TRIPS) Agreement, the World Intellectual Property Organization, the Patent Cooperation Treaty, the Madrid Protocol and The Hague Agreement concerning the International Deposit of Industrial Designs. This is further strengthened by the 2020 European-Viet Nam Free Trade Agreement whereby Viet Nam has agreed to go beyond the standards of WTO TRIPs agreement, particularly regarding enforcement provisions (European Commission, 2015[10]).

Despite the significant progress, strengthening the legal framework enforcement of IP laws and regulation could be improved. The IP Office provides, and manages at state level, services in the field of IP, including registration of industrial property rights and basic legal appraisals for dispute settlement. There are no specialised IP courts and most IP disputes are handled through administrative action rather than civil action or criminal prosecution. Vietnam ranks 43rd out of 45 countries in the annual IP index released by the US Chamber of Commerce highlighting weaknesses in the enforcement of IP rights and insufficient penalties as key areas of weakness. The fifth edition of the Global Intellectual Property Index (GIPI) ranks Vietnam's IP regime as 35th out of 43 countries scoring poorly for enforcement, with criticism for a lack of judicial guidance for assessing damages and the complexity of court procedures (International Chambers of Commerce, 2019[11]). In 2014, the National Steering Committee 389 was created to support enforcement agencies' fight against IP violations. The steering committee passed important regulation in 2020 (Decision No. 195/QD-BCD 389) which defines the modalities for co-operation between steering committees at national, ministry and provincial levels, and how steering committees should cooperate with authorities in the sharing of information and monitoring of case handling.

Despite the progress that needs to be made strengthening the enforcement environment, there is evidence that achievements to date are delivering favourable outcomes for clean energy technology transfers. The number of green technology patent applications have increased from 143 in 2000 to 886 in 2018. Japanese companies and institutions have accounted for almost a quarter of total applications, followed by the United States at 15%, and then Viet Nam at 13%. Within alternative energy production patent applications for biofuels accounted for 60%, followed by solar, wind, hydro and geothermal at 14%, 10%, 6%, and 3%, respectively. Over three quarters of applications fall under the Patent Cooperation Treaty (PCT) which means the patents apply protection for an invention simultaneously in the 150+ states bound by the PCT system of the World Intellectual Property Organisation (WIPO) (Duong, 2020[12]).

Figure 7 2. Green technology patents Viet Nam 2000-2018

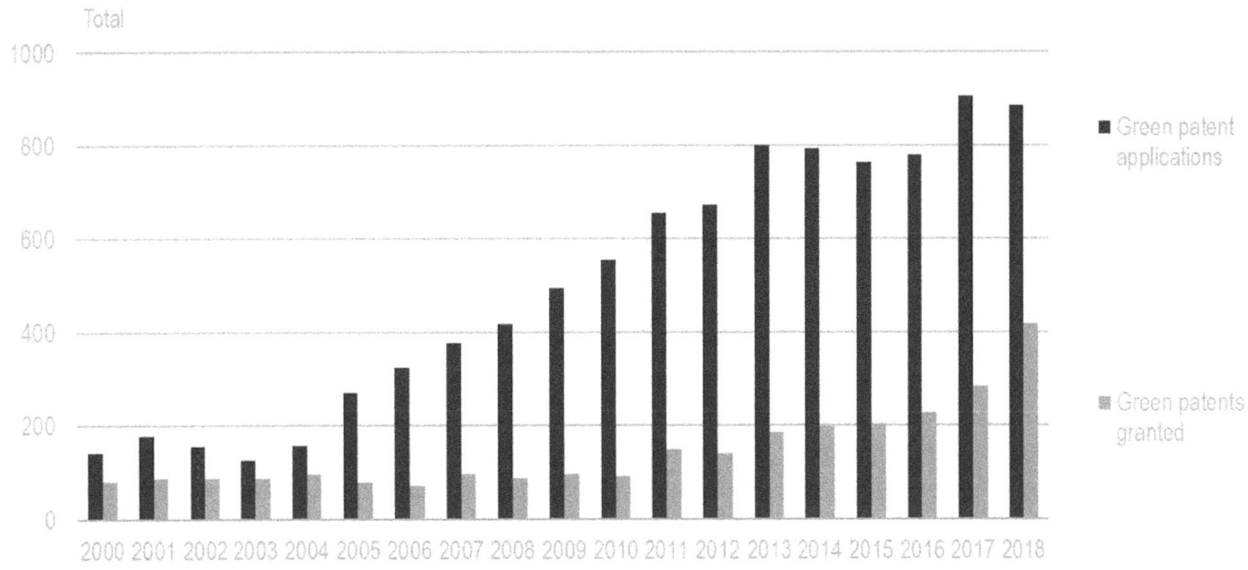

Source (Duong, 2020[12])

StatLink https://stat.link/hvlpyo

Strategic government support for innovation in the clean energy sector can drive cost reductions, technology diffusion and new value chain creation

Markets can fail when it comes to providing the socially efficient amount of resources aimed at generating new technological and scientific knowledge. This knowledge often has strong public good characteristics, implying that knowledge spill-overs provide benefits to the public as a whole, but not to the innovator (Söderholm et al., 2020[13]). This can be true in the clean energy sector particularly where local conditions necessitate localised technical solutions and processes. This is particularly relevant for the offshore wind industry where offshore project development, construction, and operation and maintenance (O&M) requires more specialised equipment and techniques. In Southeast Asia the offshore wind industry is facing new challenges due to earthquakes, tsunamis, typhoons and different ground conditions than those in Europe where offshore wind innovations have often been centred. As the industry progresses, there may be opportunities where government R&D support can reduce the cost of energy and create local value through the development of localised solutions matching Viet Nam's context (BVG Associates, 2020[14]). Establishing and supporting domestic research and development activities, in addition to international partnerships across universities, government agencies and the private sector, will be key to preparing the way for a cost competitive offshore wind industry.

Innovation in business models and sector development approaches that support wider clean energy technology diffusion are also required. This applies particularly to the biomass sector which is faced with complex and informal supply chains and the energy efficiency sector faced with various behavioural and economic barriers. Biomass feed-stocks in Viet Nam are abundant; rice husk, rice straw, coconut pith, sugar cane bagasse and coffee waste all offer great potential, however, these waste flows are diffuse and often managed in an environmentally unsound manner (NL Agency, 2013[15]). The utilisation of these resources is therefore a business opportunity as well as an environmental benefit but requires engagement with rural communities with few resources, low technical awareness, and, given their lack of capacity to cope with disruption, a natural cautiousness with new processes and technologies. Social innovation approaches where new technologies, processes, or techniques are co-created collaboratively with end-users will be relevant in exploring how farmers and local communities can be engaged. This applies both to densifying and formalising biomass supply chains as feedstock for centralised biomass to power plants and for diffusion of distributed biomass technologies such as small-scale gasifiers and anaerobic digesters.

Planning for solar photovoltaic recycling market development is a crucial element of the clean energy transition

Viet Nam's Solar PV market has grown exponentially over the last two years and large scale deployment will continue over the PDP VIII implementation period. Solar PV panels have a useful life of around 20-30 years with a small percentage of panels failing early which means the solar sector will account for a growing waste stream of failed panels and that by around 2040 panel waste will grow exponentially when the first panels reach their end of life. PV panel waste presents an environmental challenge, but also an opportunity to develop new industries, value added activities and jobs. The PV recycling industry will be essential for achieving Viet Nam's transition to a sustainable, renewables-based energy system. The recycling of decommissioned PV panels can supply both domestic and international demand for raw materials and avoid the potential environmental impacts that could be caused from landfilling. Crystalline silicon modules contain small amounts of lead and tin which can cause disturbances to soil functions, harm aquatic ecosystems, and cause development and behavioural disorders in children (Mahmoudi, Huda and Behnia, 2020[16]). Thin film modules contain small traces of heavy metals such as gallium and cadmium which are highly toxic and also require careful management. To pave the way for adequate waste management and to unlock the benefits of recycling industries, preparatory work must be completed well in advance to ensure the enabling framework is in place to support market development.

The core of an effective enabling framework is a PV specific waste policy that sets waste management targets and a supportive set of regulations which should define clear roles and responsibilities across producers, consumers, and wider society for each stage of the recycling value chain. At present, the European Union (EU) has adopted PV-specific waste regulations as one of the more advanced regional renewable energy markets. The EU Waste Electrical and Electronic Equipment (WEEE) Directive is based on an extended-producer responsibility principle and requires all producers supplying PV panels to the EU market (wherever they may be based) to finance the costs of collecting and recycling (see Box 7.2).

Box 7.2. Case Study: The EU WEEE Directive for end of life PV management

The WEEE Directive sets a common regulatory framework for solar PV end of life management across the EU with an extended-producer-responsibility principle at its core. All producers in the EU market have legal responsibilities for end-of-life management whether their manufacturing facilities are in the EU or not. The combination of producer legal liability, financing schemes, collection, recovery and recycling targets, and treatment standards is a reference point for PV waste management regulation development globally. The end of life management responsibilities enshrined in the directive cover three broad areas:

1. **Financial responsibility**: Producers are liable through a financial guarantee and insurance premium to cover the cost of collection and recycling of products sold to households.
2. **Reporting responsibility**: Producers are obliged to report on panels sold, collected and sent for treatment. Reporting waste treatment of products is also required (tonnes treated, recovered, recycled, and disposed by fraction e.g. glass, mixed plastic waste, metals).
3. **Information responsibility**: Producers must attach labels on panels to inform buyers on appropriate disposal procedures. Information must also be available to waste treatment companies on how to handle PV panels during collection, storage, dismantling and treatment.

The directive defines financing mechanisms depending on the buyer of the product. Panels sold to private households (B2C) require the producer to finance collection and recycling through a collective Pay As You Go (PAYG) approach combined with an insurance premium. For business to business transactions (B2B) either the customer or the producer are able to undertake collection and recycling. For example, a solar PV plant owner may be best positioned to fulfil the recycling obligation by using project cash flows to hire the original producer or to hire a professional third party.

Figure 7.3. Germany's business to consumer recycling finance structure

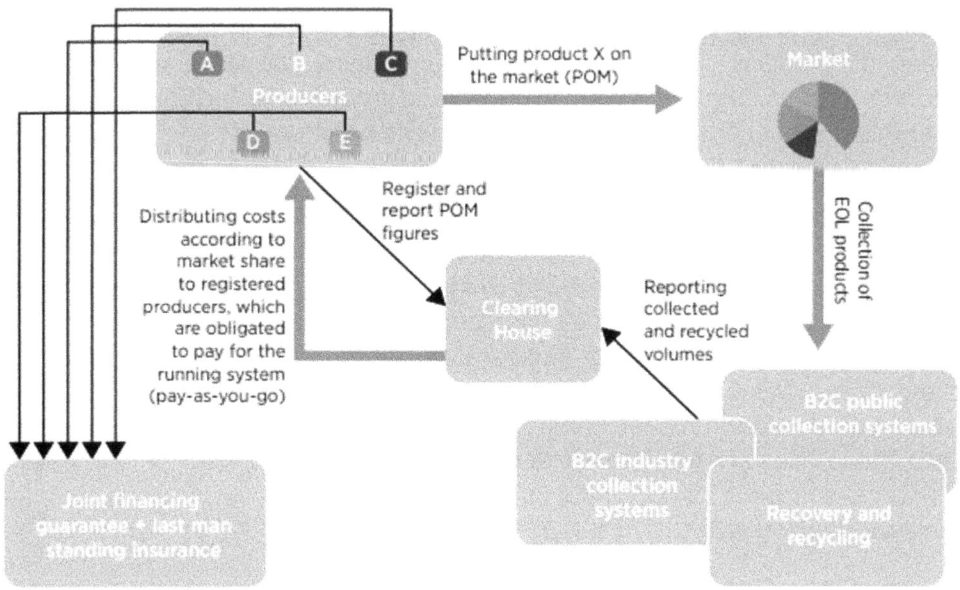

Source: (IRENA and IEA-PVPS, 2016[17])

Regulating producers to bear the cost of the full life cycle of the panel promotes innovation and cost reduction so that panels are designed with cost optimised recycling as one of the key criteria. This arrangement is also thought to be more easily monitored and enforced compared to consumer financing obligations. The regulatory framework should also set common standards for collection and recycling and for permitted contractual modalities between the producer and different customer segments (private households vs. corporates) for financing end-of-life obligations. Solar PV recycling can be commercially viable depending on appropriate incentives and fee structure.

A just clean energy transition

Policy should ensure that local communities benefit from the clean energy transition

Investment in clean energy will help Viet Nam meet its mitigation and energy security objectives, but is also an opportunity deriving wider societal benefits. The socio-economic benefits of renewable project development can be maximised through sustainable and integrated planning, which prioritises opportunities for local actors in the value chain and benefits for local communities. These should not be taken for given and require targeted policy framework and long-term strategy to be developed to ensure that communities also benefit from the clean energy transition. A number of considerations, discussed in the subsequent sections, are also relevant to ensuring a just transition. This includes the creation of opportunities for both genders, ensuring that women are not left behind, and supporting local green industries and jobs, with a focus on technical and vocational training to build human capital. Equally, it is important to ensure that an unfair burden is not placed on communities, for instance with respect to the decommissioning of solar panels or the rehabilitation of land.

Different approaches have been taken by countries to ensure that communities derive socio-economic benefits from renewable deployment. These include community co-ownership, whereby communities become a shareholder of renewable plants, allowing for a share of revenue to be retained and redistributed locally. Another approach is to include community benefits as a selection criteria in the public procurement of private renewable energy generation. This can encourage developers to look for ways to support development activities in local communities near the renewable project, for example through financial payments administered by a local body. Finally, renewable projects can learn from the experience of energy and extractives sectors which shows that developing frameworks for communication can help shape relations between large energy projects and communities and provide a channel of engagement (Box 7.3) (Clausen and Rudolph, 2020[1]) (DIIS, 2021[2]).

Moreover, local communities of renewable projects can benefit from renewable development through well designed tax structures and land fee payments. Taxes on land and housing, the transfer of land-use rights, the use of agriculture land and licences are retained by local government, as are fees on land use, land rent and registration. Dependent on the province's fiscal capacity, local and central government also share revenue from value-added tax (VAT), corporate and personal income taxes, and taxes on profits remitted abroad (Morgan and Trinh, 2016[18]). The new solar auction mechanism (discussed in chapters 3 and 5), if adopting a solar park or substation model, can allow provinces to have a forward view of revenue that will be received from these taxes and fees. This in turn can enable better planning for how these resources can be utilised for socio-economic development in local communities or for instance for implementing public energy efficiency investments.

Box 7.3. Community benefits of RE integrated into auction design: Lessons from South Africa

From 2011, community development has been a component of South Africa's national programme for renewable energy procurement, the Renewable Energy Independent Power Producers Procurement Programme (REIPPPP). Given that renewable projects have been primarily located in rural and marginalized areas, REIPPPP has created a legal framework to incentivise solar, wind and biomass IPPs to channel benefits to communities surrounding renewable project locations. Over the duration of the PPA, IPPs are required to allocate a percentage of generated revenue on socio-economic development and enterprise development projects and share ownership in the project company with local communities.

REIPPPP accomplishes this through the evaluation of bids, with 70% of the score based on price criteria and 30% on a set of social and economic development criteria, with specific percentages dedicated to components such as job creation, local content, community ownership, management control, targeted procurement from local businesses, enterprise development and socio-economic development, particularly within 50 km or within District Municipal boundaries of project sites. This includes plans for financing development projects in education, social welfare, health care, enterprise development and administration, as well as allotting project revenue towards a Community Trusts, and allocating a share of the project company to communities. To facilitate this, IPPs within the programme have tended to employ community engagement to facilitate communication and monitor implementation of community projects (WWF, 2015[19]).

Between 2011 and 2020, REIPPPP procured more than 6 000 MW of electricity from 112 wind and solar project companies leading to private investment of USD 14 billion , of which 20% was FDI. By 2020, USD 82 million had been invested in socio-economic development measures through REIPPP (DIIS, 2021[21]). It is estimated that until 2050, the programme will support marginalised communities, through 3 000 local enterprises, up to 10 000 local jobs and through 30 000 individuals benefiting from access to education-related programmes (Koffer, 2019[20]). In terms of UN 2030 Sustainable Development goals, renewable energy in South Africa aims to contribute towards SDG 7 Sustainable Energy for All, but also SDG 1 on No Poverty, SDG 4 on Quality Education, SDG 8 on Decent Work and Economic Growth and SDG 10 on Reduced Inequality. Through gender inclusive hiring targets, REIPPPP also aims to support SDG 5 on Gender Equality.

While the competitive bidding framework for renewable projects in Viet Nam is still under development, REIPPPP provides 10 years of experience in developing a competitive procurement programme that balances bankability and cost competitiveness while delivering real benefit to communities. The REIPPPP also highlights the importance of establishing coordination mechanisms between government, IPPs and communities, so that initiatives maximise the benefits of investment whilst minimising redundancy or inefficiency. For instance, although the IPP will evaluate socio-economic needs of the community to submit a plan for the tender, they may not have adequate human capacity to best identify key areas nor monitor implementation. Given the competitive environment for project tendering, opportunities for collaboration across IPPs may be missed or efforts duplicated. This is equally important for co-ordination across local communities and regional government who may prioritise different projects in line with immediate concerns and regional development planning. The creation of platforms for information sharing and collaborative learning amongst stakeholders can help local governments maximise benefits from development programmes. Although REIPPPP has helped South Africa capture local socio-economic benefits of solar and wind projects, it is important to note that ensuring a socially just energy transition goes beyond procurement practices and requires an integrated policy approach across social, economic and industrial policy areas.

A long term vision should be developed for coal regions in transition

Under the PDP VIII draft, although the planned ratio of coal-fired power capacity in 2030 has decreased from the previously revised PDP VII, it will still represent around 41 GW. In 2020, the Vietnam National Coal and Mineral Industries Group (Vinacomin) alone employed 96 000 workers (VietnamPlus, 2021[21]). Although reliance on coal imports is increasing, Viet Nam is also focusing on increasing productivity of domestic mining, which would suggest that the coal mining industry is not likely to decline in the immediate future. Nevertheless, given the position of the coal industry in Viet Nam, it is important for government to already start considering priorities around a just transition, which is the idea of a fair and inclusive energy transition that leaves no one behind.

Restructuring an industry region is a very long-term process. Historic examples show that it can take several decades for former coal mining regions to establish alternative economies, especially if the transition is to be managed in a way to avoid massive job losses or even migration out of the region (Sartor, 2018[22])This means taking into consideration the number of communities that will affected by decarbonisation, whose income significantly depends on the extraction and use of coal, particularly in the Quang Ninh basin, as well as the Red River Delta, Thai Nguyen, Backan, North Path, Da River, Ca River, Na Duong, Nong Song, Ba River, and Mekong River Delta (Mijał, 2018[23]). The government can already start laying the foundations for a just transition towards low carbon energy sources through medium and long-term planning. Other regions, such as the EU and North America are currently tackling these issues by developing just transition funds and programmes on reskilling employees and environmental rehabilitation and repurposing. By learning from the experience of other countries, Viet Nam could determine long-term and cost-effective strategies to support affected workers and communities in the coal-power-generating regions of the country, whilst also supporting growing areas of activity, such as value chains for energy efficiency and renewable energy, and by developing a pipeline of higher skilled workers[2].

Box 7.4. Overview of ILO's Just Transition Guideline

The Just Transition Guidelines include:

- social protection policies to enhance resilience and safeguard workers from the negative impacts of climate change, economic restructuring and resource constraints
- labour market policies that actively pursue job creation, limit job loss and ensure that adjustments related to greening policies are well managed
- occupational safety and health policies to protect workers from occupational hazards and risks
- skills development to ensure adequate skills at all levels to promote the greening of the economy
- the establishment of mechanisms for social dialogue throughout the policy-making processes at all levels
- policy coherence and institutional arrangements for the mainstreaming of sustainable development and to ensure stakeholder dialogue and coordination between policy fields.

Source: ILO (2019) Green Jobs and a Just Transition for Climate Action in Asia and the Pacific

Gender diversity and supporting women entrepreneurs

Gender-disaggregated data can support a more gender inclusive clean energy transition

Viet Nam should be commended on establishing the National Strategy on Gender Equality (NSGE) for the period 2011-2020, with planning for the period 2021-2030 under development. With the view of identifying gender inequalities to be addressed and to assess the impact of existing policy, the Ministry of Planning and Investment also developed a number of gender indicators in 2019. These included indicators looking at women's participation in leadership roles across government, parliament, committees and private businesses, with the view of meeting Viet Nam's Sustainable Development Goals (Circular No. 03/2019/TTBKHDT). This was followed by the National Statistical Indicators for Gender Development (Circular No. 10/2019/TTBKHDT), providing a number of indicators across socio-economic priority areas.

High-level statistics on gender portray a relatively positive picture, particularly compared to regional peers, but this also means that the debate around gender inequality in Viet Nam is often not made a priority. This may create a perception that women do not face barriers in business, despite women being disproportionately affected by underemployment, unemployment and unstable working conditions, and representing the majority of Viet Nam's working poor. The inclusion of a greater range of gender development indicators in official statistics is important, as it allows government to get a realistic measure of gender inequality and obliges line ministries to report on progress in these fields. For Viet Nam's Nationally Determined Contributions (NDC) review, the United Nations Development Programme suggested a number of indicators which would support the mainstreaming of gender development in mitigation. For example, suggested indicators look at the number of men and women employed or holding leadership positions in the renewable energy sector, or the number of men and women led businesses that have chosen to install rooftop solar PV indicators (UNDP, 2020[24]). Such information can help identify how women are participating in Viet Nam's clean energy sector and inform targeted policies supporting a gender inclusive energy transition. Currently this type of gender-disaggregated data is not being collected for the energy sector in Viet Nam.

Gender lens investing and networks can support women led businesses in clean energy

Women can play a central role in the clean energy transition but they must overcome certain challenges, such as unconscious bias, in order to have greater participation in energy and technology sectors, which have typically been dominated by men. Taking steps to support female entrepreneurs in clean energy can have the dual advantage of advancing the mitigation agenda whilst also enhancing women's employment prospects. Whilst the investment climate in Viet Nam is generally supportive for women, who own around 20% of formal enterprises, further steps can be taken to mainstream gender in finance and investment practices, and encourage banks to increase access to capital for women-owned and women-led businesses. Cultural barriers and structural gender gaps still create barriers for female entrepreneurs in Viet Nam to access capital and networks, both of which are essential for business success (Investing in Women, 2021[25]).

Despite untapped demand for credit, an International Finance Corporation (IFC) survey found that banks in Viet Nam were not actively seeking to promote gender specific lending strategies and that a prevailing bias endures that businesses are less successful when led by women (IFC, 2017[26]). Gender lens investing can help narrow the credit gap between male and female entrepreneurs, by taking into consideration the impacts on women as well the returns of the investment. Investing in Women, an Australian programme, is one example that provides support to impact investors to invest in female entrepreneurs in Vietnam and other ASEAN countries. Gender lens investing in Viet Nam is in early stages and only a limited number of funds and private impact investors are looking into this. Better data on lending practices to women led-business and women's participation in the financial sector can support investors and financiers in identifying opportunities that support both mitigation targets and tackle gender issues. Between 2017 and

2019, seven gender lens investments were identified in Viet Nam, and whilst most of the deal sizes were below USD 500 000, one very large IFC project brought the average up to USD 6 million which highlights the central role that development finance institutions can play in accelerating gender lens investing (Investing in Women, 2021[25]).

Viet Nam has seen a number of successful associations supporting women led businesses through networking, mentoring and training opportunities. Some good examples of these are the Vietnam Association of Female Entrepreneurs (VAFE), the Women's Initiative for Start-ups and Entrepreneurship (WISE), and Strengthening Women Entrepreneurship Vietnam (SWEV). This could be further enhanced by supporting networks for women working in clean energy technologies, as well as supporting this process at an earlier stage, with programmes that highlight career opportunities to girls as they are considering which academic path to take.

Education, Training and Skills Development

Driving job creation through investment in clean energy

Government spending on renewables and energy efficiency creates three times more jobs than spending on fossil fuels, with job creation up and down the supply chain (McKinsey, 2020[27]). Both sectors have a diverse set of employment needs, from highly specialised to unskilled labour, which means that job creation can take place in the short term as well as requiring a pipeline of training and skills development. Viet Nam has been one of the few countries in the world to have maintained positive growth over 2020, and is forecast to recover to a similar level of GDP growth after COVID-19. Nevertheless, this provides an opportunity to refocus policy on driving durable and resilient growth. A dollar invested in the energy transition can give three to eight times the return. Compared with conventional fiscal stimulus, well-designed projects around renewable energy assets, grid modernisation and energy efficiency building retrofits can generate higher employment and short-term returns per dollar spent (IRENA, 2020[28]).

By creating an enabling environment for investment in energy efficiency, Viet Nam creates opportunities amongst small and medium size businesses and local workers involved in efficient appliances, building materials manufacturing, industrial energy efficiency and building retrofits. Depending on the sector, USD 1 million spent on energy efficiency generate between six and 15 jobs on average, due to the labour-intensive nature of many energy efficiency upgrades. Moreover, energy efficiency investments can be rapidly mobilised, making them an attractive opportunity for government to protect existing jobs or generate new employment in moments of economic slowdown (IEA, 2020[29]).

In the renewable energy sector, employment can be linked to the development and operation of renewable projects, but also around the manufacturing of equipment. Viet Nam's solar PV workforce already stood at 56 700 jobs in 2019, of which 25 000 of these were in manufacturing (IRENA, 2020[30]). Whilst many jobs have been created around the development of plants, these tend to be temporary in nature, ending when the plant construction is finalised. Operation and maintenance jobs can extend for the duration of the plant's lifecycle, but tend to be much smaller in number. Job creation in manufacturing represents a greater long-term potential, as it is export-driven and independent of local solar PV installation. To date, modules in Viet Nam have been manufactured in collaboration with Chinese and American manufacturers, and in 2017, this amounted to 5 GW of panels, representing 7% percent of the global market. Whilst there is strong competition in the region from China, Malaysia and Thailand, Viet Nam's production factors, particularly with respect to steel, electricity tariffs and labour, give it a competitive advantage over certain components (World Bank Group, 2019[31]). In 2020, Viet Nam was amongst the top 10 employers for solar PV manufacturing, who together represented 87% of the PV jobs (IRENA, 2020[30]).

Figure 7.4. Solar PV employment in top 10 countries

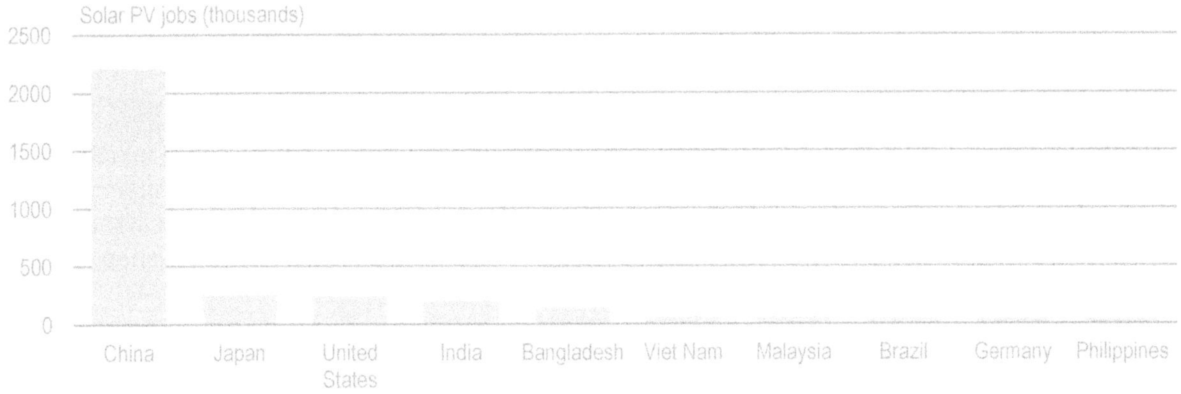

Note: Top 10 countries account for 87% of PV jobs worldwide
Source: IRENA (2020) Renewable Energy Employment by Country (database)

StatLink https://stat.link/udap4y

Modernising and greening technical and vocational educational training

Expanding technical and vocational education and training (TVET) in a strategic and cross-sectoral way will be crucial to ensure Viet Nam has the skilled workforce and capabilities to meet the needs of a greening economy. The offshore wind sector is a good example where a large pool of labour will be needed to support the development, construction and operation of multiple GWs of offshore wind farms. Operation and maintenance alone, which accounts for approximately 35% of the total costs related to an offshore wind farm, are drivers of both localised and long-term steady jobs. Building a labour pool of welders, riggers, inspectors and mariners, in addition to skilled white-collar experts, will be needed to support the long-term sector development in Vietnam and related activities ranging from port upgrades and environmental assessments to the fabrication and maintenance of engineering of infrastructure (Danish Energy Agency, 2020[32]).

TVET is explicitly prioritised in the Green Growth Strategy as well as in the Green Growth Action Plan but to date there is no integrated green skills development strategy that can guide programme formation and investment in this area. An ad hoc approach to skills development may lead to skills deficits and lost opportunities for economic development and local employment. Aligning TVET teaching institutions such as technical and vocational colleges to the needs of the greening economy is central to the process as is ensuring TVET teachers are adequately trained and hold the required competencies. There is currently a lack of competent TVET teachers in the country and curriculums and courses are not well aligned to the needs of the green economy (Mertineit and Dang, 2016[33]).

A number of development partners are working with the government in this area. For example, Agence Française de Développement (AFD) is funding five training centres to offer courses in welding, metal cutting, industrial electricity, automotive mechanics, radio telecommunications equipment installation and fibre optic networks. Supported by the United Nations Industrial Development Organization (UNIDO) and the Swiss State Secretariat for Economic Affairs (SECO), and in cooperation with the United Nations Environment Programme (UNEP), the Viet Nam National Cleaner Production Centre (VNCPC), part of the Hanoi University of Science and Technology, was established to act as a knowledge hub to build awareness and skills related to cleaner production concepts and their promotion in industrial activities. Under the Viet Nam Energy Efficiency Programme II, Hanoi University of Science and Technology has delivered training programmes for large energy users on aspects of energy management and energy efficiency auditing. The German Federal Ministry for Economic Cooperation and Development (BMZ) as funders and Deutsche Gesellschaft fuer Technische Zusammenarbeit (GIZ) as implementation agency are also very active in supporting TVET under the Vietnamese-German Programme Reform of TVET.

Building skills to promote green finance practices and the uptake of non-recourse project finance structures

The government of Viet Nam, through the Ministry of Finance and the State Bank of Viet Nam (SBV), have worked to develop the legal framework to promote green finance practices in the financial sector, particularly in the banking sector (see chapter 6). As such, Viet Nam is one of few participant countries under IFC's Sustainable Banking Network where sustainable finance is considered "established" under the sustainable banking assessment framework (Figure 7.5).

Figure 7.5. Status of green banking in selected countries

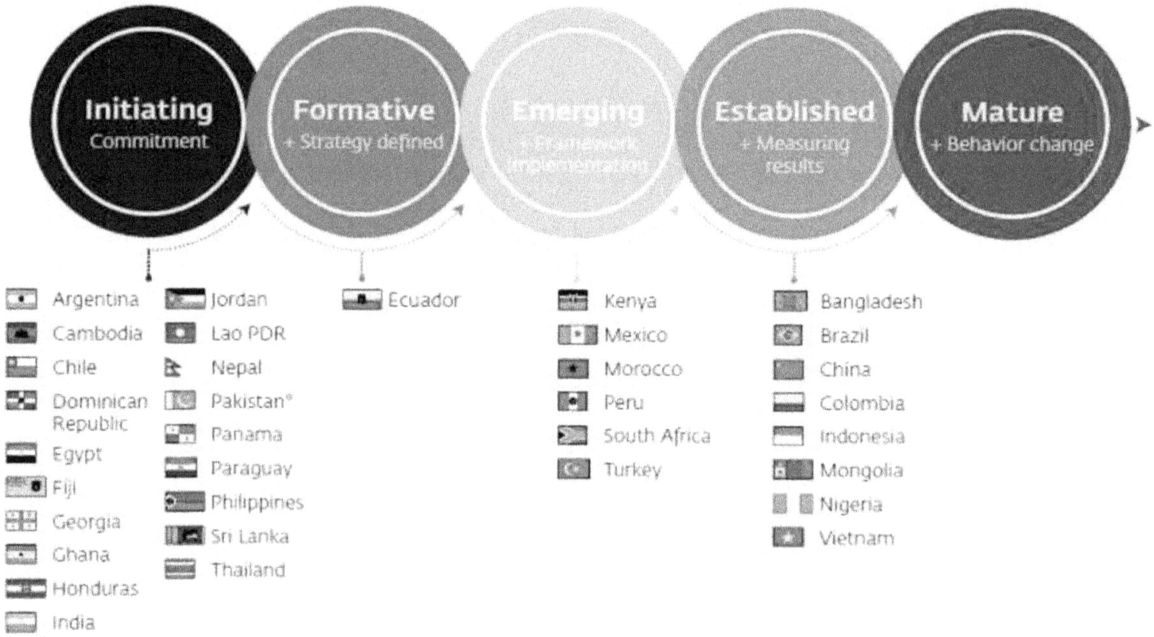

Note: All countries presented are members of IFC's Sustainable Banking Network
Source: (IFC, 2018[34])

Central to this progress has been the passing of the Directive on Promoting Green Credit Growth and Environmental and Social Risks Management (ESMS) in Credit Granting Activities. The Directive seeks to promote green economy and encourages all credit institutions to incorporate environmental and social (E&S) risks into their transactions. It also requires quarterly reporting of quantitative data to SBV covering both E&S risk management of lending activities and green finance flows (IFC, 2018[34]). SBV has implemented training workshops on this topic and a 2019 survey found 17 banks had set up E&S systems to comply with the regulation. Despite this impressive progress, ongoing capacity development and training will be required to ensure that ESMS is fully integrated and that banks have the skills and quantitative techniques to analyse and reflect E&S risks into their lending operations.

References

ADB (2020), *Projects and Tenders*, https://www.adb.org/projects (accessed on 22 December 2020). [44]

AFD (2020), *Promoting renewable energy and climate investments through a green credit line to PT SMI, a key public financial institution of Indonesia*, https://www.afd.fr/en/carte-des-projets/promoting-renewable-energy-and-climate-investments-through-green-credit-line-pt-smi-key-public-financial-institution-indonesia (accessed on 22 December 2020). [45]

Arora, A. (2007), "Intellectual Property Rights and the International Transfer of Technology: Setting out an Agenda for Empirical Research in Developing Countries", WIPO, Geneva. [9]

Bloomberg (2021), *What Does $500 Billion for Clean Energy Mean for Climate Change?*, https://www.bloomberg.com/news/articles/2021-01-21/what-does-500-billion-for-clean-energy-mean-for-climate-change (accessed on 1 April 2021). [35]

Bold Magvan (2020), *Mongolia Green Finance Corporation*, https://www.slideshare.net/OECD_ENV/bold-magvan-mgfc-mongolia-green-finance-corporation (accessed on 18 December 2020). [51]

BVG Associates (2020), *Offshore wind roadmap for Vietnam: Report for Consultation*, World Bank Group. [14]

Clausen, L. and D. Rudolph (2020), *Renewable energy for sustainable rural development: Synergies and mismatches*, Elsevier Ltd. [1]

Climate Bonds Initiative (2020), *ASEAN Green Finance: State of the Market*, https://www.climatebonds.net/files/reports/cbi_asean_sotm_2019_final.pdf (accessed on 6 April 2021). [41]

Danish Energy Agency (2020), *Input to the Roadmap for Offshore Wind.* [32]

Denimal, F. (2020), *Radical Steps Needed from Vietnam Banking Sector*, https://www.regulationasia.com/radical-steps-needed-from-vietnam-banking-sector/ (accessed on 5 April 2021). [37]

DIIS (2021), *Integrating community development in public procurement of renewable energy generation: Lessons from South Africa.* [2]

Duong, V. (2020), *Patent Landscape on Green Technology in Viet Nam*, Rouse Legal Team, https://www.researchgate.net/publication/342436180_Patent_Landscape_on_Green_Technology_in_Viet_Nam (accessed on 15 June 2021). [12]

Duong, V. (2020), *Patent Landscape on Green Technology in Viet Nam.*, https://www.researchgate.net/publication/342436180_Patent_Landscape_on_Green_Technology_in_Viet_Nam/citation/download. [54]

European Commission (2015), *Facts and figures: Free Trade Agreement between EU and Vietnam*, https://ec.europa.eu/commission/presscorner/detail/en/MEMO_15_5468. [10]

EVN (2017), *Power exchange with Laos and Cambodia: the need to ensure the technical safety and harmonious trade benefits.* [3]

EVN (n.d.), *Power exchange with Laos and Cambodia: the need to ensure the technical safety and harmonious trade benefits.* [55]

Grafström, J. et al. (2020), "Government support to renewable energy R&D: drivers and strategic interactions among EU Member States", *Economics of Innovation and New Technology*, http://dx.doi.org/10.1080/10438599.2020.1857499. [57]

HSBC, C. (2020), *ASEAN Green Finance Report 2019: HSBC & Climate Bonds launch major analysis of green investment and policy directions in SE Asia | Climate Bonds Initiative*, https://www.climatebonds.net/2020/04/asean-green-finance-report-2019-hsbc-climate-bonds-launch-major-analysis-green-investment (accessed on 6 April 2021). [40]

Hub, G. (2021), *Vietnam - Global Infrastructure Outlook*, https://outlook.gihub.org/countries/Vietnam (accessed on 5 April 2021). [38]

IEA (2020), *Energy efficiency jobs and the recovery – Energy Efficiency 2020 – Analysis*, https://www.iea.org/reports/energy-efficiency-2020/energy-efficiency-jobs-and-the-recovery. [29]

IEA (2019), *Establishing Multilateral Power Trade in ASEAN.* [4]

IEA (2019), *Southeast Asia Energy Outlook 2019*, https://www.iea.org/reports/southeast-asia-energy-outlook-2019 (accessed on 12 April 2021). [53]

IFC (2018), *Sustainable Banking Network: Country Progress Report Viet Nam Addendum to Global Progress Report.* [34]

IFC (2017), *Women-owned enterprises in Vietnam: Perceptions and Potential*, International Finance Corporation World Bank Group, https://www.ifc.org/wps/wcm/connect/86bc0493-78fa-4c7d-86ec-5858aa41fa1a/Market-study-on-Women-owned-enterprises-in-Vietnam_Eng_v1.pdf?MOD=AJPERES. [26]

Institute), G. (2020), *Potential of Green Bond in Viet Nam.* [39]

International Chambers of Commerce (2019), *Promoting and Protecting Intellectual Property in Vietnam.* [11]

Investing in Women (2021), *Gender lens investing in South East Asia: A Snapshot of Progress in Indonesia, the Philippines & Vietnam*, https://v4w.org/wp-content/uploads/2021/04/Gender-Lens-Investing-in-Southeast-Asia-Brief-MARCH-28-2021-1.pdf. [25]

IRENA (2020), *Global Renewables Outlook: Energy transformation 2050*, https://www.irena.org/-/media/Files/IRENA/Agency/Publication/2020/Apr/IRENA_Global_Renewables_Outlook_2020.pdf. [28]

IRENA (2020), *Renewable Energy and Jobs Annual Review 2020*, https://www.irena.org/-/media/Files/IRENA/Agency/Publication/2020/Sep/IRENA_RE_Jobs_2020.pdf. [30]

IRENA and IEA-PVPS (2016), *End-of-Life Management: Solar Photovoltaic Panels.* [17]

JBIC (2014), *Project Financing and Political Risk Guarantee for Sarulla Geothermal Power Plant Project in Indonesia*, https://www.jbic.go.jp/en/information/press/press-2013/0331-19526.html (accessed on 22 December 2020). [47]

Keuangan, I. (ed.) (2009), *Economic and fiscal policy strategies for climate change mitigation in Indonesia : Ministry of Finance green paper*, Ministry of Finance, Republic of Indonesia : Australia Indonesia Partnership. [43]

Koffer (2019), *Economic prosperity for marginalised communities through renewable energy in South Africa Assessing the co-benefits of decarbonising the power sector Executive report COBENEFITS STUDY*, http://www.cobenefits.info. [20]

Mahmoudi, S., N. Huda and M. Behnia (2020), "Environmental impacts and economic feasibility of end of life photovoltaic panels in Australia: A comprehensive assessment", *Journal of Cleaner Production*, Vol. 260, http://dx.doi.org/10.1016/j.jclepro.2020.120996. [16]

McKinsey (2020), *A low-carbon economic stimulus after COVID-19*, https://www.mckinsey.com/business-functions/sustainability/our-insights/how-a-post-pandemic-stimulus-can-both-create-jobs-and-help-the-climate. [27]

Mertineit, K. and T. Dang (2016), *Greening TVET in Viet Nam: Sustainable Development, Green Economy and the Role of Greening TVET*, GIZ, Hanoi. [33]

Mijał, W. (2018), *Coal Mining and Coal Preparation in Vietnam*, http://doi.org/10.29227/IM-2018-01-40. [23]

Ministry of Finance, I. (2020), *Green Sukuk: Allocation and Impact Report*, https://www.djppr.kemenkeu.go.id/page/loadViewer?idViewer=9468&action=download (accessed on 8 March 2021). [42]

Morgan, P. and L. Trinh (2016), *FISCAL DECENTRALIZATION AND LOCAL BUDGET DEFICITS IN VIET NAM: AN EMPIRICAL ANALYSIS. ADBI Working Paper 613*, https://www.adb.org/publications/fiscal-decentralization-local-budget-. [18]

Muhammed Sayed (2020), *Climate Finance Facility*, Development Bank of Southern Africa, https://www.slideshare.net/OECD_ENV/muhammed-sayed-dbsa-climate-finance-facility (accessed on 18 December 2020). [49]

NL Agency (2013), *Biomass Opportunities in Vietnam*, The Embassy of the Kingdom of The Netherlands. [15]

OECD (2018), *Making Blended Finance Work for the Sustainable Development Goals*, OECD Publishing, Paris, https://dx.doi.org/10.1787/9789264288768-en. [48]

Park, W. (2008), *Technology Transfer and the Economic Implications of the Strengthening of Intellectual Property Rights in Developing Countries*, OECD, Paris. [56]

Park, W. and D. Lippoldt (2008), *Technology Transfer and the Economic Implications of the Strengthening of Intellectual Property Rights in Developing Countries*, OECD, Paris. [8]

Rillo, A. (2018), "ASEAN Financial Integration: Opportunities, Risks, and Challenges", *Public Policy Review*, Vol. 14/5. [5]

Sartor, O. (2018), *Implementing coal transitions: Insights from case studies of major coal-consuming economies.*, http://www.coaltransitions.org. [22]

Söderholm, P. et al. (2020), "Government support to renewable energy R&D: drivers and strategic interactions among EU Member States", *Economics of Innovation and New Technology*, http://dx.doi.org/10.1080/10438599.2020.1857499. [13]

Stiglitz, J. (2010), *Risk and Global Economic Architecture: Why Full Financial Integration May Be Undesirable*, Columbia University and Brooks World Poverty Institute, New York. [7]

Sylvester, B. (2020), *About the Clean Energy Finance Corporation*, Clean Energy Finance Corporation, https://www.slideshare.net/OECD_ENV/bianca-sylvester-cefc-about-the-cefc-experience-setting-up-a-green-finance-facililty-in-australia (accessed on 18 December 2020). [50]

Thanh, V. (2015), "Vietnam's Perspectives on Regional Economic Integration", *Journal of Southeast Asian Economies*, Vol. 32/1, pp. 106-124. [6]

UNDP (2020), *Empowering Women and Delivering Electricity Access to the Off-Grid Population in Viet Nam*, United Nations Development Programme, https://www.ndcs.undp.org/content/ndc-support-programme/en/home/impact-and-learning/library/empowering-women-and-delivering-electricity-access-to-the-off-gr.html. [24]

US International Development Finance Corporation (2019), *Information Summary for the Public PT Energi Bayu Jeneponto.* [46]

VietnamPlus (2021), *Vinacomin completes 26 percent of annual production plan in Q1*, Business News, https://en.vietnamplus.vn/vinacomin-completes-26-percent-of-annual-production-plan-in-q1/199601.vnp (accessed on 17 June 2021). [21]

World Bank (2020), *Vibrant Vietnam Forging the Foundation of a High-Income Economy Main Report*, https://www.mendeley.com/reference-manager/reader/6ed9f731-3ca4-3612-aa71-6e44bbfd64c8/62e8a610-2cba-9619-5bc4-e9e19d214633 (accessed on 12 April 2021). [52]

World Bank (2019), *Unlocking capital markets for Vietnam's future development FINANCE IN TRANSITION.* [36]

World Bank Group (2019), *Viet Nam Solar Competitive Bidding Strategy and Framework*, http://www.worldbank.org. [31]

WWF (2015), *A review of the local community development requirements in South Africa's renewable energy procurement programme*, https://www0.sun.ac.za/cst/wp-content/uploads/2017/04/WWF_Wlokas_Review-of-local-community-development-in-REIPPP_2015.pdf. [19]

Notes

[1] BVG Associates. Offshore wind roadmap for Vietnam. https://ocean-energyresources.com/wp-content/uploads/2020/09/BVGA-32201-Vietnam-OW-roadmap-report-EN-r1.pdf.

[2] https://www.renac.de/fileadmin/renac/media/Projects/Co-Benefits/Vietnam/COBENEFITS-Study-Vietnam-Employment.pdf.

www.ingramcontent.com/pod-product-compliance
Ingram Content Group UK Ltd.
Pitfield, Milton Keynes, MK11 3LW, UK
UKHW051502290926
15471UKWH00008B/1372